96 GREAT INTERVIEW QUESTIONS TO ASK BEFORE YOU HIRE

THIRD EDITION

96 GREAT INTERVIEW QUESTIONS TO ASK BEFORE YOU HIRE

THIRD EDITION

PAUL FALCONE

AMACOM

AMERICAN MANAGEMENT ASSOCIATION
New York • Atlanta • Brussels • Chicago • Mexico City • San Francisco
Shanghai • Tokyo • Toronto • Washington, DC

This publication is designed to provide accurate and authoritative information in regard to the subject matter covered. It is sold with the understanding that the publisher is not engaged in rendering legal, accounting, or other professional service. If legal advice or other expert assistance is required, the services of a competent professional person should be sought.

Library of Congress Cataloging-in-Publication Data

Names: Falcone, Paul, author.
Title: 96 great interview questions to ask before you hire / Paul Falcone.
Other titles: Ninety-six great interview questions to ask before you hire
Description: Third edition. | New York : AMACOM, [2018] | Includes index.
Identifiers: LCCN 2017036087 (print) | LCCN 2017044890 (ebook) | ISBN
    9780814439166 (ebook) | ISBN 9780814439159 (pbk.)
Subjects: LCSH: Employment interviewing.
Classification: LCC HF5549.5.I6 (ebook) | LCC HF5549.5.I6 F35 2018 (print) |
    DDC 658.3/1124—dc23
LC record available at https://lccn.loc.gov/2017036087

About AMA

American Management Association (www.amanet.org) is a world leader in talent development, advancing the skills of individuals to drive business success. Our mission is to support the goals of individuals and organizations through a complete range of products and services, including classroom and virtual seminars, webcasts, webinars, podcasts, conferences, corporate and government solutions, business books, and research. AMA's approach to improving performance combines experiential learning—learning through doing—with opportunities for ongoing professional growth at every step of one's career journey.

10 9 8 7 6 5 3 2 1

*To my lovely wife and best friend, Janet,
and our two wonderful kids—Nina and Sam—more inspiration
than any writer could hope for.*

Contents

PART 1
Interview Questions to Identify High-Performance Candidates

Contents

PART 2
Selecting Candidates and Making the Offer

PART 3
Key Interviewing, Reference-Checking, and Recruitment Issues

Acknowledgments

To my dear friends at AMACOM Books, especially Senior Editor Tim Burgard and VP of Marketing Rosemary Carlough, thank you for your continued friendship and faith in me.

To my friends and business associates who added untold value to the development of this book as it made its way through the various rounds of editing—Kim Congdon, global vice president of human resources and talent management at Herbalife in Torrance, California; Travis Griffith, vice president of human resources and administration at Smashcast.tv in Playa Vista, California; Eve Nasby, vice president at Amerit Consulting in San Diego; Dr. Judith Enns, executive vice president, human resources division, Eastridge Workforce Solutions in San Diego; Sherry Benjamins, president of S. Benjamins & Company, Inc. in Seal Beach, California; and Pete Tzavalas, senior vice president at Challenger, Gray, & Christmas, Inc. California—you've all been instrumental mentors in my career, and I so appreciate your help and support with this third edition as it made its way through the various rounds of review.

And special thanks to the dream legal team that assisted me with select portions of this manuscript, especially in light of the many changing employment laws that are impacting the hiring landscape: Rich Falcone (no relation to the author), shareholder and management litigation partner with Littler Mendelson, LLP, in Irvine, California; and Christopher W. Olmsted, shareholder in the San Diego office of Ogletree, Deakins, Nash, Smoak & Stewart, PC. I can't thank you both enough for the time and effort you dedicated to helping me launch this third edition of a very special book.

Introduction

The Challenges and Rewards of Becoming a More Dynamic Interviewer and Hiring Manager

It sure can be difficult and confusing to hire. It takes a lot of time, and it probably makes you—the hiring manager—feel like you have to choose without having all the information you need to come to an informed decision. After all, candidates are often known to behave one way during an interview, only to perform in a totally different manner once they settle into their roles. The hiring process itself can seem scattered: Interview rounds, testing, reference checks, and background checks sure seem to take a long time and still don't guarantee an overall fit with your department culture or with the rest of your team. If these concerns have plagued you in the past, you're not alone. But the good news is that effective interviewing and hiring is a leadership muscle that you can begin to strengthen immediately. And once you develop confidence in your ability to approach the hiring process with a fresh sense of excitement and optimism and become known for hiring excellent contributors, your career can skyrocket.

After all, hiring top talent is where it all begins. Hire the right team members who know how to motivate themselves, hold themselves accountable for results, and demonstrate an achievement mentality in all they do, and your role as manager becomes so much easier. That's because strong performers tend to manage themselves. They share information openly, express appreciation and gratitude for the opportunity your company provides, and demonstrate an inner competitiveness to excel. Your role becomes more of a mentor and coach rather than a unilateral decision maker and disciplinarian. They thrive and find traction in their careers, and you have the opportunity to practice selfless leadership by helping them build achievement bullets on their résumés and LinkedIn profiles. The work relationship truly becomes win-win-win: As a supervisor, you thrive in developing a reputation as a solid people leader and hiring manager; your people benefit from having a supportive yet fairly hands-off boss who allows them to find new ways of contributing to your organization while building their careers; and the organization benefits from having a team that demonstrates a healthy balance of achievement, ongoing contributions, and a general sense of employee satisfaction and engagement. In short, you'll experience little or no drama, a heightened sense of awareness in terms of having each other's backs and supporting one another, and an achievement mentality that stems from a healthy sense of competition that spurs others to success.

All it takes is a change to your sponsoring thought about what leadership is and how hiring is critical to leadership success. As the saying goes, change your perspective and you'll change your perception. In other words, change your approach right now to the importance of growing and developing strong teams, and you'll very likely experience management and leadership at a much higher level. Start with the simple premise that it all begins with the people you hire and that there's a proven way to make high-probability hires—in other words, while there are no guarantees, there's a structure and approach to hiring that will generate strong contributors almost every time. With the proper hires in place, everything else about effective leadership comes together: open communication, teamwork and camaraderie, and most important, accountability and productivity. It's amazing how much easier leading becomes when you hire the right people up front: Performance management, leadership development, ethics and conduct adherence, and succession planning all fall neatly into place. It all starts with hiring the right people at the right time for the right roles. This book is designed to help you build your hiring program; get this right, and this portable skill will reap ongoing benefits throughout the rest of your career.

After all, *human capital* is your company's primary profit lever in a knowledge-based economy. *Talent* has become the emerging single, sustainable, competitive advantage that any company possesses. And it all starts with effective interviewing and hiring. Talent acquisition is a leadership muscle that can be strengthened and developed over time. Become effective at attracting and hiring strong talent, and your life as a leader in corporate America begins to soar. After all, when you hire people who excel in their careers, possess the skills, knowledge, and abilities to hit the ground running, and demonstrate emotional intelligence, half the battle is won. They'll know how to communicate proactively so you never feel like you're flying blindly, they'll motivate themselves in light of your department's changing needs, and they'll hold themselves accountable for concrete results because that's simply how they're built and how they define themselves.

Make one poor hire, in comparison, and you may be faced with someone who suffers from a victim mentality, an inappropriate sense of entitlement, or a poor work ethic. In short, you could end up spending way too much of your time addressing substandard performance and conduct challenges rather than building your department with the help of the new hire's talent and contributions. Every exceptional leader knows that it's better and more effective to manage people's strengths rather than accommodate their weaknesses. But if you rush too quickly into a new hire relationship, lack the self-discipline to interview thoroughly, or fail to get to know the individual through the eyes of former supervisors during the reference-checking process, you'll have the equivalent of a loose cannon on the deck of your ship.

What typically goes wrong in most hiring situations? Interviewers haven't defined the three or four key criteria they're looking for in their next hire, and they haven't built a strategic interview questioning process to ferret out those qualities. Managers often argue that they don't have the time to review résumés or conduct thorough interviews because they're so busy and understaffed, but think about it: If you don't dedicate the necessary time and energy to hire outstanding talent, then you'll only be perpetuating the problem. After all, the last thing you need on top of all the time it takes to train someone and bring them up to speed is a new hire with a poor attitude, a lackluster work ethic, or a penchant for needing time off (think worker's compensation and intermittent Family and Medical Leave Act time) when the going gets tough and the stakes are highest.

Now's the time to master the art of effective hiring, knowing that it will pay dividends for the rest of your career. Understand that becoming known as someone who hires great people is a learnable and portable skill: Once you get it right, once you understand how all the pieces of the hiring and onboarding puzzle come together to create high-probability hires, you'll have a key advantage that helps you stand out as a rarity among your peers. But you have to arm yourself with the right questions and the right strategy first to lead an interview effectively.

Granted, it's a skill set that will take time and dedication to master. And yes, there will be no guarantees, because when it comes to evaluating human beings, no hiring manager, test, or algorithm will provide absolute home runs each and every time. But picture this: If you develop confidence in this one critical area of your leadership skill set, if you pride yourself on excelling at candidate evaluation, selection, and integration onto your team, and if people compete to join your ranks because of your stellar reputation as a leader, you'll catapult your leadership brand to new heights. In short, if there's one critical leadership skill that's learnable and makes an immediate positive impact on your day-to-day challenges as well as your long-term career trajectory, this is it. Effective interviewing and hiring pays incredible dividends.

If you're willing to focus on building this particular muscle right now, on enhancing your awareness of attracting, developing, and retaining key talent, then so am I. I'd love nothing more than to join you as a coach and mentor in building your confidence, amplifying your talent awareness, and helping you excel in your career as a people developer and turnaround expert. After all, every time you invite someone to join your team, you create the opportunity for new achievements and accomplishments that reflect *you*—especially your leadership, communication, and team-building abilities. And that will always be the first and most critical step in leading effectively; after all, if new hires motivate themselves and find new ways of adding value to your organization, that will in turn reflect your leadership abilities and values, plain and simple.

What about all those excuses that hiring managers make from time to time?

- Dealing with the awkward silence and discomfort that come from asking unilateral questions for extended periods of time or interpreting candidates' responses to challenging questions
- Feeling that candidates are overly schooled and rehearsed in their responses so that you never truly get to know the real person behind all the interviewing hype
- Fearing that candidates may have multiple offers so you won't be competitive or that they may be interviewing with you only to fish for a counteroffer at their current place of employment

And don't forget the biggest excuse of all: Interviewing requires too much detective work, and you simply don't have the time or the inclination to invest so much of yourself in the multiple rounds of interviews or

4

reference checks to ensure you've identified the right person who's the strongest fit—especially since you might not be able to close them on the offer once the interviewing process is all said and done.

Well, fear not: You now have a blueprint—a handy guide and a guiding hand—to successfully prepare you for all sorts of hiring scenarios. This how-to book can be customized and adapted to fit all sorts of hiring situations, whether you're looking for early career, first-job workers, professionals and technicians, or midlevel managers and senior executives. It's structured by functional disciplines so you can turn right to the chapter you need, whether you're looking to interview salespeople, college campus recruits, or professional/technical millennials who represent your organization's talent pipeline.

Even better, we'll address what to look for in typical candidate responses that might point to inconsistencies or untruths that require further investigation. After all, asking the question is only half the equation; knowing how to interpret and ask for additional information after the candidate's initial response is equally if not more important in gauging the real person behind the interviewing façade. That's because the further you get away from the initial, structured query, the more you're called upon to employ your interpretative and evaluative decision-making skills. Therefore, we'll focus on what you need to know most about common and predictable responses coming your way:

- What might trip off danger signals or red flags in a candidate's response?
- What kinds of superficial responses deserve more in-depth probing?
- How can you find ways to identify each candidate's true talents and match their personal style to your department's or company's culture?

The Solution

96 Great Interview Questions to Ask Before You Hire is a practical how-to guide for any hiring situation. This book teaches you how to evaluate:

- What is the individual's motivation for changing jobs?
- Could your organization fill the person's needs?
- Is this individual committed to progressive career management or just "recruiter's bait" waiting to jump at the next offer?

- Worse, could your interview merely be a ploy to leverage more money at his current company by accepting a counteroffer?
- Does this person adhere strictly to her job duties, or does she constantly assume responsibilities beyond her written job description and attempt to reinvent her job in light of her company's changing needs?
- How well does this candidate distinguish between high- and low-payoff activities, how does he handle stress, how does he accept constructive criticism, and what kind of work ethic does he have?

The Pièce de Résistance

96 Great Interview Questions to Ask Before You Hire assumes that there are two levels of interviewing that are critical before you make a hiring decision: First, you interview the candidate who weaves a tale of past performance and achievements. That historical perspective helps you project what the future will look like because past behavior will most likely be repeated. Second, you interview the candidate's former immediate supervisors, who can verify your insights into the individual's ability to excel in your company. For only with an objective, third-party evaluation can you be sure that a candidate's historical recounting of performance is accurate.

More significantly, third-party references are one of the most valid tools available for predicting the future. Guaranteed? No. But insightful as to what it's like working side by side with this person every day? Absolutely. Discerning as to where the person will need the most support in the first ninety days? Of course. Incisive in terms of how best to manage the person either by providing lots of structure, direction, and feedback or by allowing him to be a solo flyer with lots of autonomy and independent decision-making authority? You betcha. And while we're at it, we'll develop a methodology for getting former employers to open up to you over the phone and share their feelings about a particular candidate's abilities to make a successful transition into your company.

So let's get ready to put together an interviewing and reference-checking blueprint that will catapult your candidate-evaluation skills to new heights, increase your confidence in mastering every hiring situation, and help you build better teams of coworkers who will give your organization the competitive advantage.

Best Practices in Recruitment and Selection

This book is a complete, hands-on guide to the employment process. There's not much theory to wade through—just questions to add immediate critical content to your interview and suggestions for interpreting the answers you get. Written for senior executives, front-line managers, contingency recruiters, and human resources professionals, it guides you from start to finish through the entire employment process by highlighting:

- Questions to ask candidates through multiple rounds of interviews
- Reference-checking queries to validate your insights into the person's ability to excel in your company
- Counteroffer preparation
- Job offer negotiations

The premise for this book is a simple one: The best workers have the most options. Positioning yourself and your company to identify individuals with the strongest track records and to appeal to those top performers is what the interviewing and selection process is all about. You are both buyer and seller, critical observer and attractive commodity. For nothing less than your organization's bottom line is at stake.

Legal Compliance

The primary caveat, however, is to keep your questioning patterns within legal boundaries so that you don't unnecessarily expose your company to unwanted liability. Lost-wages litigation, wrongful failure to hire, and other legal remedies exist for workers whose rights have been violated. Consequently, the queries and questioning techniques that follow will not only provide you with refreshing insights into candidates' performance and behavior patterns, but you can rest assured that they will also keep you from running afoul of the law. Just to be safe, refer now to Chapter 19, "Staying Within the Law: A Changing Legal Landscape, Plus Interview Questions to Avoid at All Costs." It will provide you with the ten most common errors to look out for.

In addition, Chapter 19 will provide you with an overview of legal and legislative challenges that may affect your interviewing and selection abilities. Feel free to read this chapter first if you prefer to familiarize yourself with the broader legal trends that may impact recruitment and talent acquisition over the coming years.

Behavioral Interview Questions

In addition, the most successful technique for adding dimension to superficial answers lies in employing a behavioral interview questioning format. Behavioral interviewing techniques attempt to relate a candidate's answers to specific past experiences and focus on projecting potential performance from past actions. By relating a candidate's answers to specific past experiences, you'll develop much more reliable indicators of how the individual will most likely act in the future. Behavioral questions do not deny that people can learn from their mistakes and alter their behaviors. They do, however, assume that a person's future behavior will closely reflect past actions.

Behavioral interview questions call for on-the-spot self-analysis. There are two main types of behavioral formats: self-appraisal and situational questions. *Self-appraisal* queries ask a candidate, "What is it about you that makes you feel a certain way or want to do something?" For example, "What is it about you that makes you get totally involved in your work to a point where you lose track of the time?" Similarly, the self-appraisal format may ask for a third-party validation of the candidate's actions: "What would your supervisor say about that?"

Other examples of self-appraisal queries include:

➡ "On a scale of one to ten (one meaning that you're lenient and understanding, ten meaning that you're demanding and critical), how do you see yourself as a supervisor? Why?"

➡ "If you had the choice of working in a marketing or a finance environment, which would you choose and why?"

➡ "In the future, how do you think you would handle an employee termination differently under the same circumstances that you've described here?"

Situational queries, like self-appraisal queries, look for concrete experience as an indicator of future behavior. The standard behavioral interviewing query begins with the paradigm: *"Tell me about a time when you took action without getting your boss's prior approval," "Describe the last time you assumed responsibility for a task that was clearly outside of your job description,"* or *"Give me an example of a time when you had to make a critical decision in your boss's absence."* Notice the specific linkage to concrete past experiences and situations.

The beauty of this questioning methodology is that it can be applied to anything: a candidate's greatest strengths and weaknesses, his supervisory and sales styles, his communication skills, or the last time he fired someone. As a result, behavioral questions ensure spontaneity since candidates can't prepare for them in advance. Rehearsed answers to traditional queries go by the wayside in this ad hoc interviewing environment where candidates tell stories about their real-life performance. And because they tie responses to concrete past actions, behavioral questions minimize the candidate's inclination to exaggerate answers. Therefore, you're assured of more accurate answers in the selection process, and you're provided with specific ammunition to use down the line in the reference-checking process.

Figure I-1 is a wishbone diagram showing the unpredictable course of a behavioral interview question. Watch where the behavioral interview questions lead this conversation. Because this technique is critical to advanced candidate evaluations, we'll employ it throughout the rest of the book.

Figure I-1. The unpredictable course of behavioral interview questioning.

"Tell me about a time when you . . . felt it important to take it upon yourself to bring bad news to your boss."

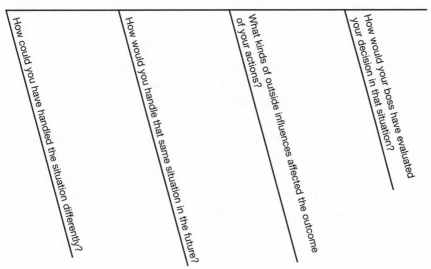

How could you have handled the situation differently?

How would you handle that same situation in the future?

What kinds of outside influences affected the outcome of your actions?

How would your boss have evaluated your decision in that situation?

How Is This Book Structured?

96 Great Interview Questions to Ask Before You Hire is divided into twenty-five chapters. Parts 1 and 2, the first eighteen chapters, contain approximately five questions per chapter. Each chapter either addresses individual characteristics (for identifying a candidate's career stability or promotions through the ranks, for example) or highlights functional interviewing strategies (for evaluating secretaries, senior managers, salespeople, or professional/technical staff).

Although every attempt has been made to include the most practical queries for a specific hiring need, no topic is all-inclusive. For example, although there are ten primary questions to ask sales candidates, other areas of the book will complement those ten key questions. You might logically pull information out of the chapters on career stability, achievement-anchored questions, or likability and compatibility to round out your sales interview. Similarly, you could employ traditional queries with holistic interviewing questions when evaluating professional/technical candidates like accountants, programmers, or paralegals. The point is, it's up to you to mix and match the questioning techniques as you see fit. One thing is for sure, though: Talent doesn't exist in a vacuum and has to be benchmarked to your style of doing business. Consequently, you'll have plenty of latitude to customize the information for your particular interviewing situation.

You'll note as well that many of the questions are two-pronged queries that require the candidate to make logical connections and provide greater background depth in response. Those connectors not only measure how well the individual breaks down information into its component parts but also force the candidate to tie together all the loose ends when concluding. Two-pronged questions are also beneficial because they allow you, the interviewer, to be more specific in your queries. The old one-liners don't go far enough nowadays in gathering the in-depth data necessary to make a hiring calculation. By stating your questions more specifically and intimating how you want the candidate to interpret your query, you'll automatically increase your control of the hiring situation.

High-Performance Questioning Techniques for a Competitive Business Environment

The "Why Ask This Question?" section after each query attempts to crystallize why the question is indeed valid. It addresses what you are attempting to measure in a candidate's response. It also specifies the ideal circumstances for employing the question in sales, secretarial, professional/technical, or senior management interviews.

The "Analyzing the Response" section after the query is typically much longer because it attempts to highlight:

- What you should expect to hear in a typical candidate's response
- What variations on this questioning theme exist to perhaps rephrase the query in a slightly different manner
- What danger signs you should look out for in evaluating candidate responses
- How you could employ behavioral interviewing techniques to add concrete, historical dimensions to the individual's response and thereby avoid canned and rehearsed answers
- How you could look for contrary evidence that further challenges candidates to develop or defend their answers
- How you would subsequently verify a candidate's responses via a reference check

A key advantage to this book therefore lies not only in the cataloging of high-yield questions for various hiring situations but also in the quick and insightful interpretations of expected responses. After all, once you're forewarned about the hot buttons and danger zones that could spell subpar performance or an unacceptable work ethic, you'll be better equipped to avoid marginal hires. And since no human being is perfect, you will be in a better position for damage control if you understand each candidate's shortcomings. You will gain these critical insights through information that the candidate volunteers during your interview and through external verifications (reference checks from past employers).

Finally, Part 3 (Chapters 19 through 25) provides practical information in terms of getting the most for your recruitment dollar while minimizing your legal exposure.

Chapter 19, "Staying Within the Law: A Changing Legal Landscape, Plus Interview Questions to Avoid at All Costs," will help you and your

11

management team steer clear of the interviewing snare of ten key questions that could land your company in legal hot water and suggests suitable alternatives for deriving the information you want to know. The legal and legislative updates included will point out broad overviews of trends that could impact the laws of your state or city.

Chapter 20, "Telephone Screening Interviews: Formats and Follow-Ups for Swift Information Gathering," takes a practical look at phone assessments in order to determine whether a candidate is qualified for an in-person meeting. Such screening interviews are exceptionally effective at guarding your time, since a ten-minute up-front investment could potentially save hours of your (and a candidate's) time. Employ the matrix in this section to quickly and efficiently determine a candidate's viability.

Chapter 21, "Getting Real Information from Reference Checks," will show you how to structure the reference-checking telephone call so you can build immediate rapport and honest communication with the prior supervisor.

Chapter 22, "Background Checks," includes critical information on how to select background-checking firms, how much to expect to pay for their services, and the liability your company may face in terms of theft, violence, and wrongful-hiring and retention claims if you fail to conduct criminal background checks. We'll also explore newly evolving areas for investigation, including civil records checks and social networking checks.

Chapter 23, "Interviewing and Evaluating Freelancers and Remote Workers: The New Frontier of Hiring Just-in-Time and Virtual Talent," will survey numerous questions you may want to use when selecting and hiring individuals for these types of roles. The trend in hiring freelancers and remote workers is significantly on the rise, and the questions suggested will help you make stronger selection decisions when evaluating talent for these types of roles. Note that this chapter lists the questions only, without delving into the "Why Ask This Question?" and "Analyzing the Response" sections since these areas are so broad and full of variety.

Chapter 24, "Effective Onboarding to Maximize the Chances of Initial Success and Create True Believers," discusses the importance of transitioning new hires into your organization and department over an extended period. It's a smart way to protect your investment and ensure that new hires aren't left to sink or swim. Mapped over ninety days, with suggestions for six-month and one-year follow-ups, this chapter will help you develop a blueprint for new hires to ensure a smooth integration into a new company, onto a new team, and sometimes even into a new industry or sector of the economy (think military to the private sector).

Chapter 25, "Maximizing Your Recruitment Resources," provides a cost-benefit analysis for choosing contingency recruitment versus retained search firms. It also addresses the critical role that recruitment process outsourcers provide to help companies scale up quickly. Finally, it highlights one of the best-kept secrets in town for locating talented candidates for free: your local outplacement firm's job-development and research department.

So pick up a pencil and a highlighter and join me for a behind-the-scenes look at sophisticated candidate-evaluation techniques that will maximize all your recruitment and selection efforts.

What's New in the Third Edition

So much has changed across the hiring landscape over the past few years, thanks to social media advances, the meteoric rise of the just-in-time labor market with freelancers and remote workers, and legal updates introducing ban-the-box legislation and fair-pay initiatives, among other things. Rest assured that you can rely on *96 Great Interview Questions* to bring you up to speed on some of the most important technological, social, and legislative changes that we've seen in decades and that may significantly impact your recruitment and selection practices from this point forward.

From a more practical standpoint, however, we want to focus on building greater trust and rapport during the interview. So look to information on the anatomy of an effective interview, the coaching interview, and icebreakers to shortcut introductory formalities and get to know the real candidates and their job-search needs at this point in their careers. Help candidates come to realize why your organization and opportunity may make sense for them over the long haul in terms of building their résumé and career portfolio, and you'll have employees who appreciate your advice and transparency in serving as a selfless career mentor and coach *during the preemployment stage* of your working relationship. You may just find that such goodwill and selfless leadership on your part come back to you in countless ways over your career as you develop strong teams of healthy, career-minded individuals who focus on codifying their achievements and holding themselves accountable to the highest performance standards because of the respect and admiration they hold for you.

And while the first two editions focused on millennials, sales associates, and senior executives, we've now added a chapter (10) on middle management—those high-level individual contributors and managers and directors who represent your organization's future talent pipeline. After all, if you're not hiring with succession planning in mind when it comes to your manager and director openings, you may be missing a key opportunity to link your talent acquisition to your talent-management strategies.

Two other new chapters, 23 and 24, focus on interviewing freelancers and remote/virtual employees as well as implementing an effective onboarding program so you can ensure a smooth transition into your organization and into the candidate's new role. In all, we've attempted to provide you with the tools to build rapport and establish your cultural values from the very first contact to evaluating midlevel management candidates and freelance talent to providing legal insights that will help your company keep abreast of critical developments in the hiring space. Thanks to you, *96 Great Interview Questions* continues to educate and motivate hiring managers all over the world on one of the most—if not *the* most—critical leadership competency today: assessing, developing, and retaining top talent.

Legal Caveat

Bear in mind that this book is not intended as a legal guide for the complex issues surrounding candidate selection, reference and background checking, and other aspects of hiring and employment practices. Because the book does not purport to render legal advice, it should not be used in place of an attorney when proper legal counsel and guidance become necessary.

The Anatomy of an Effective Interview

Finding the Magical 80-20 Balance in How Much You're Talking vs. How Much the Candidate Is Telling

Training front-line leaders how to interview effectively typically starts with role-playing to establish a baseline and understand where you are now as a team. Human resources (HR) professionals, recruiters, and trainers often begin by assembling small groups of ten to fifteen leaders for an interviewing workshop and then handing out a sample résumé that's common to the types of hires the organization typically makes. The trainer asks everyone in the workshop to review the résumé for several minutes and then requests that they begin interviewing her as if she's the candidate. They're collectively the "one voice" of the hiring manager, and she'll field their questions as the candidate in this mock interview scenario. Trainers typically find that the group's questions are fairly scattered and lack any sort of alignment. Initial questions from the audience bounce around from "Tell me about yourself" to "What's your greatest strength?" to "Give me an example of a time when you've had to overcome a significant obstacle at work." Often there's little consistency in the team's questioning techniques, there are no icebreakers to ease into the interview, and the strategy for what the hiring managers are looking for gets lost in the shuffle.

The interviewing relationship isn't quite ready to dig into details right off the bat. Going from zero to question-and-answer mode in any interview situation misses the opportunity to build rapport, establish some common ground, and make the individual feel welcome, which are all critical to the relationship-building process that's supposed to happen during any interview. If you move too quickly into a formal question-and-answer format, you'll likely create an expectation of formality where candidates are hesitant to reveal their true selves. In reality, your goal should be to establish trust and allow candidates to feel comfortable sharing some vulnerability in a positive sense. You'll know you're there when a candidate occasionally says, "Well, Paul, I wouldn't normally say this during an interview, *but* . . ." Vulnerability builds trust, and your ultimate goal will be to get to know the real candidate behind all the interviewing hype.

But how do you get there? What types of questions typically make candidates feel comfortable and at ease sharing more about themselves—their short-term goals, their longer-term career objectives, and their ultimate willingness to join your organization versus the others out there that are competing for talent? Before we launch into the discussion of icebreakers and other initial interviewing queries that allow candidates to feel more comfortable discussing their wants and needs, it's important to understand how the interview should be structured. A consistent interviewing construct will ensure that you, the interviewer and talent evaluator, can focus on your keys to hire, compare apples to apples in terms of your selection criteria, and make candidates feel welcome while providing them with insights into your leadership style.

Here's a roadmap that may help you develop your own interviewing format and move seamlessly into a discussion that helps candidates assess themselves in terms of their potential fit with your organization, department, and team. After all, talent-based hiring always relies on the overall fit factor: the candidate's career and personal interests matching the challenges of the role you're attempting to fill. Assuming a one-hour interview, compare your current interviewing style and structure to the model that follows and see where you complement versus deviate from this typical interviewing time frame:

Step 1: Icebreaker (three minutes)

Step 2: Career interest questions (five minutes)

Step 3: Résumé review: company and prior-role exploration (ten minutes)

Step 4: Discipline- and role-specific interviewing queries (ten minutes)

Step 5: General questions relating to fit factor, personal and career interests, and overall compatibility match (fifteen minutes)

Step 6: Counteroffer role play (two minutes)

Step 7: Salary expectations and next steps[1] (three minutes)

Step 8: Information sharing regarding the company, role, and team, as well as challenges awaiting the new hire (ten to twenty minutes) → your opportunity to talk and sell

Note that the interviewer really shouldn't begin sharing information about the company or role until Step 8. Too many interviewers jump right into the company's history, its players, its historical achievements, its corporate philanthropy mission, and many other aspects of the organization or role at the very beginning of the interview, allowing candidates little input other than to nod their heads with understanding. Likewise, if the interviewer shares too much information initially about the challenges of the role, it will likely tip off candidates in terms of how they should frame their responses to the questions that follow. Instead, in almost all cases, interviewers should follow the 80-20 rule in letting candidates talk 80 percent of the time at the beginning of the meeting. Interviewers can then share their 20 percent—opinions, words of wisdom, career advice, and the like—once the questioning is complete (i.e., around Step 8).

Note as well that many interviewers begin the questioning process at Step 3. They launch an interview by jumping right into technical questions about the candidate's résumé without giving the individual a chance to settle in, share a bit about herself, and discuss what interested her about the role initially and why she initially applied. While Parts 1 and 2 combined only last five to ten minutes in most cases, they go a long way in building trust and camaraderie. Don't shortchange this critical part of the interview because, as the saying goes, you never get a second chance to make a first impression. Discipline yourself to re-invent your interview to focus on the candidate's interests and career needs and desires before jumping into the technical and tactical portions of the interview.

Speaking of the technical and tactical, Step 4 provides you with the opportunity to discuss discipline-specific issues with candidates to gain a sense of their depth and know-how. This step is not covered elsewhere in this book, because it's too specific to particular roles. You'll have different sets of questions for nurses; graphics designers; HR, finance, and information technology (IT) professionals; sales and marketing associates; safety specialists; mortgage bankers; claims adjusters; and whatever other specialty roles your company hires. No book could cover all those discipline-specific specialties, so you have the discretion at this point in the interview to ask whatever questions you feel are pertinent to the role at hand.

For example, you might choose to ask the following types of discipline-specific questions to job candidates in these specialty areas:

◆ REGISTERED NURSE

"How do you protect the rights and confidentiality of patients?"

"Tell me about a time when a patient was agitated and refused care. How did you handle it?"

"What is your current nurse-to-patient ratio?"

"What percentage of patients is unvaccinated or on a delayed/selected vaccination schedule?"

"What are your views on alternative/natural/holistic medicine?"

"Can you explain the meaning of 'triage' and how that plays itself out in your experience in terms of prioritizing patient care?"

◆ PARAMEDIC

"What originally drew you to the field of emergency medicine?"

"What do you find most challenging and rewarding about your work as a paramedic?"

"What was the most difficult situation you've faced in the field so far?"

"What was the last emergency situation you faced, and how did you assess your priorities?"

"If you could invent one piece of technology to help emergency medicine specialists in the future, what would it be?"

"If you weren't a paramedic, what would you be doing right now career-wise?"

"What optional basic life-support medications are you most familiar with?"

◆ INSURANCE AGENT

"How do you personalize the process of buying insurance for each client?"

"What questions should you ask to evaluate a prospective client's needs?"

"When is it advisable to replace one policy with another?"

"What specific follow-up actions do you take after you have sold a policy?"

"What's the most successful sale you've ever made?"

"Which upselling techniques have you employed successfully with your clients?"

"How do you keep track of the policy plans you've sold?"

◆ GRAPHIC DESIGNER

"What types of designing projects are you most interested in?"

"What's your philosophy about producing effective visual communications?"

"Tell me about your approach to design research. How do you decide to employ a particular tool, technique, or strategy to make a client happy and to achieve the ultimate result you're looking for?"

"What was the biggest design achievement of your career?"

"What are the three most unusual projects in your portfolio?"

"What's your approach to designing clean, functional, and search-engine-optimization-friendly websites that are easy to navigate?"

"What was the most challenging design project you've worked on, especially one that required a lot of thought and sensitivity?"

"At what point do you look for additional technical support when programming becomes more complex? Does that typically occur at the level of layout, search-engine-optimization integration, or final site upload?"

"How do you judge the success of a campaign? What milestones or metrics do you typically focus on?"

"How would you rate yourself in terms of your ability to produce appropriate work for a broad range of clients?"

And the list goes on and on. If you haven't discussed situation-specific questions and scenarios to ask of prospective hires, simply sit down with your peers and develop a short list of questions that you all agree are important to know. After all, successful residential property appraisers may have to be willing to jump fences, climb on roofs, and face down aggressive dogs. It may sound menial or trite at first, but incorporating these types of practical and commonsense questions into your candidate analysis could go a long way in helping you identify the right fit for your organization.

Icebreakers

Putting Candidates at Ease and Building Rapport

Once you have a structure in mind for approaching each interview in a purposeful and strategic way, it's time to build rapport, set the mood of the meeting, and launch into some initial questions. But how do you ask the right questions that get candidates talking and fully engaged right from the start? Simple: Start by asking them about themselves. The question is, what types of questions typically make candidates feel comfortable and at ease sharing more about themselves? Start with something business related that also allows candidates to put their best foot forward, like:

➡ "Tell me about your job search up to now. What's motivating you to look for a new opportunity, and what have your experiences been as a candidate in the open market?"

➡ "Before we launch too deeply into your career experience and background as well as what we're looking for in our next hire, tell me what criteria you're using in selecting your next role or company. What's really important to you at this point in your career?"

➡ "Not to limit you in any way, but besides us, which would be the two or three leading companies that you'd want to pursue now if you could, and why are they on your short list?"

Icebreakers are helpful in creating a relaxed and personalized atmosphere. People tend to be comfortable talking about themselves and their experiences without having the formal question-and-answer format coming their way right off the bat in the interview evaluation process.

21

Openers are meant to establish the tone and tenor of the meeting, and richer discussions stem from more personalized and transparent invitations to connect on a more personal level.

If a candidate is entry level or hourly, you can adjust your opening question to build rapport and trust by asking something a bit more humorous and friendly like:

➡ "So, let me ask you the most important question before we begin: Do you enjoy interviewing for a new job, or would you rather stick needles in your eye than have to interview?"

➡ "Most surveys will tell you that there are only two things that people hate more than interviewing: dying and paying taxes. Does that describe you fairly well, or do you actually enjoy interviewing a bit more than that?"

With more senior candidates, you might want to defer to their hiring expertise or understanding of organizational design by asking questions like:

➡ "Let me switch roles with you before we begin. When you hire people at your own company, what do you generally look for in terms of their backgrounds, experiences, and overall style? And what do you like or dislike about interviewing candidates from my side of the desk?"

➡ "Explain the internal structure of your current department and where your role fits into the organization chart, including direct and dotted line reports and immediate vs. extended staff that you oversee, so that I have a contextual understanding of how your organization is set up."

Clearly, you can open with questions that reflect your style, personality, and individuality. What's important, though, is that you're comfortable in your own approach and try to make the candidate feel at ease in answering questions transparently and in a spirit of healthy sharing. Too many times, employers engage in formal question-and-answer discussions without ever letting the candidate talk about their true selves. Candidates really want to know what it's like working for you. Don't underestimate the power of a strong bond or interpersonal relationship in terms of its power to serve as the ultimate swing factor in the candidate's accepting your job over someone else's.

Of course, vulnerability and trust go two ways; as an employer, you'll want to share your true perceptions about the job in terms of its advantages and shortcomings. No candidate is a perfect fit, and no job is a perfect opportunity either. But establishing trust and rapport in the very first meeting goes a long way in getting the relationship off to a good start and establishing an expectation of transparency in a potentially new hiring relationship. In essence, you'll be giving each candidate a glimpse of how you value and handle professional and career development in the workplace. To do that in the preemployment stage may come as a bit of a surprise to some candidates, but it will certainly help you stand out among your competition because of your selflessness and goodwill. Considered another way, you'll actually be transitioning the career and professional development process to the preemployment stage, which will help candidates appreciate your approach to finding the right match for both parties.

Combined with additional interviewing queries focusing on what candidates' ideal opportunities might look like in terms of role, responsibilities, and learning curve, you'll be setting a foundation for longer-term success. After all, how many candidates are asked career-introspection questions that force them to think about their career progression out loud, their key motivators in selecting a new organization, and this position's link to career opportunities three to five years from now? No, they're not easy questions, but most candidates will walk away from an interview like this with a solid impression of the organization and your leadership style. Open your interviews with questions like these, and watch candidates' interest grow exponentially as they reveal more of their true selves during the interviewing and selection process.

For Openers

Inviting Questions to Launch into the Formal Interview

If the icebreaker questions set the mood, then a smooth transition into the first formal interview questions will go a long way in cementing a spirit of trust and transparency between the hiring manager and the candidate. Not all of the questions that follow need to be asked at the onset of the interview; some can be saved for later in the process, toward the end of the meeting. Feel comfortable experimenting with some of the following questions to gauge candidates' responses and ensure your own comfort with the timing and placement of the questions throughout the interview. At least one or two of these questions, however, serve as logical introductions into more in-depth conversations and exploration that allow both of you to get to know one another better from the beginning of the meeting.

> **BONUS QUESTION A:** "Walk me through your progression in your career, leading up to how you landed in your current role at your present company."

Why Ask This Question?

There are several advantages to asking this opener question once the "real" interview begins. First, it avoids the awkward alternative of "Tell me about yourself." That question isn't a terrible interview opener, but it's all over the place, and candidates usually don't know where to start. Besides, they may inadvertently share private (a.k.a. "protected") information that you simply don't want or need as an interviewer. ("Well, I'm a cancer survivor, but I'm very proud of everything I've been able to do in my career over the past five years since I recuperated.")

Second, it gives the candidate a chance to emphasize some key achievements and landmarks that may have gotten him to this point in his career. Such a response might sound like this:

➡ "I graduated from college four years ago in Spokane, Washington, but always wanted to live in a big city. I relocated to Chicago because my older sister went to school there and graduated three years earlier than me, and now we live about five blocks from one another. I was fortunate enough to find the position with my current employer within three months of relocating here, but it looks like my position may be in jeopardy because of a pending merger with a competitor, and I want to get ahead of the curve and explore opportunities before my position gets eliminated."

Allowing candidates a chance to bring you up to speed on what's going on in their current situation is a smart place to start because it gets you on the same page quickly, while allowing them the chance to share some personal and professional background information that may be relevant to their reason for meeting with you today.

Third, asking this question gives you a chance to review their résumé in real time with them. In many cases, you won't have had time to really study the résumé in depth just before the meeting, and it may be two weeks since you first saw the résumé and conducted a telephone-screening interview with the individual. Giving them a chance to walk you through their career progression in large blocks of time and events will help bring you up to speed and allow you to pick up your interviewing questions at any point along the way.

Analyzing the Response

The one caveat is that this is only meant to be a quick overview question. You might want to add to or rephrase the question, such as saying, "Let's start with a brief overview of your career progression, leading me up to how you landed in your current role. *Just maybe a minute*

25

or two working backward on your résumé from the past to the present so that I understand how you've progressed in your career and gotten to this point." This should ensure the candidates don't get lost in their own details. It's interesting to see, however, whether they can explain their backgrounds in ninety seconds or less. Much like an elevator-pitch introduction, you're looking to see how well they can compartmentalize information, let their personality shine through, put their best foot forward, and personalize their message to make you feel comfortable getting to know them.

If candidates stall by getting stuck spending too much time at one point in their career, politely say something like, "That's okay—I don't need too much detail at this point about that particular position. Why don't you keep going and bring me up to speed from that point forward, getting me to how you landed in your current role at XYZ Company?" That should be enough to jump-start a stalled conversation opener and reorient individuals to complete their response to your original question. After all, this is simply meant to be an open-ended and inviting question to allow them to share a brief career overview and invite you into their world, so to speak. If someone can't stop talking, however, or keeps going down rabbit holes, it could give you cause for concern in terms of their communication style and abilities. In such cases, you might want to consider shortening your interview if the opener is that difficult for the candidate to get through. Like all else, it depends on the nature of the role you're attempting to fill and the communication style of the individual you're trying to bring aboard. (Don't judge too harshly—it's only the opener question, and candidates may be nervous.)

BONUS QUESTION B: What's your primary reason for leaving your current organization, and what are your criteria for selecting your next role, company, or industry?

This question is the equivalent of "What brings you here today"? but is framed in a way to link candidates' responses to their career needs and career growth plans. It's a safe general opener that invites candidates to give you a sneak peek at their priorities and immediate needs, which keeps them talking and you listening—exactly where you want to be at the onset of an interview.

Why Ask This Question?

It's reasonable to expect candidates at all levels—from entry level to senior executive—to be able to answer a basic question like this. What will differ is the level of detail and finesse contained in their responses. As we'll discuss elsewhere in the book, especially in Chapter 4 on the importance of career stability, their reason for leaving must be fulfilled by joining your organization. Otherwise, it may appear that they're running from a problem or simply making a change for change's sake. What you're looking for is a level of business maturity and career introspection that tells you they're managing their careers wisely, have healthy career and professional values, and possess the business acumen to know when job change is a healthy alternative to staying put.

Analyzing the Response

Then again, it's not always an easy question to answer and can be challenging if the candidate hasn't thought the job search all the way through. That's why asking it on the front end is typically a good starter: It's a fair question, it provides an immediate indication of the individual's career management abilities and thought processes about his working life, and it helps you assess whether the person sitting in front of you may be a potential match and fit for your team. While not a trick question, it can reveal some serious shortcomings if an individual isn't able to articulate a mission and vision for his own career path that's gotten him to the point of sitting with you in your office that day.

Note as well that it's a two-part question. Part one focuses on the candidate's reason for leaving her current company. Clearly there are certain responses that are healthy signs of career management and career movement, while there can likewise be unhealthy or premature signs that might spell only a short-term stay at your organization. Part two of the question asks about the selection criteria that the individual is focusing on to justify leaving one company and joining another. (It works just as well if the candidate is currently unemployed.)

In essence, you're asking about the ingredients that need to go into the recipe mix that will inspire the individual to say yes to a prospective offer. This part may surprise you: You'll likely find entry-level workers who can answer a question like this with distinction, while you'll also find 27 more senior-level professionals who may not have thought this all the way through. Here's how a college senior answered the question during her on-campus interview:

➡ "Having studied business as a major and human resources as a minor, I realize there are a number of directions I can take. The position will likely be something around an analyst level. I love the idea of metrics and analytics, and I think Big Data is the wave of the future for HR and so many other corporate disciplines out there. I enjoy looking for trends in patterns in the work I do and finding new ways of solving problems that may not have been thought of before. But the bigger issue for me is the industry that I choose. I've spent a lot of time with the Bureau of Labor Statistics' *Occupational Outlook Handbook*, and I believe the industry you choose is the most important predictor of future career success these days. The healthcare, hospital, and home-health segments are growing exponentially faster than just about anything else because of the retiring Baby Boomers, and I want to give my myself the greatest advantage by working in an industry that's in strong demand now, is changing rapidly, and has excellent potential for a successful career trajectory over the long term. That's why I was so excited to meet with you today."

What do you think? Would you be interested in pursuing this young lady a bit further as a potential fit for your organization? Are you excited about the level of sophistication of her response and enthusiasm about knowing what she wants via her in-depth research leading up to the interview? More important, is your opportunity in her target sights because your position is exactly what she's looking for? Well, she's not alone: You may just find equally impressive responses from entry-level candidates as well. So go ahead and give them a chance to shine and impress you. Setting up candidates to provide answers that will knock your socks off is a great way to approach interviews, especially at this early stage of the meeting.

BONUS QUESTION C: Let's say you were to get this job with our organization. If you were happy in your role and excelling in your job one year from now, what would it look and feel like?

28   While I'm not a big fan of hypothetical questions during the interview process, this one has some merit. Like some of our previous questions,

it looks for a certain level of career introspection and ties to longer-term goals. This one is different, however, in that it indicates an individual's level of passion and excitement. The candidate-desire factor can be a critical issue when selecting one finalist over another. Giving candidates a chance to shine by tying in their desire to the opportunity at hand may go a long way in helping you find the best talent fit for the position you're trying to fill.

Why Ask This Question?

Desire factor isn't something that's typically discussed or addressed during an interview. It's a silent motivator that either drives someone to accept an offer or to reject it. But injecting this type of criterion into your interview-questioning practice can have real benefits. After all, who wouldn't want to know about how excited someone may be to join your firm? Why shouldn't this factor be escalated and included as a valid point of discussion and consideration? And why do we tend to let candidates come to their own decisions about this in silence rather than sharing their feelings throughout the hiring process?

Yes, this question can be saved for some other point later in the hiring process when the candidate has more knowledge upon which to formulate a response and draw a conclusion. But remember that candidates are typically drawn first to companies rather than to jobs. Not to take away from the significance of the role they're about to play, most candidates will feel more motivated by the organization they're about to join than by the specific role they'll play in it. What is it about a company that motivates them so much? Typically, it's the organization's stellar reputation. The opportunity to brand their résumé with an employer of choice is a significant motivator in the selection process. It can also be based on the organization's mission and purpose—especially common for nonprofits. But don't underestimate other factors like the firm's reputation for corporate social responsibility—whether as a green company, a firm known for its ethics and goodwill, or a company ranked as a best-place-to-work organization.

Analyzing the Response

In short, you won't know their motivations unless you ask. And you have every right to ask since you truly want to understand each candidate's key

29

motivations and drivers. A typical response from a manager-level candidate or above might sound like this:

➡ "If I'm looking back a year from now on my drive home from work and thinking that I'm really liking it here, it's because I feel appreciated for what I do. I want my peers to think of me as someone who welcomes their input and believes in teamwork and selfless leadership. I want them to think of me as the go-to guy to develop creative and innovative solutions. The fun of working is all about building the leadership muscle of the groups that I supervise and paying it forward—in other words, creating strong leaders in their own right who will one day become someone else's favorite boss.

"I've got a healthy sense of competition in that I think it inspires others to do their best and find new ways of contributing. And developing an achievement mentality can only come when your people feel like you've got their backs—that you support them and trust them to use their judgment and discretion to do the right thing. If all those things were happening at the same time—a strong sense of team, an appreciation for what I do, and a reputation as the go-to guy who gets things done—then I'd know I was hitting on all cylinders and as happy as I could probably be in a job."

Well said. Enough said. You've gotten through to the true essence of who this person is and what she wants to be. It's now up to you to decide whether you want her to join your team. Interestingly enough, you've done this all without the help of personality tests and assessments aimed at getting candidates' true sentiments about themselves, their work, and the relationships with those around them. There's nothing wrong with candidate testing so long as the tools themselves are validated. But even if you test, there's no reason not to get to know the real person by altering some of your questions to allow for honest sharing and healthy vulnerability.

Establishing trust and rapport in the very first meeting goes a long way in getting the relationship off to a healthy start and establishing an expectation of transparency in a potential new hiring relationship. In essence, you'll be giving each candidate a glimpse of how you value and also handle professional and career development in the workplace. To do that in the pre-employment stage will likely help you stand out among your competition because of your selflessness and goodwill. In short, open your interviews with questions like these, and watch candidates' interest grow exponentially as they reveal more of their true selves and bond with you while establishing an immediate sense of trust.

Caveats and Red Flags

Finally, there are a few practical rules that you'll want to follow when you begin building rapport and a successful relationship with a candidate.

1. Hold all calls and interruptions as much as possible. Program your phone to go directly to voicemail without ringing, and if there's a call that you absolutely have to take during your interview, let the candidate know about it up front.
2. Don't keep candidates waiting. People are sometimes more nervous at interviews than they are at doctors' appointments, and you know what an unpleasant feeling that is. Stay on target schedule-wise, and if you're going to be later than ten minutes for any reason, be sure to introduce yourself to the candidate with a quick handshake and explanation of the delay, along with an estimate of how long it will be until you're ready.
3. Avoid controversial topics in your opener. Besides the "Tell me about yourself" common error, don't assume that politics or sports teams are areas for common ground, no matter where you both grew up or went to school.
4. Don't assume that you know the candidate's name just because you have a résumé. There are plenty of Robert/Bob and Katherine/Kathy combos out there, and you can't know which one is which until you ask. Also, you never know when that Katherine actually goes by Katie or Kat or some other preferred name, so just ask to be on the safe side. Oh, and don't be embarrassed if you can't figure out how to pronounce a candidate's name. Simply ask for the pronunciation and jot down the phonetic transcription in the margin.
5. Finally, be wary of weaving potentially illegal topics into your conversation. "How was your Christmas?" is probably not a wise way to initiate an interview and could easily be replaced with, "How did you enjoy your holidays?" Similarly, avoid references to personal or family situations that may leave a funny feeling in your stomach: "Oh, I see that you're a soccer coach. Do you have kids of your

31

own or do you just coach for the fun of it?" Likewise, "I see you speak Spanish. Did you learn that in school or is that your mother tongue?"

You'll find more on this topic of inappropriate interview questions in Chapter 19, "Staying Within the Law." Just remember that these rules extend to the initial icebreaking conversations that kick off your interview as well.

PART 1

INTERVIEW QUESTIONS TO IDENTIFY HIGH-PERFORMANCE CANDIDATES

1.

Five Traditional Interview Questions and Their Interpretations

Let's begin by examining the most often used interview questions and putting a new spin on their interpretations. These questions have stood the test of time, and we should consequently recognize their value in the candidate-assessment process. Their inherent weakness, of course, lies in their overuse. Most of us can remember being asked these questions during our own interviews. And job-finding books and career magazines abound with suggested responses to help candidates steer clear of the interview-questioning snare vis-à-vis these popular queries waiting to trip them up.

Our exercise in this first topic, however, isn't to employ questions just because they've been around for a long time. And it's certainly not to offer candidates an opportunity to practice their well-rehearsed lines. We will, instead, offer new interpretations in reading candidate responses.

Tell me about your greatest strength.
What's the greatest asset you'll bring to our company?

Why Ask This Question?

The "greatest strength" question works well as an icebreaker because most people are fairly comfortable talking about what makes them special and what they like. Every job candidate is ready for this one because it gets so much attention in the career press. Job candidates are also aware that this query is used as a lead-in to a natural follow-up question (which is much tougher to answer): "What's your greatest weakness?" Still, the greatest-strength question isn't a throwaway, because it can reveal a lot about an individual's self-perception. So let's open it up for a moment.

Analyzing the Response

There are two issues to watch out for in measuring a candidate's responses. First, candidates often give lofty answers with lists of adjectives that they think you want to hear and that actually add little value to your meeting. Second, a candidate's strengths may fail to match your unit's needs and thus could weigh as a negative swing factor in the selection process.

Watch out for people who give long inventories of fluff adjectives regarding their nobler traits, such as *hardworking, intelligent, loyal,* and *committed.* Adjectives are nothing but unproven claims. They waste time and delay getting to what you really want to get out of this meeting, which is concrete proof of how the individual will fit in and contribute to the team. Consequently, you'll have to keep the candidate on track by following up on these adjective lists with requests for practical applications. For example, when a candidate says she's proudest of the fact that she's a hard worker, you might respond:

- ➡ "Hard workers are always good to find. Give me an example of how hard you work relative to your peers."

- ➡ "Hard work usually results in above-average results. How has your hard work paid off in terms of the quantity of your output or the quality of your work product?"

- ➡ "Hard work in our company boils down to working late hours fairly often and occasionally coming in on Saturdays. How does your present company define hard work?"

- ➡ "How has your boss recognized your hard work? How would she say that you could have worked smarter, not harder?"

The idea here is to *qualify* this person's generic response. The second red flag issue occurs when a candidate's strengths fail to match your organizational needs. For example, a candidate may respond, "I guess I would say that I'm proudest of my progression through the ranks with my last company. I was promoted four times in as many years, and I feel that a company's ultimate reward to its people can be found in the recognition it gives via promotions and ongoing training." That's an excellent response. The position you're filling, however, may offer few vertical growth opportunities because you need someone who would be satisfied with repetitive work. This is a classic case of right person—wrong opportunity, and the greatest-strength query will have done its job of identifying a candidate's motives and expectations. Consequently, you might opt to disqualify the candidate for this particular position.

2

What's your greatest weakness?

Why Ask This Question?

Other variations on this theme include:

➡ "What would you consider to be your occasional fault or over-strength?"

➡ "Of your past supervisors, who would give you the weakest reference and why?"

➡ "What one area do you really need to work on in your career to become more effective on a day-to-day basis?"

You would think that most job candidates have planned responses to these often-asked queries. That's not always the case, however. A surprising number of people out there still give little advance thought to this common self-evaluation query. You could use that element of surprise to your advantage.

Analyzing the Response

The greatest-weakness question is somewhat unnerving because it causes discomfort. After all, no one wants to discuss shortcomings. Although the purpose of the question is certainly not to make anyone uncomfortable, many unsuspecting individuals will use this entree as an invitation to come clean and bare their souls to you. That's when you'll learn that they sometimes run late getting to work, feel intimidated in any kind of public-speaking forum, or tend to be overbearing with coworkers.

Note as well that it's a poor answer for candidates to respond that they have no weaknesses. After all, interviewing, to a large extent, is a game to see how deftly a person lands on her feet. By admitting no weaknesses, the person refuses to play the game. In that case, you'll need to provide a gentle nudge along the lines of, "Oh, Janet, everyone has some kind of weakness. What should I expect to be your shortcomings if we work together on a day-to-day basis?" If that coaxing fails to produce a response, beware the precedent that is being set toward poor communications and a lack of openness.

Good Answers. In contrast, what are acceptable responses that place a candidate in a favorable light? Look for replies that center on the person's impatience with her own performance, inclination toward being a perfectionist (which could slow the individual down but guarantees quality results), or tendency to avoid delegating work to others for fear that it won't get done to the candidate's high expectations. In short, the wisest "weaknesses" are strengths taken to a fault. After all, people who are impatient with their own performance typically have high expectations of themselves. Neatniks can't bear the possibility of sending out letters that contain errors. And those who have difficulty delegating are results-oriented, focused individuals who generally don't watch the clock.

How to Get More Mileage out of the Question. Once again, the key to adding a broader dimension to the candidate's response lies in employing a behavioral interviewing format. Try looking for *contrary evidence* that focuses on the negative impact of the person's actions. For example, typical comebacks you could use to the reply "I have problems delegating work to other people because I find that the end result doesn't meet my expectations" might include:

➡ *"Tell me about the last time* you didn't delegate work to a subordinate and you were left handling a disproportionate amount of the workload. How did you feel about that? How did you handle that situation differently the next time?"

➡ *"Give me an example of a time when* your not having delegated work to a direct report left that person feeling that his career-development needs weren't being met."

➡ *"Share with me a circumstance in which* you were frustrated by your boss's inability to delegate work to you. How did you eventually gain that person's trust?"

The variations are limitless. Candidates have no way of preparing canned responses to behavioral interview questions, and therein lies the true beauty of the behavioral query.

3

What was your favorite position, and what role did your boss play in making it so unique?

Why Ask This Question?

Much like the greatest-strength question, this query invites the interviewee to reflect on positive and comfortable emotions. It also prepares the stage for the related question to follow (which is much harder to address), "What was your least favorite position or company?" Still, there are telling clues in the individual's response, so let's look for the salient issues.

Analyzing the Response

Human-resources professionals and executive recruiters will attest to how warm and cozy this query generally makes candidates feel. Their shoulders will often totally relax, and a warm smile will appear. Their responses, however, could indeed knock them out of consideration for a job when they sell a love for a particular aspect of a past position that you are not offering.

Take the case of a marketing representative named Joan. When the question about favorite jobs came her way, she mistakenly mentioned one that was extremely creative and got her out of the office a few hours a week. She had worked

39

for an international firm that offered the opportunity to entertain foreign dignitaries, and she had been responsible for giving tours of the company's solar energy plant.

Granted, that may be why that particular job stood out in Joan's memory. However, because the job she was applying for didn't offer those nontraditional perks, she ended up selling her love of tasks that she wouldn't be handling on the new job. She consequently weakened her case because the company felt that she was overqualified—in other words, the organization couldn't offer her the glamour and variety she was accustomed to and felt she wouldn't be stimulated in its nine-to-five environment.

Note as well that statistically, a majority of people leave their jobs because of personality conflicts with their boss. No matter how well the company fares, once that key interpersonal relationship sours, there's little opportunity left for a subordinate to assume greater responsibilities, earn significantly more money, or remain part of the unit's succession plan. Therefore, you want to connect what role a boss played in making a job a favorite position, just as you want to tie in the supervisor's role in making a job a least-favorite position.

4

What was your least-favorite position or company? What role did your boss play in your career at that point?

Why Ask This Question?

Body language changes quickly when candidates are presented with an invitation to criticize or censure a former boss or company. After all, this query baits individuals to complain about the people to whom they should be most loyal. The ideal candidate response avoids subjective, personal interpretations that force respondents to defend their past actions. Instead, a solid response will address objective issues that place an impersonal distance between the candidates and the external factors that interfered with their ability to reach their personal best. In short, look for job candidates' abilities to objectively evaluate a situation rather than irrationally react to it.

Analyzing the Response

Little needs to be said regarding candidates who shoot down past bosses. These people automatically place themselves in a victim posture by assigning blame to others. They also show little interviewing sophistication because they fail to realize that you are taking their answers with a grain of salt; after all, most managers can relate to being the brunt of a subordinate's criticism. Why, therefore, should candidates expect you to choose sides when only one side of a complaint is being described? Besides, the candidate's former boss isn't even there to present the other side of the story, so why should you be forced to show empathy to one party and not the other? No doubt about it—talking poorly about a past employer is one of the worst things candidates can do in the interviewing process.

Good Answers. In discussing a least-favorite position and the boss's role in making it so, candidates will usually address the interpersonal challenges they had with bosses who stifled their career growth. Here's how certain positive responses might sound:

➡ "What I disliked most about my former company is the fact that it offered little risk and reward. It was a very mature company with exceptionally long staff tenure. I respect any company that can build loyalty and longevity in the ranks, but my boss, the CEO, was preparing to retire, and we senior managers were not expected to 'step outside of the box,' so to speak, when it came to taking risks. That wasn't the type of corporate culture that I wanted."

➡ "My least favorite position is unfortunately the position I now hold. My boss, the chief operating officer, inadequately prepared for a change in the business environment. The firm made hay while the sun was shining when interest rates were their lowest in thirty years. However, he put all the company's eggs in the refinance basket and developed few contingency plans for the inevitable increase in rates. That kind of quarterly profit mentality went against my better business judgment."

➡ "If I had to critique a past employer's performance, I would have to say that working for Jay Porter, the senior vice president of sales at XYZ Company, had the most challenges. We worked very well

41

together personally, but Jay needed to be much more proactive in terms of anticipating the workload. He prided himself on putting out fires. My style, conversely, was to forecast potential problems before they arose. It got very tiring after a while and took the fun out of coming to work every day."

➡ "My least favorite boss was probably Denise because she was so cynical. She provided our team of front-line supervisors with little structure and direction in our day. Her door was closed most of the time, and she was openly uncomfortable hearing about our problem issues and concerns. That made relying on her as a resource fairly impractical. Worst of all, she spoke poorly about the firm often and was renowned for causing an overactive grapevine."

These solid responses share objective evaluations that place no blame on anyone while gently probing realistic organizational or individual weaknesses.

5

Where do you see yourself in five years?

Why Ask This Question?

This question is a known showstopper because it triggers a candidate's wishful-response mechanism. You'll hear about people who want to be retired on a desert isle. You'll see flower-stand owners in the making. Those who want your job five years from now might even make you a little nervous. And what about those respondents who say that five years from now, they want to be holding the same job they're applying for today? So much for healthy career ambition.

If it seems as if anything and everything candidates say will weigh against them, you're realizing the pitfalls of this question. The fact that candidates simply seem to throw caution to the wind may provide some interesting insights that might not otherwise surface during your meeting. After all, if the candidate's five-year goals have absolutely nothing to do with the job you're offering, how could you build long-term plans around the person?

Analyzing the Response

First, when candidates respond with a far-out answer like retiring to Tahiti or opening a bowling alley, note that. Then bring them back to reality by requesting that they tie their responses in to the business world and your industry. Second, when candidates name a title other than the one they are applying for (i.e., speaking prematurely about promotional opportunities), ask: "How long would you expect to have to work in our company to realize that goal? What skills and experiences would you have to master in order to make that five-year dream a reality?"

Good Answers. A realistic response will typically show that a candidate's long-term goal will be attainable only after three or four years. Getting the prospective new hire to commit to that number of years sets up your long-term expectations and minimizes the chances of premature turnover due to a lack of sufficient growth opportunities. It's not uncommon, after all, to see new hires leave a company after six months and decry the lack of promotional opportunities at the firm.

In addition, a smart response will avoid naming job titles other than the position the candidate is applying for. The proper candidate response will, instead, place more emphasis on the assumption of broadened responsibilities at the current position. So instead of listening to a staff accountant address her desire to attain her first divisional controllership with your Fortune 500 organization, you'll hear more about the candidate's desire to assume broader duties as a staff accountant that allow her to make a positive impact on your department:

➡ "Ms. Employer, I believe I can make the greatest contribution to your company by focusing on my general staff accounting skills. That's where my total focus lies. Where it leads me in five years, I hope you'll eventually tell me. But I want you to know that I'll be open to adding value to your organization in whatever way you see fit."

Voilà—a balanced, logical, and realistic self-assessment that addresses your organization's needs and that person's ability to provide solutions to those needs.

2.

Achievement-Anchored Questions

Measuring Individuals' Awareness of Their Accomplishments

No issue is more telling in the candidate-selection process than measuring individuals' assessments of their own achievements. Not all people in the career-change process will suddenly develop newfound insights into their individual accomplishments and ability to affect a future employer's bottom line. Still, any candidates mounting a realistic job-search campaign in today's survival-of-the-fittest workplace should realize that corporate executives are taking a harder, more judgmental line on new hires. Therefore, the career introspection that ideally belongs at the onset of all candidates' job-search campaigns should mandate that all interviewees create a personalized mission statement to identify how and where they can bring about change in a future organization.

That being said, reality bears out a different truth. Fewer than 25 percent of candidates will be able to articulate clearly what distinguishes them from their peers.

What makes you stand out among your peers?

Why Ask This Question?

44   At first glance, such a simple query appears to offer only a modest challenge to the average candidate preparing for a job change. However, the

simplicity of the question doesn't necessarily equate with the difficulty and demand it places on the candidate struggling to identify a response. Although that response can take myriad forms—for example, increased revenues, decreased operational costs, streamlined work flow, or creative achievements—most job applicants give scant thought to the value they've brought to past companies. It's exactly that work-for-a-paycheck entitlement mentality that you want to avoid in your quest for high-performance, high-velocity career candidates.

Beginning with the premise that only 25 percent of the working population will be able to articulate its uniqueness as corporate assets, you'll begin your selection interview with a tool to identify proven performers who have healthy levels of self-esteem. Bear in mind that not every opening in your organization will necessitate a high level of self-confidence. Still, when it comes to winnowing the chaff from the wheat for higher-profile positions, this query is the sine qua non of all final hiring decisions.

Analyzing the Response

This simple litmus test that measures self-esteem will generate myriad answers, from "I have no idea—I just sit in a room with other staff accountants crunching out numbers all day" to "I took it upon myself to reconfigure our existing software systems to increase our customer-satisfaction index by 32 percent." The latter response obviously begs for clarification: "What motivated you to rethink your existing way of doing business? How did you involve your department and get it to buy in to your idea? How did you come up with that 32 percent figure?" and so on. But it sure is refreshing to find candidates prepared to articulate the particular nature of their achievements.

The former response, though, is problematic. You shouldn't necessarily expect bells and whistles in a candidate's reply. After all, the majority of people most likely won't have single-handedly saved their organization from financial ruin or earned it a spot on *Forbes* magazine's list of the best companies in America. You should, however, expect the candidate to accept your invitation to respond to this challenging question. A response like, "I don't know—I've never thought about it before," refuses your invitation to engage in the conversation. It's fine if the person never thought about it before, but now's the time for him or her to articulate a response.

So if the candidate backs off from you this early in the interview process, it sets a tone for the rest of the meeting: You may have to extract answers from this person like pulling teeth. That precedent impedes open and insightful communications focusing on how the individual is ready to make a contribution to your organization. If you're able to find that out five minutes into your interview, you'll have saved yourself lots of time and energy.

Good Answers. Candidate responses could be as simple as:

- ➡ "I'm totally dedicated to my work and define myself by the great job that I do."

- ➡ "I have a track record for assuming responsibilities above and beyond the call of duty, and I'm always willing to go the extra mile to get the job done."

- ➡ "I'm proudest of the fact that I was hired to grow a region of ten sales offices within a year and successfully met my target goals by the end of the third quarter."

These kinds of comebacks reveal focus and direction. A sense of strength and determination arises merely from the candidate's accepting the challenge of responding to this daunting question. You should applaud those who don't flinch in coming up with an on-the-spot answer, no matter how simple or even awkward it sounds. Bear in mind that right and wrong answers have no say in this particular questioning scenario. What's critical is the timing of the response and the conviction with which it's stated. You'll have plenty of opportunities throughout the rest of the interview to gauge factual information. Your measuring rod here focuses on eye contact, posture, and confidence; the candidate either backs off from your challenge or rises to the occasion.

What have you done in your present/last position to increase your organization's top-line revenues?

Why Ask This Question?

At first glance, it appears that this query belongs in the section of this book dedicated to sales professionals. And you may very well want to employ this question in dealing with line candidates who have a direct impact on your company's bottom-line profits. The reason this query appears here, however, is that any members of an organization—line or staff—are capable of generating revenue for a company. It may not be in the traditional sales sense, but they make money nonetheless.

Analyzing the Response

Good Answers. An administrative assistant, for example, may come up with the idea of adding a response mechanism to the back of a fund-raising letter so that donations could be returned immediately (rather than waiting for a fund-raiser to follow up with a phone call). A corporate travel coordinator might find that he's able to offer travel services to another company, thereby earning small commissions that can offset expenses in your travel budget. Or a training director might see a valuable market for her training programs outside of her company and generate add-on business revenues by offering on-site training workshops to other companies in the field. However you look at it, these nonsales employees have made money for their past employers and will probably bring similar creative insights to your firm.

What happens if nonsales candidates are unable to come up with an answer to this challenging query? Then use an alternative query that will help them identify how they've benefited a previous company from a cost-savings standpoint.

8

What have you done to reduce your department's operational costs or to save time?

Why Ask This Question?

Staff employees typically identify their achievements via their ability to reduce operational expenses (as opposed to generating revenues). Staff departments like human resources, accounting, office services, and IT are noncore segments of a business that support the revenue-raising activities of line departments. Staff workers, therefore, focus on increasing the efficiency of the organization by building a stronger infrastructure to get things done. The more efficient the systems used to bring a product to market, the more time saved. As the saying goes, time is money. So asking a support or staff worker to identify decreased costs or saved time provides the candidate with a comfortable alternative if the question about generating revenue fails.

Analyzing the Response

This question is critical if your goal is to identify economic advocates who view your company as if it were their own. Economic-advocacy theory proposes that employers totally involve their workers in the costs of running business operations and the revenues and profits currently being generated. Companies that espouse this theory practice a policy of open financials to empower workers with the necessary information to conduct the business as if it were their own. After all, sharing the monthly costs of office space, supplies, and parking passes with employees goes a long way in developing a sense of appreciation for the costs of doing business. Likewise, sharing revenue goals builds camaraderie among informed and empowered workers.

Regardless of whether (or to what degree) your particular company espouses such financial-disclosure practices, finding people who look beyond their immediate functional areas to reduce costs will have a direct impact on your bottom line. Committed employees generate ideas to increase the work flow and suggest improvements outside of their departments. Such a profit-and-loss orientation should prove a significant benefit to any company wanting to redefine itself in a quickly changing marketplace.

Good Answers. A human resources manager might talk about reducing annual cost-per-hire expenses (hiring costs divided by the number of new hires) by implementing a successful employee-referral program. A production-control coordinator might discuss increasing unit output by eliminating minor costs associated with rework. A corporate recruiter might focus on lowering the company's overall cost per hire, time-to-fill rate, or first-year turnover.

How to Get More Mileage out of the Question. If candidates have a difficult time coming up with ways to prove their economic-advocacy tendencies, take them through a miniquestioning scenario that helps them mentally move from the features of their jobs (what they merely do to earn a paycheck) to the benefits they provide their employers. Let's look at three candidates to see how you could encourage people to attain a higher realization of their achievements:

Step 1: "I assume, Mary, that as an office manager/plant engineer/controller, your job is to coordinate a large workload and meet specific deadlines for your department. How do you measure your productivity?"

◆ **INITIAL RESPONSES**

> *Office manager:* "By the number of billable hours that I process."

> *Plant engineer:* "By the quality of the repairs I make so that problems, once fixed, don't interrupt production again."

> *Controller:* "By output of my payables, receivables, and payroll staff."

Step 2: "And how does your company, in a broader sense, benefit from your achievements?"

◆ **ENHANCED RESPONSES**

> *Office manager:* "I facilitate communications and get the proper information into the hands of decision makers so that business gets carried out."

> *Plant engineer:* "I support the manufacturing-production process by calibrating test instruments to ensure that the liquids and powders flowing through the production cylinders are distributed equally."

> *Controller:* "I ensure that payroll is met each pay period and maintain the integrity of our credit rating."

Step 3: "Then I would ask you to go even beyond that in terms of your ultimate impact on the company's bottom line. How have your activities reduced your company's operating expenses or saved time by increasing the work flow?"

◆ **ULTIMATE RESPONSES**

Office manager: "I've been able to juggle a higher volume of billable-hour statements without error, so I've cut down on unnecessary phone calls, increased our department's monthly production numbers, and made my boss's life a lot easier."

Plant engineer: "The calibration mechanisms in the testing instruments that we used to measure powder and liquid distribution were refined to increase efficiencies. Those increases in efficiency measures helped the company control the production process and reduce costs associated with inaccurate container injection."

Controller: "I've been able to keep the financial end of my company running smoothly. I never missed a payroll deadline, I increased the effectiveness of our accounts receivable program by training my people to become actively involved collectors, and I ensured that our creditworthiness was untainted."

Voilà—a simple three-step questioning method to help uncover candidates' achievements by questioning them on a benefit-to-solution level as opposed to a more traditional evaluation that focuses strictly on the features of their respective jobs.

9

What has been your most creative achievement at work?

Why Ask This Question?

Creativity in this case has nothing to do with "artsy" stuff or candidates' needs for aesthetic satisfaction at work. Instead, it centers on coming up with unique solutions to existing challenges that companies face every day. Individuals with penchants for reframing problems and customizing solutions deserve a special place in your organization. The question is, how do you make people feel comfortable discussing their discoveries when cultural and personal barriers get in the way? After all, lots of candidates will equate discussing their achievements with bragging about themselves.

Analyzing the Response

How to Get More Mileage out of the Question. A prudent way to get candidates to open up to you regarding the creative solutions they've offered their past employers is to apply a technique from the behavioral psychology realm called *appropriate sharing*. Appropriate sharing is a therapeutic technique to overcome so-called blocking tendencies where respondents have difficulty answering questions that make them personally uncomfortable. The premise of the technique lies in sharing personal anecdotes that show the candidate that you've been there, too. Once that mutual level of understanding is established, candidates will hopefully feel more at ease exchanging personal information about themselves.

Here's an example of an introduction into this sharing technique:

➡ "Marlene, one of the things we value most in our company is people who look at problems more creatively and try to find solutions to issues that impede our growth. When I originally interviewed here, the employer asked me how I creatively solved problems at work. Well, I didn't quite understand what she meant until after the interview was over. And then I kicked myself for not being able to give her an answer on the spot. But I'd like you to think about one problem—no matter how minor it might seem—that slowed down your department or created extra work with very little payoff. Then tell me what you did to make the situation better. Or even if you did nothing, tell me what you possibly could have done to change the situation."

Obviously, there's no need to go overboard in creating a comfortable environment to encourage open responses. After all, you don't want to coddle the candidate. Still, painting a picture of how you responded to the question—for example, how you ordered Post-it notes to replace fax cover sheets—when it was asked of you during a past interview should allay a shy candidate's fears about revealing creative achievements that maximized the work flow.

Unfortunately, many candidates don't even realize the positive impact of their actions. Although your role in the interview process certainly

51

isn't to build strangers' self-esteem, it's exciting to watch the lights go on as candidates play out their achievements before your very eyes. Swapping tales about creative achievements might be an excellent place to start when dealing with self-effacing individuals.

What would your current supervisors say makes you most valuable to them?

Why Ask This Question?

Your final query in this section should focus on mapping out the direct benefits of candidates' actions. In the preceding examples, you've probed individuals' impact on the company or department via increased revenues, decreased operating expenses, or time saved. An alternative lies in questioning interviewees' impact on their bosses. Although senior managerial and professional/technical candidates will typically be able to affect an organization's bottom line via the breadth and scope of their responsibilities, lower-level employees might feel intimidated at having to address such grand and global issues. Provide them with an alternative by setting their sights on a much more definable and concrete result—namely, making their bosses' lives easier.

Analyzing the Response

How are bosses' lives made easier? Well, for the typical administrative support or light-industrial worker, aiming to please a supervisor could very well define the individual's overriding career philosophy. After all, junior-level employees typically don't see their contributions recognized in the monthly newsletter or on the company's 10-Q quarterly report statement. Still, having relieved the boss of time-consuming tasks or having electronically organized a former paper-trail system might have been the primary accolade on the candidate's last performance appraisal.

How to Get More Mileage out of the Question. As a matter of fact, the key to generating a realistic response centers on the performance-evaluation process. If a candidate has difficulty articulating how her boss's job was made easier, then question what the boss focused on during the last performance review. In particular, the sections on a typical performance review template titled "Strengths" and "Areas for Development" target tasks that the individual already performs particularly well or should focus on developing to an even greater degree. Similarly, ask questions about where the individual may be expected to train coworkers. If an employee assumes quasi-supervisory or lead responsibilities, even for limited projects, that's usually enough to lighten the supervisor's workload.

3.

Holistic Interview Queries

Challenging Candidates to Assess Themselves

Holistic questions assess how individuals see themselves fitting into your corporate team. Holistic queries attempt to measure the whole person— the candidate's work patterns, career goals, and ability to see the global impact of his or her actions. They are usually broad, open-ended queries that candidates find challenging to answer on the spot because of their all-encompassing nature. However, they successfully measure people's broad perceptions of their self-worth, self-esteem, and potential abilities to contribute.

Holistic questions aim to surface candidates' self-admitted short-comings, their interest in the technical and analytical aspects of their occupational specialties, their capacity for self-critical insight, and their inclination to distribute time and energy in proportion to the payoff potential of a given task. Moreover, beyond engaging candidates in assessing their overall job responsibilities, these questions will also help you more clearly define your needs when attempting to fill a newly created position.

For example, let's say you're creating a new position for a programmer analyst to aid in the transition from your in-house loan-servicing program to an off-the-shelf software application. You know what you want to achieve in creating this new position, but you're not exactly sure what pedigree or background orientation you'll need in the ideal candidate. You may want someone who understands the pressures and protocol inherent in the data-conversion process. Maybe you need someone with a strong background in artificial intelligence, or perhaps an individual with an exceptionally strong understanding of mortgage-banking processes (making the position a hybrid of programmer analyst and business analyst).

Whatever your emphasis, it's clear that not all programmer analysts will possess the desired orientation. People out of mortgage banking may lack the requisite artificial intelligence orientation. Candidates who are currently working in your target application may know nothing of the mortgage loan process. And individuals who have successfully mastered conversions from a more strategic vantage point may lack the desired hands-on programming and coding background that will ultimately make this transitional project a success.

More than anything else, therefore, holistic queries help you define how candidates see themselves and their brand of programming and analysis. Armed with the individual's self-evaluation, you'll be better positioned to select the most appropriate orientations, experience histories, and skill sets in the candidate-selection process. Following are some of the more popular applications of holistic interviewing techniques. See which ones apply most to your immediate needs.

What are the broad responsibilities of a [job title]?

Why Ask This Question?

Defining broad responsibilities is somewhat cumbersome, but it should challenge a candidate to do some out-loud brainstorming that helps differentiate and order primary and secondary job responsibilities. It will dovetail nicely into amplifying the person's résumé highlights, and it will also paint a picture for you of the person's comfort zones. (Those areas will typically surface first in the response.) See whether the candidate's feedback matches the critical elements that encompass your opening, and probe for details regarding areas that the candidate initially overlooks in his or her response.

Analyzing the Response

One common mistake employers make is to list an opening for an administrative assistant with an employment agency and then provide little critical detail regarding the desired candidate's work habits, primary duties, and track record of achievements. "A secretary is a secretary is a secretary" goes this flawed line of thinking, and few examples provide better insight into the usefulness of this interviewing question. Watch how various candidates will paint much different pictures of their jobs in response to your query regarding their broad responsibilities:

Candidate 1: "The broad responsibilities of an administrative assistant include lowering the company's operational costs by saving time, representing the company in her boss's absence, and making decisions that further the company's interests. I've achieved these goals, Ms. Employer, by putting together correspondence with pinpoint grammatical and contextual accuracy, by screening phone calls with a true customer-service attitude, and by doing everything else necessary in a business office to keep my boss one step ahead of the game. I totally automated her agenda using a personal information manager. I also set up all of my departmental work logs on shareware software so that my boss could spot-check where I was on any specific project without leaving her desk. In short, I see the secretarial role as quasi administrative, quasi personal, quasi technical, and quasi managerial."

Candidate 2: "The broad responsibilities of an administrative assistant center on being one step ahead of all your projects so that your boss can remain proactive in keeping his end of the business plan running smoothly. No management by crisis, no putting out fires are allowed. I feel that being able to look beyond the functional boundaries of your department and envision the whole organizational picture is the key to keeping your input in perspective and maintaining what I call organizational forecasting ability. That's why I read my company's annual reports, 10-K statements, and 10-Q statements, and I follow the stock performance. The administrative assistant is a right-hand function to an executive who's responsible for coordinating one department's actions with the goals of the whole company."

Candidate 3: "My current job as an administrative assistant to the vice president of investor relations entails heavy word processing, and its broad duties consequently focus on meeting deadlines with accuracy. My present boss doesn't rely on me for screening calls, and I have an assistant who handles all the office filing. That leaves only one thing for me:

heavy-duty production on my Mac. From the day I was hired, we agreed that my primary responsibility would be to focus on putting together mutual fund prospectuses, annual reports, and 10-K filings. I work on a project-by-project basis and get a lot of satisfaction from developing a library of my work. Of course, I would welcome the opportunity to handle other tasks in addition to heavy word processing. That's why I'm so interested in this position."

Obviously, these administrators define themselves very differently vis-à-vis their personal business missions, their ways of impacting their companies, and their relationships with their bosses.

Also, beware the candidate who replies to this query with generic lists of duties, like this: "Well, I'm a secretary, so I type, answer phones, and file. What else would you like to know?" Such bulleted lists (many poor résumés, by the way, are written like this) reveal absolutely no self-confidence, pride in work, or inclination to see the broader implications of one's actions. Chances are you'll have to drive home lessons with this person about being a team player and taking a greater interest in her own career as well as your needs.

12

What aspects of your job do you consider most crucial?

Why Ask This Question?

This query is a logical follow-up to the previous question. If the former question sets up a broad perspective of a candidate's primary and secondary responsibilities, this add-on forces specific identification of a candidate's key strengths and areas of interest. Once again, if you're hiring someone for a newly created position in your organization and you're not sure what criteria you'll need in selecting finalists, ask this question of your first interviewees to gain clearer insight into your own needs. It should quickly provide you with concrete data regarding their current work experiences. While you view this question from the perspective that it will help you match those areas the candidate is familiar with to your opening, you should keep in mind that many job seekers are open to and capable of learning additional skills and developing new interests.

Analyzing the Response

Typical applications of this query result in lists of black-and-white specialty areas that either match your needs or fall short of your expectations. For example, when hiring a human resources manager, you may need someone with lots of background in compensation, benefits administration, and employee relations. If the HR manager you're currently evaluating comes from a stronger recruitment and training background, then this candidate's brand of HR management will most likely fail to provide a solution to your specific needs.

As a case in point, when the individual responds to your question regarding what she considers to be the most crucial aspects of her position, she'll initially link her ability to reduce company expenses to reduced costs per hire and a highly trained workforce, not to more competitive workers compensation insurance premiums and reduced 401(k) plan administration fees. Consequently, you should look carefully at the candidate's initial response to identify her comfort zone and her plans for initially attacking the new job.

How to Get More Mileage out of the Question. The response that candidates generate at this juncture will typically get to the heart of their bottom-line responsibilities. Salespeople, for example, will demonstrate whether they are more money-motivated or driven to please customers regardless of the sale. Top producers who define themselves as closers will say that the most crucial aspect of their position lies in getting the prospect to say yes. You might reply:

➡ "I've found that people who define themselves as closers are often more apt to *debate* than they are to *persuade*. Therefore, they're inclined to impress clients rather than try to gain their confidence. They also sometimes have a tendency to talk when they should be listening, and they have a low tolerance for detail that makes them cut far too many corners. Could anyone ever accuse you of having any of those characteristics?"

On the other hand, a salesperson who sees the most crucial aspects of her job as developing long-term relationships with clients might avoid even mentioning closing the sale in her response. Such candidates are willing to get to the sale more slowly in an effort to gain a prospect's confidence and become an informational resource for that customer. Although these are certainly noble intentions, you might reply:

➡ "I've found that people who are willing to go slowly in terms of closing the sale sometimes have an inability to distinguish sound sales approaches from ineffective ones. They can waste time on nonworkable leads by trying to win over people who are just price shopping, and there is an inclination to be run ragged by demanding customers. Could anyone ever accuse you of having any of those characteristics?"

The purpose of these responses is not to discourage an otherwise optimistic candidate who is secure in her style of doing business. Instead, it shows a point-counterpoint reverse strategy for challenging the candidate's beliefs about what she feels are the most crucial aspects of her work.

13

How many hours a week do you find it necessary to work in order to get your job done?

Why Ask This Question?

This is obviously a critical question revolving around your hidden agenda of workplace expectations. If a candidate works 8:00 a.m. to 8:00 p.m., and you happen to pride yourself on completing your daily tasks by 4:59 p.m., then your business styles don't match. You may very well reason here that overly optimistic candidates can spread themselves too thin by starting more than they could realistically hope to finish. If that's the case, you would probably view that inability to complete work in a timely and consistent manner as poor business judgment.

By contrast, if you're at a stage in your career where you're working twelve-hour days and you expect a new hire to keep you company, then the fact that the candidate intends to leave at 5:00 sharp may become an overwhelming obstacle because it shows a lack of dedication to the job.

Analyzing the Response

Good Answers. So what should you expect to hear in a given candidate's response? If someone has after-hour commitments via night school or a second position, then you'll probably get a direct response limiting the person's overtime commitments. In contrast, if the candidate wants your particular position at all costs, you'll most likely hear that he is willing to do whatever it takes to land the position. But what if the candidate isn't sure what your needs are? An astute candidate would probably provide you with a response that avoids limitations and keeps the lines of communication open:

➡ "Mr. Employer, I've worked jobs that have required unlimited time commitments on an ongoing basis, and I've worked for companies that looked down on anyone who worked beyond normal business hours. I'm capable of excelling in either type of environment. Which style do you envision for this job?"

In this case, the candidate will have bought herself some time by responding openly to a closed-end query. She could now take an offensive position to a question that was meant to throw her into defensive mode. Ideally, along the way you will have gained some valuable insights into this individual's plans for dedication to long office hours. After all, time in the office is often an indicator of future commitment. Remember that certain people live to work while others work to live. Those willing to dedicate long hours and sacrifice personal life for business fall into the live-to-work category, which may bode better for your business.

14

**How does your position relate to the overall goals
of your department or company?**

Why Ask This Question?

This one is self-explanatory. If you're looking for someone who ties individual performance to the bigger picture, then this global query will be your best bet. This question can be used at the clerical or senior management level. The key to its interpretation, moreover, lies in the *degree* to which the candidate sees his own impact on areas outside of his immediate department.

Analyzing the Response

Let's take an example. Say you're interviewing candidates for a vice president of finance position. When you ask this question to a very progressive career builder (approximately in her mid-thirties, six years of experience with a Big 4 accounting firm before going inside with a client about two years ago, and master-of-business-administration certified-public-accountant credentials), you soon learn that this person actually defines herself by medium-scale victories. In other words, you find out that her brand of vice presidency relies more on a heavy-handed chief financial officer (CFO) calling all the shots while she implements those decisions: It was the CFO who took the company public. The CFO created the organization's accounting and finance infrastructures. And the CFO does all the road shows presenting the company's stock to Wall Street analysts and brokers.

So you ask yourself, where does this young vice president of finance actually make the biggest impact on her current company? And you realize that it is as an implementer of someone else's decisions, not as a creator of her own strategic objectives. So, if you're looking for someone with an exceptional track record for the development and design of systems to lead your company's finance function, then the fact that this candidate's brand of finance has more to do with following the chief financial officer's lead may make you steer clear of this hire. It's a classic case of right person—wrong opportunity, and this query will hopefully have brought that issue to the surface.

On the other hand, if your CFO wants to maintain a fair amount of control over the corporate finance function, then hiring a lesser-experienced VP of finance who's used to reporting upward for ultimate sign-off on key decisions might be a logical and prudent choice. Therefore, when assessing candidates' responses regarding how they relate their position to the overall goals of the department or company, gauge the responses with concrete examples of their responsibilities and their ultimate authority to make and enforce decisions.

15

What area of your skills do you need to improve upon in the next year?

Why Ask This Question?

Self-critical insight is a necessary trait shared by all high-performance job candidates. Without self-admitted shortcomings, a candidate will most likely require a greater deal of feedback from you about his mistakes to make sure that he learns from them. He may also border on cockiness and abrasiveness because he may be the type who finds fault in others without objectively looking at himself to find solutions to problems. In short, you may need to cultivate a greater sense of objectivity in this individual by helping him focus on *what* is right rather than being unduly concerned about *who* is right.

In comparison, candidates who openly accept their shortcomings from an objective third-party point of view will put you and your management team in a good position for damage control once those admitted weaknesses surface. The issue then becomes monitoring the new hire's performance and adding structure and support from a positive standpoint to enhance the individual's overall effectiveness.

Analyzing the Response

Short-term, tactical goals keep people balanced and focused on their present needs. Long-term, strategic goals, in contrast, make up a vision of achievement and a framework of purpose in one's life. A very acceptable answer to a short-term, tactical query can easily focus on technical skills, since most employees at any given time can bone up on some aspect of their technical abilities. Secretaries, for example, might address their shorthand having become rusty because of scant use. Programmers might address their not being totally familiar with client-server applications. Controllers might address their concerns about having limited exposure to initial public offerings if that's one of the immediate issues ahead of you. These are indeed legitimate concerns, but they are fixable from the standpoint of simple exposure to new systems and activities.

On the strategic side, areas for improvement become more difficult for candidates to defend. Candidates who choose the strategic route in answering this question risk painting themselves into a corner and damaging their candidacy. For example, candidates might point out poor career management skills as the strategic flaw they need to improve upon. Such individuals might not have developed the necessary discipline to harness their energies toward productive ends in a well-organized, consistent, and persistent manner. As a result, they are not as far along in their careers as they would like to be.

Therefore, there is a lot of job hopping, evidenced by premature reasons for leaving past positions. Such candidates will often address the obvious lack of career stability evident from their résumés and then emphasize their need to make a long-term commitment to the next company they join. It's your call, and it's not an easy one when taking a leap of faith that the candidate will change past patterns of behavior once a part of your company. Still, you might optimistically view this recognition as a positive sign that the individual is volunteering such a critical concern so openly.

The important thing is that the candidate gets invited to address tactical or strategic weaknesses and present solutions for self-improvement. Again, this holistic interviewing question tests the individual's ability to recognize flaws in judgment, past performance, career management, and the like. Beware the candidate who fails to accept your invitation to criticize herself. A lack of openness will deny the possibility for self-improvement. And anyone who shies away from self-critical insight shows little ability to learn from past mistakes. That penchant will offer little to your company, which is in turn making its own mistakes and relying on its management team to steer new courses into uncharted waters.

4.

Questions About Career Stability

Your likelihood of objectively evaluating a candidate's potential to influence your organization rests squarely on your ability to discern the individual's motivations, values, and career goals. Employment longevity is often a function of a candidate's reason for leaving past positions—the link in the individual's career progression. Our simple premise here is that people tend to repeat patterns of change in their careers over time. Therefore, if you can identify what trips a candidate's internal job-change mechanism, you'll learn two things:

1. The person's capacity for making long-term commitments
2. Whether the opportunity that you offer will satisfy the individual's needs

Accordingly, the key to determining the slippery issue of candidate career motivations will lie in examining the most important line on an employment application: the reason for leaving.

Aggressively probing a candidate's motivation for changing past positions will address the motivation behind the moves that drives the individual's career philosophy. Your ability to account for these *silent motives* will spell success or failure in the candidate-selection process because reasons for leaving are the clearest indicators of a person's career motivations, realistic goals, and tolerance for adversity. They consequently reveal the true person behind all the hype.

Of course, the swift changes in economic cycles after the merger-and-acquisition craze of the 1980s followed by widespread economic stagnation in the early 1990s have blurred the lines of measurement for employee longevity and loyalty. You obviously don't want to hold it against candidates if they were caught up in layoffs beyond their control. Your goal, consequently, will be to distinguish between candidates who were laid off through no fault of their own and those who purposely orchestrated their own moves.

Qualifying the Layoff

Unprecedented layoffs have plagued corporate America in recent decades and indiscriminately and adversely affected many hardworking individuals who happened to be in the wrong division or department of an underperforming company. Slashing of the balance sheets meant that thousands of workers could be cut from the payroll simultaneously. And many disenfranchised workers witnessed a breach of the American dream, wherein increased corporate profitability stemmed from job slashing, watered-down benefits, and depressed wages. Worst of all, complementing this new harsh economic reality was the traditional belief that anyone laid off was a poor performer or underachiever. That traditional assumption is no longer generally held, but too many layoffs in too short a time still remains a challenge for a significant percentage of the white-collar population.

On the other hand, not all layoffs occur because of massive divisional downsizings. It is also the case that "layoff" for too many workers has become a convenient umbrella excuse for glossing over individual failures. People unable to reinvent their jobs in light of their companies' changing needs are often simply displaced nowadays. Rather than structuring progressive disciplinary measures to eventually justify terminating the worker, employers sometimes decide on a no-fault layoff and agree to pay severance (in exchange for a release agreement) and unemployment compensation as a path-of-least-resistance maneuver. Your first step in qualifying any downsizing, therefore, is to distinguish between individual and group layoffs.

16

How many employees were laid off simultaneously?

Why Ask This Question?

This query focuses the candidate on his former company's actions and automatically links his layoff to a particular business need. If the candidate was individually laid off (and possibly fired), there was probably a reason he was chosen to leave. It may simply be a matter of tenure: The LIFO (last-in, first-out) method dictates that employees with the least amount of tenure be let go first. However, that's typically the only occasion where the individual layoff is justified. Shy of that scenario, workers who are laid off individually are many times jettisoned for lack of production, interpersonal problems, or core competencies and requisite technical skills that have become obsolete.

Analyzing the Response

How to Get More Mileage out of the Question. When a candidate was indeed individually laid off, you'll want to ask these questions:

➡ "Was it logical for you to be the individual chosen to be laid off? How so?"

➡ "Could your individual layoff possibly have been related to your performance or level of production and output?"

➡ "Is there anything your boss didn't know about your performance that could have perhaps changed her mind about choosing you to begin the layoff process?"

➡ "Was anyone else laid off immediately after you were? If so, how many people, and from what departments?"

➡ "Do you feel that the decision to let you go had anything to do with your interpersonal relationships with your boss or any of your coworkers? Could politics have adversely affected you?"

A second corollary that relates to qualifying the layoff and that mirrors this query is:

17

How many people survived the cut?

Why Ask This Question?

The phrasing of this question allows the candidate to assess the layoff from a different business angle, namely the organization's need to retain certain people to keep the work flowing. As such, it complements the preceding query by forcing the candidate to objectively come to terms with the past company's actions. Furthermore, the response you get should again link this individual's fate to an objective business reason for having been let go.

Analyzing the Response

How to Get More Mileage out of the Question. If a particular department or division was eliminated, then the only people who survived were outside of those ill-fated areas. Again, that's totally beyond a candidate's control and shouldn't weigh as a negative swing factor in the selection process. However, if the individual was laid off from a department that is still intact, there may have been a problem.

Therefore, ask the individual to account for why particular individuals survived the cut:

➡ "How did the organization decide who in the marketing department would remain and who would be let go?"

➡ "What criteria were used in determining your department's new staffing configuration?"

➡ "Were you surprised to find out that anyone in particular was kept or let go, or did the layoffs occur as you expected?"

Inviting candidates to assess how the company decided to dismantle a particular business unit will provide you with insights into their abilities to view problem areas with global objectivity. You'll also see if they react negatively and personally to unfavorable outcomes in their lives.

Finally, a third issue for qualifying a layoff lies in asking:

67

How many waves of layoffs did you survive before you were let go yourself?

Why Ask This Question?

Surviving multiple rounds of cuts can be an exceptionally attractive attribute. Only the most consistent performers are asked to wind down an operation. And when all is said and done, not only did they stick it out in terms of helping the company through a very difficult and emotional time, but they never let up in production or output. Although they knew that their eventual reward for their efforts was nothing more than their own layoff, they found new ways of adding value in light of their organizations' changing needs. As a matter of fact, this is often one of the first issues that contingency recruiters mention to prospective employers in the candidate-presentation process. After all, helping businesses wind down their operations usually spells loyalty and high performance.

Analyzing the Response

How to Get More Mileage out of the Question. Allow interviewees the chance to explain, round by round if necessary, why they were chosen to stay aboard as others were let go. How many hats did they have to wear to keep their jobs through those layoffs? Where did they receive their cross functional training? How did they cross-train their peers? What prompted their managers to choose them to help wind things down, and how did those managers solicit their support? You'll be surprised at what valuable information you could develop in examining a candidate's approach to aiding an organization's downsizing.

Keep in mind as well that there is a difference between Chapter 7 and Chapter 11 bankruptcies. Chapter 7 total liquidations leave no survivors; there's typically only the carcass of a company left. Chapter 11 bankruptcies are restructurings where the courts hold creditors at bay to give companies a chance to raise revenues to a point where they can eventually emerge out of bankruptcy. In those situations, a core staff of employees remains to carry on the business. As you guessed, it could be a very big plus in a candidate's column to be among this core of survivors mandated with returning the organization to profitability.

How do you document this information during your interview? Simply by taking notes that explain the circumstances surrounding each layoff. For instance, if the candidate writes "layoff" in the "reason for leaving" the last job space, jot down your qualified reason for the layoff as shown by the examples in Figure 4-1.

Obviously, the answers you'll generate might open a whole new can of worms in terms of the individual's suitability at your firm. And that's exactly what delving into these reasons for leaving is supposed to do. At the very least, gathering this type of information on the front end will point out which areas need to be more fully explored through the use of a reference check a little farther down the road. Congratulations—you've just learned to dramatically enhance your candidate-evaluation skills.

Figure 4-1. Qualifying and documenting layoffs as a candidate's reason for leaving past companies.

Layoff: Company underwent Chapter 7 total Liquidation.

Layoff: Company underwent Chapter 11 restructuring: 300 employees reduced to 60. Only Loan origination division kept while loan servicing portfolio was sold off to another bank. Loan servicing staff totally let go.

Staff reduction: West Coast pharmaceutical manufacturing division relocated to corporate HQ in Chicago. Candidate unable to relocate for family reasons.

Layoff: Four people let go out of a staff of 18. LIFO (Last-in, First-out) syndrome: candidate had only one year of tenure.

Downsizing: Candidate individually laid off. Feels it's because her boss personally disliked her.

Layoff: Candidate individually laid off. Never quite felt like she belonged due to a corporate culture mismatch. Left on bad terms. Employer probably won't give a reference.

The last three questions should provide you with invaluable insights into one of the most overlooked areas in candidate evaluation: qualifying the layoff. Remember, however, that there is another type of reason for leaving that you'll want to examine to gain a thorough feel for candidates' goals and motivations, namely, when individuals deliberately make their own moves.

Qualifying Individually Orchestrated Moves

Although movement from company to company can happen for good reasons, too much movement in a candidate's background—especially when it's movement for movement's sake—should throw up a red flag for you. Bearing in mind our premise that people tend to repeat patterns of change in their careers over time, you need to identify what trips a candidate's internal job-change mechanism. The most effective way to do that is by challenging the most hackneyed and overused excuse in corporate America: no room for growth.

"No room for growth" translates into bored, tired, and unmotivated. Unfortunately, too many job candidates wear it as a badge of honor showing that they've mastered and consequently outgrown their positions. In certain circumstances, it may be true that they've outgrown their current job responsibilities, but the real question is, how much growth and advancement should job candidates realistically expect, especially in terms of the challenging economies and job markets they face? When confronted with a generic "no room for growth" reason for leaving, ask the individual:

19

What does growth mean to you?

Why Ask This Question?

The term *growth* is one of those slippery words in the job-hunting world. To some, it means (vertical) promotions up the ladder. To others, it means increased responsibilities gained through (lateral) broadened experiences. To still others, it simply means more money. Don't assume that you know a candidate's true motives when "no room for growth" is the stated reason for leaving. Instead, use this as an opportunity to gauge how realistic the candidate is, what true motives exist, and how much capacity for dealing with adversity the person has.

Analyzing the Response

How to Get More Mileage out of the Question. Let's role-play this one together. I'll be the candidate; you be the interviewer.

Situation 1

Employer: Paul, I see that you marked "no room for growth" as your reason for wishing to leave your present company. What exactly does growth mean to you?

Candidate: Well, I really want to work in an organization where I can make a difference. I'm not looking for quick advances and promotions up the proverbial ladder, but I do want to know that my contribution has a positive impact on my company. My present company is an excellent organization in terms of the tenure of its senior management team, but it's exactly that paradox of tenure that creates a corporate culture that refuses to keep up with the times. Besides, it's a mature company in a descending life cycle. I see working for your firm as an opportunity to join a dynamic company with a lot more risk and a lot more reward. And it's exactly that risk-reward relationship that makes me feel that I could hit a home run by joining your firm.

Well, what do you think? I don't know about you, but I'm sold. I understand this candidate's career goals, and I also understand how those goals would naturally be met by joining my company. This person passed this hurdle. Let's look at another example.

Situation 2

Employer: Paul, I see that you marked "no room for growth" as your reason for leaving your last company. What exactly does growth mean to you?

Candidate: As a senior vice president of loan servicing, I'm overseeing a loan-service portfolio of 100,000 loans worth approximately $10 billion. We've built that up from 10,000 loans worth about $1 billion nine years ago. If we were still on an aggressive expansion track, Ms. Employer, I wouldn't be in your office today. But our bank was recently bought out by a huge finance company that put us on its balance sheet simply to diversify its portfolio. Accordingly, the word's out that we're going into a mode of maintenance and stasis. Working with your company would allow me to oversee a significantly larger portfolio—450,000 loans worth about $45 billion. And that would just about allow me to reach the brass ring in my career. I'm ready for that level of responsibility, and I'm hungry to make it happen. That's why I'm here today.

71

Now what do you think? Yes, I agree. This candidate has a legitimate motivation to make a job change, and I admire his awareness of his accomplishments and realistic self-assessment of his ability to contribute. He passes this test.

Situation 3

Employer: Paul, I see that you marked "no room for growth" as your reason for leaving your last company. What exactly does growth mean to you?

Candidate: I would say that "growth" means having the opportunity to make more money based on my contribution to the organization. I need a challenge. I also need to know that my ideas are supported by senior management. After all, if you're not going to be appreciated for doing your job day in and day out, why bother? I'm not saying that the owners of my present company owe me a living, but their management style is sorely lacking in that they just don't seem to care. There are simply too many problems at that company, and they can't seem to get their act together. As a matter of fact, a number of people are looking to make a move right now. That's why I left.

Okay, I set you up. I know you realize that Situation 3 is a problem candidate. But why? Besides the whiny attitude, why is this candidate a poor risk?

There are two reasons. First, he lacks a critical quality that sets high-performance career candidates apart from the rest: the ability to remain an objective, third-party evaluator of his career. What's important to him is what his company can do for him—not what he can do for his company. He's subjectively and emotionally entangled in a situation that he refuses to try to change. In his response, he never addresses his attempts to confront the problems that are making that organization (in his opinion, at least) stall. It's exactly that lack of trying that makes him appear whiny and complaining.

Second, and even more significant, keep in mind that whatever problems made a candidate decide to leave his last job must be solved by your company. If you can't offer him a solution to his problems, then there's no reason why his joining your firm would make for a more successful outcome. His problem is that he's simply not motivated at his present job, and there's no reason to believe that a new situation will make him act any differently. After all, he'll be expected to motivate himself once aboard your company. Additionally, your organization, like all others, has its own dysfunctionality quotient. Since he's only a taker and not a giver, you'll have nothing to offer this gentleman once the novelty of the new job wears off six months down the line. Consequently, he's probably got nothing to offer you. Move on to your next interview.

20

What will you do differently at your present company if you don't get this position?

Why Ask This Question?

If a candidate's response to "What does growth mean to you?" appears self-centered or shows a lack of global reasoning, but the individual otherwise shows promise, then press the issue further. Force the candidate to come to terms with how she'll make her work life more palatable once she returns to reality back in the office. Look again for creative ways in which a benefit will result for candidate and company. After all, practically any situation can be enhanced with a renewed commitment to success, whether at the company, department, or coworker level. Besides, even if the candidate isn't wholeheartedly committed to bettering her employment relationship, she should at least be smart enough to show you that she's a team player willing to put her company's needs ahead of her own.

Analyzing the Response

 Beware the respondent who refuses to entertain this issue. If life is so bad back at the office that nothing can salvage even parts of that employment relationship, then you're looking at a "mentally unemployed" individual who has perhaps given up too easily on fixing problems in her career. In such cases, the response (or lack thereof) should suffice to convince you that the candidate doesn't belong in your company.

By the way, many employers consider it a major ding against a candidate when the person leaves a job without having another position firmly in hand. It points to a lack of business maturity and a low tolerance for adversity when an employee unseats himself without another firm offer of employment secured. In today's employment marketplace, it's hard to

73

believe that conditions are so bad that people would rather go on unemployment than wait it out at their present jobs while looking for a new one. Besides, they should know that their marketability goes way down when they're in transition as opposed to when they're employed. It's a rookie mistake, and it shows a lack of business savvy.

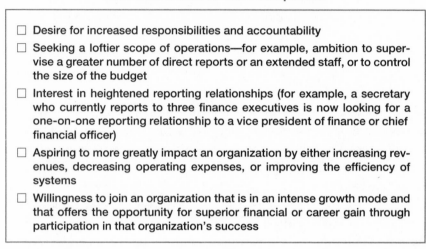

Figure 4-2. Realistic reasons for candidates orchestrating their own moves to leave companies.

☐ Desire for increased responsibilities and accountability

☐ Seeking a loftier scope of operations—for example, ambition to supervise a greater number of direct reports or an extended staff, or to control the size of the budget

☐ Interest in heightened reporting relationships (for example, a secretary who currently reports to three finance executives is now looking for a one-on-one reporting relationship to a vice president of finance or chief financial officer)

☐ Aspiring to more greatly impact an organization by either increasing revenues, decreasing operating expenses, or improving the efficiency of systems

☐ Willingness to join an organization that is in an intense growth mode and that offers the opportunity for superior financial or career gain through participation in that organization's success

Therefore, knowing how to effectively press the no-room-for-growth issue in your selection interview will clearly reveal an individual's career values and motivations—a critical insight into the person's ability to make an impact on your company. Now that you've examined the pros and cons of candidates who have orchestrated their own moves from company to company, look at the brief checklist of favorable reasons for leaving shown in Figure 4-2. Again, when you know what you're looking for, it makes the whole recruitment and selection process that much easier.

5.

Searching for Patterns of Progression Through the Ranks

A critical characteristic of high-performance job candidates may be found in individuals' progression through the ranks. *People who show progressive demonstrations of increased responsibilities understand how to add value to their companies over time.* These are the proven performers who are capable of reinventing their jobs and assuming responsibilities above and beyond the call of duty. The fact that their achievements have been noticed and rewarded by their superiors makes these individuals capable of contributing to your organization over the long haul. (Promotion through the ranks, after all, is usually a function of longevity. You have to stay long enough in a company to receive recognition and added responsibilities.)

There's a unique way to bring out a candidate's progression through the ranks during the interview process. Most employers begin an interview by saying, "So, Janet, tell me about what you do in your present job." Yes, that's an icebreaker, and it should get the candidate talking freely. However, the information you derive from asking that question adds little value to your meeting: You simply end up getting a laundry list of duties that are already highlighted in the résumé. Also, you typically end up with only a generic job description that would fit anyone with that person's title.

Instead, try opening the question by using a progression indicator that invites candidates to describe their present duties in light of their historical advancement:

21

Can you describe how you've progressed through the ranks and landed in your current position at ABC Company?

Why Ask This Question?

This technique adds a historical context or perspective to the individual's current duties. Instead of simply focusing on her responsibilities as an accounting manager, for example, the candidate would address her various promotions leading up to her role in accounting management. All of a sudden, you have a much deeper understanding of this individual's abilities to assume broader responsibilities via her progression through the ranks.

Analyzing the Response

Remember, many job candidates don't reveal progression on a résumé. Instead, they simply list their last position held at each company. So if you don't ask for the history leading up to the person's present job, you'll lose that added dimension of progression. Here's how it works: Imagine you're sitting down with an accounting manager whose résumé shows that she oversees a staff of eight people in payables, receivables, and payroll. Saying, "So, Janet, tell me about your present job as accounting manager" will reveal the following information, which you jot down in your notepad:

➡ Oversees 8 in A/P, A/R; general ledger; multistate payroll in 7 Western states for 100 employees

➡ ADP-generated quarterly tax reporting

➡ A/P—$12MM/mo; A/R—$14MM/mo

➡ Reports to controller; dotted-line reporting relationship to VP Finance

That's not bad information in terms of gathering technical reporting data and scope of responsibilities. But most of that information is probably already on the résumé or employment application. So what clearer insights have you gained into this candidate's abilities to influence your company's future? Unfortunately, not too much. You have nothing more than historical facts.

How to Get More Mileage out of the Question. Now, let's see how this can become more valuable and telling simply by rephrasing and using the progression indicator: "So, Janet, describe how you've progressed through the ranks and landed in your current position at ABC Company." Janet's feedback sounds something like this:

➡ "Well, I began with the organization six years ago as a staff accountant. I did that job for about three years, but in that time my supervisor relied on me to handle a lot of work in his absence. I guess I took on what I'd call a team-leader role in terms of running the office in his absence, and people generally came to me with the tougher questions that no one else seemed to be able to answer.

"After that, I was promoted to accounting supervisor and did that for the next two and a half years. The accounting supervisor to whom I originally reported left for an early retirement. He determined that I would be his logical replacement, and I was very happy to receive that promotion.

"Finally, about six months ago, we had some turnover, and the controller asked me to take on additional responsibilities as accounting manager. Since then, I've been overseeing a staff of eight people in accounts payable, accounts receivable, and payroll. I report directly to the controller with a dotted-line relationship to the vice president of finance, and I helped take our company through a software conversion that we completed just last month."

Do you hear the difference that the progression indicator makes? You'll still end up with a thorough understanding of Janet's current primary and secondary responsibilities, reporting relationships, and scope of authority. But now you have time frames and accomplishments by which to measure them. In taking your notes on her employment application, your comments would look something like this:

1. Staff accountant (three years)—assumed team leader responsibilities
2. Accounting supervisor (two and a half years)—after incumbent retired
3. Accounting manager (six months)—asked by controller to oversee staff of eight in A/P, A/R, and payroll; general ledger; directly reports to controller; dotted-line to VP Finance

Historically reframing a candidate's career progression will add insights and dimensions to your evaluation. It should make your life easier when recommending this candidate to another member of your organization. And it will certainly facilitate your hiring decision seeing that another employer in a different company placed that much value in this individual.

But what if the candidate wasn't on her last job long enough to progress vertically through the ranks? Or what if she was there for six years and held the same job title over that entire period? Should that be held against her? If you ask a candidate to detail her historical progression over time and you get a response of, "Well, I started as an accounting manager, so I didn't really progress anywhere," then follow up your initial question like this:

22

How have you added value to your job over time?

Why Ask This Question?

Every employee is hired to achieve one of three benefits for a company: (1) increase revenues, (2) decrease expenses, or (3) save time. Although vertical progression through the ranks is admirable, long-term commitment to one position is equally necessary in running a successful business. Still, no job remains static over time, and phrasing your question this way forces candidates to account for the changes necessary to maintain output or increase production.

Analyzing the Response

How to Get More Mileage out of the Question. Candidates may struggle with this question because it's so broad. When that's the case, question how the company, division, or department has changed over time. When a company is rapidly expanding, for example, revenues typically have to be maintained for an extended period before full-time staff is added to accommodate the greater workload. Consequently, productivity per employee must increase to produce more product with the same number of people. Reciprocally, when companies are downsizing, employees lucky enough to survive a layoff are typically forced to maintain the work flow with fewer staff members to support their efforts. Once again, we have a case for increased productivity per employee.

In either case, framing candidates' value-added achievements around a changing business environment will usually aid those individuals in redefining how work was redistributed to meet increased production demands or how work was reallocated because of new staffing configurations. By examining how the company had to change over time, candidates should find it easier to address their roles in the unit's new direction.

To delve further into this issue, you should ask candidates to address specific steps taken to reach their unit's production goals. In this case, follow up your question about added value like this:

23

How have you had to reinvent or redefine your job to meet your company's changing needs? What proactive steps did you have to take to increase the output of your position?

Why Ask This Question?

Phrasing the follow-up question this way forces candidates to see themselves in terms of the company's bottom line. The ability to increase revenues or decrease costs is an absolute litmus test of an employee's track record of influencing an organization. Many people fall into the routine of going to work and performing a job. They consequently lose perspective about the bigger picture. Therefore, crafting a question that forces individuals to account for their "macro" impact in their immediate area of responsibility forces them to come to terms with their value as corporate assets or as "human resources."

Analyzing the Response

How to Get More Mileage out of the Question. Asking people how they've added value to their companies by reinventing their jobs over time is a challenging query. There's usually an uncomfortable moment of silence when candidates ponder a question that seems to offer meaning to everything they do in the working world but that they'd never thought of before. And so, after a few shuffles in the chair and awkward clearings of the throat, generalities come spewing forth regarding their commitment, dependability, and dedication. Those fluff adjectives do little, however, in terms of generating the concrete information you want.

79

"Nice try," you might say, smiling, "but that's not what I mean." Give them a moment to regain their composure and continue with such questions as:

➡ "How did your role as an accounting manager change over time?"

➡ "Were you the architect of your changing responsibilities, or did your immediate supervisor direct your revised focus?"

➡ "In terms of your company's changing needs, did your department take on a new mission? And if so, what was your role in redefining your department's new direction?"

➡ "Would you say that the scope of your responsibility increased or decreased in terms of the size of the staff you oversaw or the budget under your control?"

And so goes the questioning pattern. It's a challenge indeed for candidates to articulate their overall capabilities to make a positive impact on an organization, as opposed to performing the day-to-day generic duties that earn them a paycheck. You'll no doubt see some of them walking away from your interview scratching their heads about their roles in business. Of course, not all positions in all companies require high levels of self-esteem and global-reasoning abilities. Still, when you need a superstar candidate for a demanding position, these questions should help you identify individuals who look proactively at their own performance and find ways to increase the work flow and efficiently streamline operations.

Bear in mind that there are two types of progression in people's career histories. Individuals either assume greater responsibilities and move vertically up the ladder with higher titles and pay, or they horizontally expand their jobs by assuming broader responsibilities. In the latter case, although candidates retain the same title, their broadened responsibilities add a depth of knowledge and experience to the company (and to their résumés). To amplify both types of career changes, ask:

24

Can you distinguish between your vertical progression through the ranks at your last/present company and your lateral assumption of broader responsibilities?

Why Ask This Question?

It's fairly well known that U.S. organizations are flattening out by reducing the levels of management necessary to carry out business. Consequently, far fewer jobs are available up the proverbial corporate ladder. Instead, many workers are seeking cross functional experiences to broaden their expertise in their organizations' line units. Similarly, many executives are looking for international assignments to gain the broader knowledge of doing business overseas.

Analyzing the Response

As discussed under Question 21, documenting vertical promotions is a fairly straightforward task. The key to evaluating lateral movement, on the other hand, lies in understanding the candidate's motivation behind those moves. When workers assume broader responsibilities by relocating to another plant or related business unit, it is either at their request or the company's. Both reasons are telling.

How to Get More Mileage out of the Question. Employees who deliberately seek out cross functional opportunities will most likely increase their chances for promotion later on at their current firm, or they will improve their marketability elsewhere. The answer regarding the individual's motivation can be gleaned by asking things like:

➡ "When you switched from human resources to corporate human resources, what ultimate goal did you have in mind?"

➡ "And what prompted the move: Were you asked by management to transfer to the corporate office, or did you put in for the transfer yourself?"

➡ "In retrospect, what was the ultimate benefit to the company?"

Employees who relocate or take on lateral assignments at the company's request show loyalty and flexibility—two admirable traits in today's business world. After all, what greater test of an employee's commitment is there than accepting an assignment overseas for a year and relocating the entire family? Moreover, in a study conducted by the national outplacement firm Right Associates in conjunction with the University of Tennessee, it was estimated that 41 percent of employee relocations were

81

for lateral moves, whereas only 39 percent were for promotions. Consequently, there is a marked shift away from the traditionally accepted transfer-equals-promotion paradigm. What that means to you is that lateral relocations and cross functional training represent a new barometer for measuring employee commitment and adaptability.

Discussing the ramifications of individuals' career movements within their companies can clearly serve as an accurate indicator of people's needs and motivation. It's equally important to look at career progression from a job-change perspective as candidates consider leaving their current company to join yours. When employed candidates interview with you and express a generic reason for wanting to leave their present position like, "I'm looking for added responsibilities and more challenge," it's time to gain a more accurate understanding of their *real* motivation for change. You can gather a more realistic response by asking:

25

What would be your next logical move in progression at your present company?

Why Ask This Question?

Let's face it: No one wants to talk about a derailed career. After all, upward movers and fast trackers will stay with a company as long as they can still make a positive impact on the organization and their interpersonal relationships remain strong. Once that win-win relationship gets compromised, however, the job search begins. Still, as a savvy and sophisticated interviewer, you're responsible for getting to the heart of the matter, and few questions work as well as this one in forcing individuals to candidly come to terms with their current limitations.

Analyzing the Response

The "next logical move in progression" query surfaces candidates' immediate career goals—namely, their next step in added responsibilities, influence, and compensation. Something is blocking their attainment of that brass ring—a superior who refuses to retire, a change in senior management that threatens job stability, or a level of achievement that seems to elude them—and they may not be comfortable admitting it to themselves, much less you, the prospective employer.

How to Get More Mileage out of the Question. A gentle probing question regarding the nature of this career block might sound something like this: "Chuck, the company is healthy, your track record with the firm is apparently solid, yet you're looking outside for increased opportunities. Share with me what's blocking the road ahead for you. And what would have to happen for you to remove that roadblock from your path?" Your caring tone should go a long way in encouraging the candidate to open up regarding his actual concerns. More important, your targeted question will have pierced a wound that you have every right to explore before passing final judgment on this individual's candidacy.

To encourage the candidate further, you might ask questions like these:

➡ "Where exactly on the organization chart would you be if you made one vertical move upward?"

➡ "Whose job would you have, why would you want it, and what would you typically have to do to get there?"

➡ "What would you have to add to your background to receive that promotion?"

➡ "How long would it take for you to see that game plan through to completion?"

➡ "From a relationship standpoint with your boss, what's the key factor keeping you from reaching that rung on the ladder?"

All shooting stars eventually burn out. Interpersonal relationships fluctuate as personnel changes take place. And the heir apparent to the throne may get passed over for someone else who is possibly less capable but more politically fit. These are all natural occurrences that encourage workers to explore opportunities with other teams in different leagues. You are ultimately responsible, however, for ensuring that the malady plaguing the candidate isn't chronic and going to carry forward to your company.

When you're not sure that you're getting the whole story regarding the candidate's motivation for leaving the current company and joining yours, apply the pressure-temperament-recognition triad to explore common problem areas that candidates usually prefer to hide from prospective employers. These three issues should be applied as rapid-fire queries to swiftly identify a candidate's hot buttons that could trigger negative re-actions. A dubious response in any of the three following areas should be probed more deeply for fear that the problem will infect new employees in your organization. For example, you could use this questioning strategy as follows:

➡ "Vic, I sense that you're holding back from me regarding what's really standing in your way at your current company."

➡ "Tell me about the level of *pressure* on your job: Did you ever find yourself complaining about management's inability or unwillingness to relieve the pressure, and could that have anything to do with your decision to look elsewhere?"

➡ "Would you say that your *temperament* complemented your boss's, or were you cut from a different cloth? In other words, did the interpersonal relationship with your immediate superior demotivate you or encourage you to reach your personal best?"

➡ "How could the company have done a better job of *recognizing* your contributions?"

How could these problem issues carry over into your organization? Someone who complains about management's unwillingness to better the working environment is most likely conditioned to place blame on the organization rather than accept responsibility for the company's short-comings. In addition, having a different outlook or opinion than your supervisor is in itself no great sin, but this query may trigger some deep resentment that the candidate holds against his superior. Thus, your spe-cific mention of this issue could open a floodgate of complaints against the person's boss. Finally, feeling inadequately recognized for your con-tributions isn't at all uncommon—unless the candidate placed unrealistic expectations or demands on his previous company.

In short, these rapid-fire queries could release pent-up tensions lying just below the surface. A candidate with chronic issues regarding stress, interpersonal relationships with the boss, or the need for praise and rec-ognition may stir up similar latent feelings in coworkers. Again, many candidates have such issues to some degree, but if they seem dispropor-tionately strong, proceed with caution.

6.

Likability Equals Compatibility

Matching Candidates' Personalities to Your Organization's Corporate Culture

The majority of hires in corporate America are based on a personality match: how well the two people get along and immediately establish rapport with each other. We all tend to hire in our own image, so when we see someone who appears to think and act as we do, we often build a case in our minds for finding reasons to make that placement happen. Our immediate comfort and confidence create a feeling that this person will bring out the best in us and that work will become a lot more bearable with a soul mate to share the burden.

Sometimes we see candidates whom we admire for having achieved accomplishments that we wish we had ourselves, so we become inclined to delve more deeply into their backgrounds to see how they attained that brass ring that's eluded us thus far. Maybe the person graduated from Harvard. Perhaps the individual has a master of business administration (MBA) degree in finance, which still remains only a distant dream for you. Or possibly the person worked at a very high-profile company where you always wanted to work. Whatever the cause of these immediate attractions and affinities, it is important to understand that these are all totally natural human responses that bond us to others very quickly.

Unfortunately, too many managers in business today use this likability factor as the prime criterion for bringing someone aboard. They regretfully admit later down the road that they "felt it in their gut" that a certain candidate would make a successful contribution to the company, only to find out later that the person's management approach or technical orientation wasn't compatible with their style or the organization's needs. So, is it wrong to hire on the basis of initial gut feelings and personal affinities? Absolutely not. But it is certainly a mistake to make decisions solely on a likability factor without employing other diagnostic, more objective tools in the selection process.

The purpose of this topic is to supply you with such diagnostic, impersonal tools to help you clearly delineate your needs and a candidate's potential solution to the immediate challenges you're facing. Therefore, you're cautioned to rely on your gut feelings only *after* you've objectively diagnosed the candidate. The bottom line to keeping your gut feelings in check is that initial *likability* must be matched by future *compatibility*—compatible business styles, management techniques, and tolerance capacities. Then, once you've determined the individual's approach to work, you can evaluate where you'll complement each other and balance each other out.

26

What kind of mentoring and training style do you have? Do you naturally delegate responsibilities, or do you expect your direct reports to come to you for added responsibilities?

Why Ask This Question?

Some people inherently have a high level of interest in training and motivating others. They are naturals at teaching and derive a psychic income from sharing their expertise and helping others grow. These types of managers often speak of the excellent mentors who guided them through their own careers, and they now see a chance to give back to others what was so generously given to them: time, patience, and guidance. Other managers readily admit to having little patience for holding other people's hands. They are independent types who expect their direct reports to operate solo. Whatever the case, you can often gauge this personal orientation via the individual's willingness to delegate responsibilities downward.

Analyzing the Response

Compatibility in the staff-development area is critical because coworkers in discord about the amount of time to spend mentoring others will sooner or later have a falling out. Training is the largest drain on time in business, and if you disagree with someone you hire about the priority level that staff training should receive, then you'll more than likely be at odds regarding project completion dates and work flow continuity.

In general, there are two types of delegators in business. People who are more control oriented typically have a need to hold on to their possessions—whether power, information, or authority. They are often uncomfortable passing responsibility down the line for fear that they will later be challenged by a subordinate with ideas for getting things done differently. Perhaps there is a fear that if they do not hold all the cards at any given time, they may be faced with a question to which they have no answer—obviously an uncomfortable position that would test anyone's feelings of insecurity. Of course, these traits don't necessarily make anyone a bad manager; they just make it more difficult for subordinates to exert autonomy and independent decision making.

Reciprocally, individuals who consistently pass responsibilities down the line—and who operate from more of a shared, participatory management style based on consensus building—naturally offer subordinates more opportunities for creative self-expression and empowerment. Such managers often employ policies of openness in information sharing, a greater sense of partnership with their coworkers, and increased accountability.

Still, you have to be aware that managers who too readily pass responsibilities down the line may sometimes be criticized for delegating work that rightfully belongs on their own desks. In addition, you could end up with chaos on your hands by injecting this type of manager into a department that needs more autocratic rules. Decentralized power placed in the hands of a loosely formed, immature team of workers will necessitate that you step in to impose the discipline that the team lacks. In short, you'll end up managing a high-need problem unit with a departmental head who is not well suited to that team's needs.

Again, there is no right or wrong delegation style, but simply a level of success associated with that manager's ability to motivate and empower staff to reach a department's goals. If this question successfully delivers the information you want, you'll be better able to identify various types of managerial candidates: those who keep their people on a short leash and who oversee even the minute aspects of a given project and those who expect their people to assume additional responsibilities without asking permission. That is, you'll differentiate the more autocratic controller (who will guarantee a targeted output) from the enlightened manager

87

(capable of creating an empowered, creative worker team). Both types of managers may dedicate themselves to making your company more efficient and profitable; it's simply a matter of how to get there.

27

Every company has its own quirks—its dysfunctionality quotient, so to speak. How dysfunctional was your last company, and how much tolerance do you have for dealing with a company's shortcomings and inconsistencies?

Why Ask This Question?

Tolerance for a company's shortcomings and inconsistencies is definitely an area that calls for compatible business styles. If you're fairly patient and realize that the hands of time turn slowly, then matching yourself up with a bull in a china closet who's used to issuing mandates that force immediate change will probably irritate both of you pretty quickly. You'll feel that she's too aggressive and makes overly optimistic assumptions by overcommitting herself. She'll feel that you're much too laid back and lack the necessary sense of urgency to steer the ship in a new direction.

Signs of dysfunction within a company include an overactive grapevine, compartmentalization, the need for total control, a deterioration of company ethics, isolation by function, and cynicism. Every company shares these characteristics at any given time—only the *degree* of dysfunctionality varies. Engaging a candidate to objectively address these corporate weaknesses demands that the individual ride a fine line between outright subjective criticism and an objective, evaluative critique of organizational shortcomings. With this question, you'll want to assess candidates' insights into the problems they've faced battling bureaucracy as well as the solutions they've provided in attempting to overcome those organizational flaws.

Analyzing the Response

If a candidate places himself in a victim posture by identifying weaknesses that negatively affected his performance, then beware this individual's capacity for dealing with adversity. As long as there are people in a company, there will be personality conflicts, power plays, weak leaders, jealous peers, and apathetic subordinates. Placing blame on the company for not controlling these universally human issues spells weakness and poor stamina on the candidate's part.

How to Get More Mileage out of the Question. If a candidate fails to understand the point of this question and bluntly responds that her current company isn't dysfunctional at all, clarify your question by asking one of the following:

➡ "Could your company be characterized as having an overactive grapevine? In other words, do the people standing around the water cooler know more about the power plays and machinations at the executive level than they probably should?"

➡ "Do you find that departments work more independently of each other than they should? After all, without constant interaction among functional units, it's possible that not all players will be tugging in the same direction at any given time."

➡ "Would you describe your senior management team as tight fisted and autocratic, or does it have a policy of open financials and full disclosure so that employees feel that they own the company rather than just work there?"

➡ "Were any particular departments or any of your immediate reports consistently cynical about working in the company? More important, how justified were they in their complaints?"

Not even the most balanced company will meet all of these criteria, so pointing these areas out should help communicate what you want the candidate to address.

Once you've gotten the candidate to identify an organizational shortcoming (which shouldn't be too hard after providing such a varied menu to choose from), employ this follow-up query: "Tell me what role you played in solving some of these problems." By their very nature, organizational or cultural weaknesses are systemic issues beyond the control of any one employee. Therefore, you can't expect one person (shy of the CEO) to have a serious impact on an organization's cultural shortcomings. Still, you may find that this person started a grassroots, bottom-up movement that encouraged interdepartmental communications.

89

For example, a sales manager who invites human resources recruiters to spend a day in the field to get a better feel for the types of challenges facing the account executives will open up the lines of communication between two otherwise isolated units. A vice president of finance who holds a management training workshop on how to read the firm's annual report likewise breaks through such barriers. And anyone who persuades other employees around the water cooler to stop spreading rumors is doing his share to better the work environment. A small step, yes, but a positive step nonetheless. And if you're cut from that same cloth and share similar beliefs, you'll complement each other's work styles and business objectives.

28

How would you describe the amount of structure, direction, and feedback you need in order to excel?

Why Ask This Question?

People typically need more supervision when they're new to a company and learning the ins and outs of new computer systems, work styles, and company expectations. Once they've completed their initial ninety days or even first year, they naturally become more self-confident and independent. Still, some folks really thrive on feedback for a job well done. No matter how long they've held their current position, they need that ongoing pat on the back to bolster their morale and keep them on track. Others truly resent any kind of structured, ongoing feedback, believing that the supervisor's close attention implies that they're not self-sufficient on their jobs. Few areas of compatibility are as critical and immediately evident as this issue regarding feedback and structure.

Analyzing the Response

How to Get More Mileage out of the Question. Eighty percent of respondents will say that they want a combination of feedback and independence. After all, no worker really wants a boss who will oversee every aspect of every step of a given project. That scrutiny would make any of us feel paranoid about our work and limited in our abilities because of a lack of trust. On the other hand, all of us like praise for a job well done and, from time to time, concrete feedback regarding our performance.

Because so many candidates will fall into this generic and comfortable answer, you need to force the issue to the extreme to really get at the candidate's true feelings regarding supervisory feedback. If necessary, reword the question this way:

➡ "Mary, if you had to choose between one extreme or the other, would you want a manager who totally leaves you alone to get your work done independently and only wants to hear from you if there's a problem, or would you prefer someone who meets with you regularly to help you focus on your production goals for the day or for the week?"

Again, there are no right or wrong answers; it's simply a matter of gauging your compatibility ratio. If you're more of a career mentor and you take pride in growing your people, then you'll probably want a more intimate relationship with subordinates because you'll want to measure their progress and contribute to their growth. On the other hand, if you're a hands-off manager and don't particularly relish the thought of helping staff members find their way through the woods, then a candidate who wants extra time from you will probably appear to be a high-need employee. Find this out before you say "I do" to anyone you'll be spending long hours with—it's worth the effort on the front end inviting individuals to assess their expectations of your time.

29

**In terms of managing your staff, do you expect
more than you inspect, or vice versa?**

Why Ask This Question?

Expectation versus inspection can certainly conjure up a picture of a candidate's management philosophy. As you guessed, there's nothing wrong with either style. It's simply a matter of matching the candidate's natural inclinations to your departmental needs. A fairly disorganized unit with a majority of neophytes will benefit from a general who inspects a lot. A mature team of independent technicians or artists will benefit more from a management style of freedom and creativity so that as long as deadlines are met, the workers have autonomy to complete the work as they see fit.

Analyzing the Response

How to Get More Mileage out of the Question. Candidates will readily admit if they are more inclined to inspect than to expect subordinates' work. The initial answer you get, however, is limited because it only superficially identifies the person's supervisory orientation. The key lies in unraveling the *degree* of inspection or expectation. For example, you might ask:

➡ "Dennis, you define yourself as someone who inspects his subordinates' work more than he expects good work from them. My next question for you is, what is the average tenure of your sales team? Are these folks all new to the business, or are they fairly seasoned?"

When Dennis responds that he's got a fairly green sales team with one year of experience on average since college graduation, his inspection management style makes lots of sense. If, on the other hand, Dennis had a lot of senior account executives under his wing, then you'd have to wonder whether his overbearing style didn't detract from the team's potential. Yet a third query in this string would be, "Dennis, how successful is your team compared with other sales teams within your organization?" If his team ranks toward the back of the line because its members are young and inexperienced, then that inspection style again makes sense. Similarly, if his team of senior account executives ranks at the front of the polls, then his inspection style works, so don't mess with it.

Whatever the case, beware the ramifications of the individual's supervisory inclinations. If he's optimistic and altruistic by nature and expects his people to perform out of pure self-motivation, then his underperforming junior sales team may lack the proper discipline for success. If he's a taskmaster and his mature sales team shows only lackluster performance, then he may be riding them too hard and squelching creativity.

Ask, "Given the nature of your sales team, might it make more sense to inject a greater level of [discipline/freedom] into their work environment? How would you do that, and how long would you expect it to take to see concrete results?" Such an invitation might just take the conversation into a new direction of self-admitted weaknesses, and that in turn could lead to honest introspection regarding a too harsh or too lenient supervisory approach.

30

How do you approach your work from the standpoint of
balancing your career with your personal life?

Why Ask This Question?

This is an open invitation to engage in a person-to-person values session. No
work-related accomplishments. No self-admitted weaknesses. No "When
was the last time you had to bring bad news to your boss, and how did you
handle it?" This is a purely human communication that transcends everything "business-y" about an interview. Although it borders on getting a little
too personal for a typical business meeting, it does open the lines of communication by taking the interview to a deeper, more humanistic plane.

Analyzing the Response

Because of the lighter nature of this question, it typically won't turn into a
knockout factor in the candidate-selection process. However, because certain companies do expect employees to live for their organizations, this query
might reveal certain expectations toward commitment that could hinder your
relationship. For example, some companies expect their employees to come in
to work before 7:30 a.m., leave after 8:00 p.m., and come to work on Saturdays.
A staunch reply from a candidate intimating that "My private time is not to be
messed with" might cool off an otherwise hot interview.

In contrast, a self-proclaimed workaholic might leave you feeling am-
bivalent about an otherwise successful interview if you personally believe
that work is a means to an end and that working to live is preferable to
living to work. Again, if you strongly espouse either theory or work in a
company with stringent expectations regarding employee time commitments, then add this query to your arsenal to see whether any extreme
emotions will surface that could eventually clash with your personal expectations or corporate culture.

31

Paint a picture of the corporate culture you'll create if we
hire you. Do you operate under a more paternalistic agenda
with power centralized in the hands of a few, or do you
constantly push responsibility and accountability down the line?

93

Why Ask This Question?

You often hear of a company's corporate culture when in fact any given organization will have multiple cultures in different departments. The marketing manager may be well schooled in progressive human resource principles like empowerment, quality circles, and cross functional teams. The manufacturing manager may have come from an environment where you're expected to do your job, say yes to your boss, and collect your paycheck. Trying to describe a single corporate culture in such a company would be well-nigh impossible. Labeling the marketing or manufacturing unit's cultures, on the other hand, should be fairly easy to do. The bottom line, therefore, is that individual managers dictate the way a unit does business. You need to know a candidate's vision of how work will get done and how people will interact in order to avoid surprises down the road.

Analyzing the Response

How to Get More Mileage out of the Question. If a candidate has trouble putting her hands around this question, you could follow up with a brief explanation to clarify what you want to learn:

➡ "Mary, what will life as we know it now turn into ninety days after we hire you? How will the work flow, how will people react to one another in your unit, how many weekly meetings will be going on, and how will our customers know that there's been a change?"

Obviously, the answers you get will be cast in the most positive light possible. Still, by requiring specific answers, you'll generate details regarding the candidate's personal style and expectations.

Let's take the case of Emma White, a candidate for IT manager at a plastics manufacturing organization outside of Springdale, Arkansas. She was applying for a position that would oversee a staff of ten programmer analysts, technical writers, and PC-user support reps. Her mandate, if hired, would be to increase morale in a department with lots of tenure but little enthusiasm for change and within one year transition the department from an HP3000 to a Windows client-server environment.

Here's how Emma responded to the query about how things would change after she was hired:

➡ "I like to hold a lot of meetings. It's important to me that everyone in my unit feels tied in to the bigger picture, and without that added element of human interaction, I find it difficult to bring a staff of people together in a coordinated effort. Not only do those meetings keep us all abreast of what's going on at a more global level, but they also give the staff a chance to surface new and creative ideas to make operations run more smoothly. After all, a roundtable brainstorming session gets my creative juices up and running, and I've found that it works well for others, too.

"In terms of increasing morale, those two or three roundtable meetings each week would make up step one of a plan designed to improve morale. I would also designate certain members of the department to lead meetings—depending on their areas of expertise—and depend on them to raise others' morale. Finally, I would propose holding companywide meetings to sell our IT services to the rest of the organization. For example, we could train company employees in word processing, spreadsheet, and email skills. We'd cost out how much an outside service would charge for such training, and then we'd deliver those cost savings to senior management as part of our formal proposal to begin training.

"In the meantime, I would enroll my staff in Windows client-server courses that would enhance their technical skills, so that by the time we came to the conversion start date next year, their confidence and competence would smooth the transition process. That plan should work to increase departmental morale; have spillover, morale-boosting effects for the rest of the company; and simultaneously ease our transition to the new software applications."

So how did Emma score? She made an excellent case for empowering her staff by pushing responsibility and accountability down the line. Her desire to tie staff members into the more global picture seems attainable because she'll get her IT people (a staff function) focused on profit and loss line considerations by having them cost out external training programs and then delivering a cost-benefit analysis. And her commitment to her staff's broader educational goals shows that she'll make good use of her first year on the job because the planned transition to the client-server platform won't begin until her second year.

The response to this question can provide some valuable insights into a new and improved departmental corporate culture that may be compatible with the company's style of doing business. And if the candidate's answer isn't compatible, then this detailed picture of life ninety days into the job should provide you with enough information to confirm that you want a different style of manager at the helm of your IT team.

95

7.

The College Campus Recruit

Interviewing newly minted graduates has its own unique challenges because so little of their experience has any relevance to real life in the business world. That's not to say that these students haven't worked hard to maintain a solid grade point average or to finance their educations. Nor does it in any way minimize the skills they've developed through team sports, fraternity leadership, or travel abroad. It's just that their university experiences don't easily lend themselves to measurable business criteria, and therein lies your challenge.

That being the case, many interviewers find themselves in the land of hypothetical questions. And hypothetical "What would you do if . . ." questioning formats reveal little insight into how candidates will perform on the job. Indeed, if there is one area of interviewing that can be rehearsed and memorized, it's the hypothetical situation. That's because hypothetical questions test the candidates' abilities only to theorize about their potential performance. Also, candidates are given so much freedom to express themselves that their responses are prone to exaggeration.

So instead of asking candidates to hypothesize about life in the business world, you're better off meeting them at their level and asking behavioral questions regarding their reality: life on campus. For what you need to measure in the new graduate is the same as what you gauge in a timeworn businessperson: the quality of the person's character. After all, any new hire is simply a bet that you make in terms of the individual's potential to give your company a competitive advantage someday. That's why you can justify the fact that you'll most likely take a loss in the new hire's first year while you're putting all that training into the person.

Still, characteristics like common sense, tenacity, reliability, and leadership go a long way in making your company a more successful operation. And everyone's got to start somewhere, so targeting eager and hungry graduates ready to make their mark on the world may make sense for you. You've just got to be sure of two things: first, that the candidates are somewhat aware of what they want in life (otherwise your company becomes one of the frogs that need to be kissed before they find their prince), and second, that the graduates' strengths can readily be translated from an academic to a business context. Following are some questions that should help you make more accurate assessments of recent graduates' abilities to have a solid impact on your company over time.

Why did you choose your [college/major]?

Why Ask This Question?

Let's be practical, because most larger universities probably offer close to one hundred majors from which to choose. The four with the most direct real-life practical application are engineering, premed, computer science, and business. Does that mean that those political science, anthropology, communications, and geography majors have little to offer? Of course not. Keep in mind, however, that unless you're hiring for one of the Big 4 accounting firms, you'll have about a 95 percent chance of interviewing students with majors that have little relevance to your direct line of business. So employing this query will allow you to tunnel inside their heads for a moment and gauge what interests them and why.

Analyzing the Response

This is obviously an opening query to get the candidate talking freely. It's no doubt the most often asked question in the on-campus interview, but it serves its purpose because it puts candidates at ease while providing you with a framework from which to judge the rest of their responses. Bear in mind that 80 percent of the hire is determined in the first few minutes of the interview. Candidates with clearly defined responses to such a macro issue will place themselves at the top of the pile right from the get-go.

Your goal in evaluating the response will be to look for career managers and career builders in the making.

Good Answers. For example, if someone chooses a university because it has one of the best academic programs in that individual's major field of study, there is a strong chance that the candidate had her eye on that college while still in high school. If so, you might ask, "What did you have to achieve in high school to make the final cut to get into this university?" Such long-term insights on the candidate's part reveal a commitment to project completion and a high tolerance for adversity. In short, this person reaches the goals she sets for herself.

Furthermore, if a candidate chooses an economics major because he feels that the lateral thinking skills developed in those studies would prepare him better for studying law, then similarly view that person as a long-term career builder who will most likely finish what he starts. What about the German major who wants a chance to study abroad and understand the psychology of a people by studying their literature and poetry as opposed to their history and politics? Ditto. Does it matter whether the economics major decided against law school or the German major against a career in foreign diplomacy? Of course not. The point is that these students reveal a quality of character difficult to find nowadays: a premeditated devotion and an unceasing follow-up to academic areas that mean a lot to them. Look for these macro visionaries ten years later, and you'll find leaders in all fields of business.

33

How does your degree prepare you (a) for a career in industry or (b) to excel as a [job title]?

Why Ask This Question?

Moving deductively from the generic to the specific, this query asks candidates to make a causal connection between their academic majors and their targeted first positions out of college. It will not only justify why the candidates have chosen to interview with your firm, but it may also provide insights into graduates' inclinations to research a situation before committing to it.

For example, before conducting on-campus interviews, you would typically forward your annual report and public relations materials to the university placement center. Candidates who research your organization in advance and ask questions related to your organization's market niche, short-term challenges, or the outside influences that have a direct impact on your business operations clearly separate themselves from their peers. And since most universities offer Internet services, even if you haven't provided your company's annual report in advance, there's little excuse for a graduating senior—even in the midst of finals—not to have taken ten minutes to visit your company's website or otherwise perform some advanced research on your company.

Analyzing the Response

How to Get More Mileage out of the Question. Asking graduates "How has your degree prepared you for a career in advertising?" or "How has your degree prepared you to excel as a staff accountant at our Big 6 accounting firm?" should reveal the link in the candidate's career progression from academia to business. Here again, you'll be faced with something of a jump in imagination as candidates relate their theoretical studies to real-life future performance. Your challenge will be to equate excellence in general skill categories with specific functions back at the office.

For example, a graduate who worked as a research assistant is probably inquisitive and resourceful enough to handle a position that requires investigative skills. Similarly, someone who writes for the school paper reveals a creative bent. Editors of that same school paper are probably more inclined to analysis. And student tutors probably have more of a knack for public speaking and customer service. There's no absolute matrix that will clearly place certain college-related activities into a business context, so translating from academia to business isn't a cut-and-dried science. That's why interviews are in essence opinions about an individual's ability to provide you with a profitable return on investment over time. And that's also what makes the evaluation process fun and challenging.

34

What experience do you have beyond academics that qualifies you to make a successful transition into business?

Why Ask This Question?

Students with a broad base of extracurricular activities and community involvement show a high capacity for dealing with changing priorities and balancing multiple tasks. That's not to say that students who do little beyond their expected course work can't perform as well in an environment with last-minute changes and competing demands. As a matter of fact, the competition among premed students is so intense that one-tenth of a point's difference on their grade point average could determine which graduate schools accept or reject them. So if you're hiring doctors, then you'll probably value academic genius above all else.

Still, most businesses require well-rounded individuals with lots to give in terms of networking with other businesspeople, attending industry-related functions, and finding time to make a presence in the community. Therefore, extracurricular activities say a lot about graduates' inclinations to make broad-based contributions to multiple organizations.

Analyzing the Response

Only you can determine how much extracurricular activity is enough as far as your organizational hiring profile is concerned. And only you can discern what grade point average will suffice to predict success in your company. But there obviously has to be a practical trade-off between the number of nonacademic activities and candidates' final grade point averages because they can't be studying when marching around the football field, playing the trumpet, or working in the neighborhood grocery store thirty hours a week to finance their educations.

Extracurricular qualifications consequently come in two varieties: (1) school-related and community-based activities and (2) working arrangements to finance an education. Both are noble in terms of their broadening the depth of students' appreciation and heightening the whole experience of advanced learning. Additionally, some crucial issues may surface that provide clearer insights into the candidate-evaluation process.

Those students who participate in the same school-related activities for all four years reveal a level of commitment and discipline that is not easily shaken. The continuity in their actions also shows that they have fairly well come to terms with their strengths and interests and pursue them steadfastly. Others explore multiple activities and disciplines before (if ever) committing to one that can apparently hold their interest. Again, there's nothing wrong with that; not everyone will be a four-year letterman on the football team.

 But it is interesting to see how diverse and eclectic those students' elective activities turn out. For example, someone who's tried everything from swim team to chess club to sorority membership may appear somewhat flighty and inconsistent. If you notice that each of those memberships lasted no more than a semester, then you might logically reason that the individual has difficulty committing to longer-term organizational relationships. Whether that's enough to ultimately serve as a negative swing factor is up to you. The inconsistency, however, is telling.

How to Get More Mileage out of the Question. In comparison, students who work flipping hamburgers, waiting tables, or tutoring other students will most likely appreciate the value of their educations from a dollars-and-cents standpoint. These are the self-made, independent types who typically rely on no one other than themselves for their success or failure. What they lack in terms of enriching extracurricular experiences they make up for in a heightened sense of self-reliance and self-determination. Accordingly, you might ask:

➡ "What particular business skills did you develop while working your way through college?"

➡ "How might you have an advantage over a peer who was enjoying fraternity life and other fun activities while you were employed in a less-than-glamorous job?"

➡ "How could the adversity you faced from the pressure of meeting your financial obligations affect your work ethic and approach to business?"

In short, look for the skills, values, and work ethic developed from hard labor. As they say, hard work never killed anybody. Combined with the pressures of meeting demanding academic performance standards, such a rigorous agenda of activities portends a particularly successful transition into business.

Do you think your grades are a good indicator of your ability to succeed in business?

Why Ask This Question?

Ah, tough question. But it certainly gets right to the heart of the matter. After all, every interview deserves its challenging moments. As a matter of fact, some employers choose to really lay on the pressure with queries such as, "Why are your grades so erratic? Why didn't you get better grades? Did you really think that a psychology major would qualify you to land a job in a company like ours?" These pressure cookers, however, can unnerve even the most self-confident candidates. Unless you're looking for someone who can really take rejection and deal in a boiler-room environment, you're better off leaving these nasty questions out of your interviewing agenda. They build little goodwill and test nothing other than the candidate's ability to tell you what you want to hear.

Analyzing the Response

Are grades in and of themselves clear indicators of potential job performance? To answer that, think about your own career experience. If you were clearly a C student and now rank within the top fifth percentile of sales producers in your company, then your need to locate a straight-A student will probably be negligible. If, on the other hand, you were a straight-A student and made a stellar transition into an insurance company as an actuary, then you might logically reason that academic grades necessarily correlate to logical thought patterns and self-imposed discipline.

The point is that most people hire in their own image. Grades, consequently, may reflect an individual's potential performance, but that's not guaranteed. What's more important in the interview process, though, is how the student feels about the correlation between grades and work potential. If the candidate immediately begins to apologize for less-than-stellar grades, beware: You might end up with someone lacking self-esteem and confidence in his abilities. On the other hand, if the individual fails to come to terms with his flagging academic performance, then you may be faced with a graduate who fails to assume responsibility for his actions and who bends the truth to subjectively paint pictures in his favor.

What's the ideal answer? An open admission of the individual's short-comings. Few graduates sport straight-A grades. For example, consider someone who responds like this:

➡ "I was a B-minus student and took five years to complete my degree, but I worked thirty hours a week to finance my education, and I was the first in my family to attend college. I'm proud of my performance and did the best I could with the time and resources available to me."

This individual accepts her shortcomings and reveals a healthy ego. Similarly, a response like the following accounts for what the student was doing when not studying:

➡ "I had a C average as an English major, but I was awarded the Freshman of the Year Award in the marching band and served my fraternity as president in my senior year."

There's a very healthy trade-off between time at study and time holding leadership roles on campus, so that balance atones for a less-than-perfect grade point average.

By contrast, beware the student who blames others for her failures. A nagging and complaining tone like "Well, I could've had better grades if I didn't have to work all the time," or "My 2.5 GPA corresponds to a 3.5 GPA if I hadn't participated in so many community-based activities and had as much time to study as everyone else" portends poor performance. After all, no one needs to apologize for less-than-perfect grades. More important, no one should blame others for circumstances beyond her control. That's a trait that definitely translates from academia to business, and it's a headache that you need to avoid.

36

What other types of positions and companies are you considering right now?

Why Ask This Question?

This question helps you accurately assess what kind of expectations a graduate has for himself. If those plans are realistic and logically tie into what your organization has to offer, then there's an excellent chance you won't be one of those frogs that many recent grads have to kiss before they find their prince. If the individual's plans are too casual or undeveloped, on the other hand, there may be a serious lack of commitment to starting a business career.

Analyzing the Response

Whenever possible, most college grads will attempt to find a position that ties into their majors. Foreign-language majors apply to the diplomacy schools to ultimately become ambassadors to the United Nations; film majors send their résumés to the major Hollywood studios; physical education majors contact professional and collegiate football, basketball, and baseball franchises; and physical anthropology majors apply to become docents at the nearest museum of natural history. So what should it tell you when a film major is applying to your plastics manufacturing organization for an entry-level sales position? Probably that the heavens are out of sync and the individual isn't totally dedicated to making your company a lifelong pursuit.

How to Get More Mileage out of the Question. To gather more data, ask questions like these:

➡ "Mary, you were a film major. If you could rub on a magic lamp and apply your studies directly to the working world, what would you ideally be doing? Why are you interviewing for positions other than those in the film world? How long would you realistically expect it to take to land your first job in the film industry, and what will you do in the meantime while you're waiting for your first break?"

Your assumption in this situation is clear to the candidate: Why aren't you seeking to use immediately the knowledge and skills you worked so hard to gain over the past four years?

Your assumption to yourself will be equally lucid: "There's some reason why this person isn't looking for a job in the film business. I've got to find out, though, before I tempt fate and bring her aboard." You are entitled, after all, to continuity in the positions you fill. If a candidate wants to get her feet wet in the business world, she should temp for a while rather than accept a full-time position with a half-hearted commitment.

Next, it's critical that you gauge the caliber of companies and industries that the candidate is pursuing in addition to your opportunity. If all the positions are in the financial services arena in some capacity related to customer service, then you're safe in assuming that the individual's consistency reveals her true desires. If the candidate is interviewing all over the map, with meetings set up for retail positions, office administrative work, and product manufacturing, then she probably lacks direction.

Having eclectic tastes and an inquisitive, experimental nature can be a virtue in certain circumstances, but it's a disadvantage when searching for a first job. Simply ask the candidate:

➡ "Doris, I see that you're exploring very diverse opportunities. What criteria are you using in selecting your career path? How would you rank the various opportunities in terms of your interest level?"

Forcing the situation could cause the candidate some discomfort, but it will help clarify for you exactly where your opportunity stands in her pecking order. And that will help ensure that the bet you're making regarding this individual's potential minimizes the downside risk that she'll be gone before you've had a chance to recoup your investment in training.

College campus interviewing is one of the most exhilarating areas of career evaluation because of the candidates' excitement and eagerness to open a new chapter in their lives and to make a contribution that will lead to serious income and independence. Evaluating candidates correctly will help you learn which ones are apt to influence your company most positively. Your skilled questioning techniques will also serve to teach them more about themselves—their desires, strengths, limitations, and motivations—on their way to new career paths.

8.

Millennials

The Newest Generation of Your Workforce

Between 2011 and 2029, seventy-seven million baby boomers will transition into retirement. The natural offset will be found in the seventy million or so millennials taking their place. Workplace demographics in the United States are usually categorized into four segments:

1. *Traditionalists*—born prior to 1946
2. *Baby Boomers*—born 1946–1964 (who began retiring in 2011)
3. *Generation X*—born 1965–1980
4. *Millennials*—born 1981–2000

It's this fourth group that seems to be getting the most press coverage because it represents the future of corporate America. Being the largest generation since the baby boom, millennials represent a huge economic and social force and may already be the most-studied generation in history.

The millennial generation—also known as generation Y, the Net generation, and the IM generation—is the most tech-savvy generation that's ever graced our planet. And navigating generational politics in the office has never been as critical as it is today, thanks to this workforce that has no recognition of life without cell phones, the Internet, social media, instant messaging (IM), email, text messaging, and personal electronic entertainment.

Millennials grew up in a society where children's self-esteem was consciously nurtured, and they've benefited from the longest economic boom in history. As a result of their experience, unique values have developed that make them different from generations that came before. And due to their sheer size and the key responsibility that's befallen them—picking up where the baby boomers will leave off—they've become a force to be reckoned with, both in terms of hiring and retention.

This generation is known for its confidence—not just the natural confidence of youth but an assuredness that comes from growing up in prosperous economic times. They demonstrate high levels of trust and optimism and can balance ambition with practicality. They're socially conscious, focused on achievement, diverse, and fairly street smart. In short, most demographers would sum them up as bright, ambitious, concerned, and amazingly connected through technology.

That said, millennials represent specific challenges to employers. Negatively characterized as narcissistic and entitled, these newcomers have been accused of demonstrating a penchant for self-indulgence, IM shorthand illiteracy, and shorter attention spans. In addition, you'll be faced with a generation that is used to getting a lot of praise and not much censuring, so the traditional understanding of what constitutes constructive criticism may become a common workplace issue—and one that needs to be addressed during the interview process.

In addition, remember that millennials tend to blur private and public communication. Because of the availability of technology that's allowed them to post their innermost secrets on Facebook or SnapChat as well as videos of themselves on YouTube, their level of sensitivity toward protecting company confidential information may not be well developed.

Most important, remember that this generation communicates differently. Shorthand IM and text messages don't require a lot of face-to-face negotiation, and they may be less inclined to communicate in person. This is particularly an issue when there is conflict. So you may need to provide special care when it comes to the appropriate amount of structure, direction, and feedback they'll require on a daily basis, as well as guidance in terms of face-to-face communication with customers and older coworkers.

You may also find that these young newcomers are looking for more appreciation and open communication than you're normally used to giving—especially during the initial interview process. And maybe they're right. Perhaps it's time to simplify the interviewing equation on both sides so that the interview itself becomes an exercise of value rather than a game of wits, strategies, and defenses that simply provides gateway access into a company.

The key to this kind of simpler, more open interviewing style lies in engaging candidates' hearts as well as their minds by employing an open and honest dialogue that focuses just as much on their needs as on the needs of your company. If you tend to hire lots of workers under age thirty, this chapter is for you. Let's look at some interview questioning strategies that may identify the best that these younger workers have to offer while avoiding some of the potential pitfalls that may come your way.

37

If you were to accept this position with us today, how would you explain that to a prospective employer five years from now? How would this job provide a link in your future career progression?

Why Ask This Question?

If millennials are looking for employers to meet them halfway in providing a work experience that truly benefits both parties, then it's critical to begin the interview by understanding how candidates see the job helping them over the long run. It's a tougher question for candidates to answer at first glance because it demands a fairly significant amount of career introspection and individual insight, but the selfless nature of the question will help them understand your desire to make it a mutually beneficial relationship.

Analyzing the Response

Forcing someone to make the link between accepting a position now and its benefit to their career five years from now places you into the role of executive mentor and coach, which in itself portends well for the relationship. Few interviewers employ this technique, which forces the candidate to sell himself on accepting the position or self-selecting out of the process. Think of the beauty of the query, however: You'll have shifted the career development paradigm to the preemployment process, which makes for a positive impression of your company. And the candidate will naturally think, "Wow, if they challenge you with these kinds of questions during the interview process, they're obviously serious about career development and growing their people once you're on board."

And you certainly can expect candidates to think, "Wow, I've never been asked that before and haven't really given it much thought." However, you'll end up with a great opportunity to observe candidates talk through their immediate career needs and longer-term goals out loud and on the spot. Talk about getting to know the real candidate during the interview process.

Let's look at an example. A senior financial analyst from a competitor firm is interviewing for the same position at your company. He's been at his current company for three years and has a total of five years of experience as a senior financial analyst and senior staff accountant. You're thinking, "Why would he want another senior analyst role right now? Why isn't he looking for a manager-level position, and what's blocking his progression at this current company?"

The candidate responds to your initial five-year impact question as follows:

➡ "Well, I haven't quite thought of it that way. I feel blocked at my current company from getting ahead, but you're right [wincing]: If I were to accept this lateral position right now, it really wouldn't do all that much for my résumé five years from now. I guess maybe this wouldn't be the right position if I want to grow in my career and assume greater responsibilities and title progression."

And voilà, your career-counseling skills thrust the interview into a whole new direction, allowing you to help this candidate get to the real reason behind his job search and the ultimate fit within your organization. In this case, it didn't work to your advantage in terms of hiring the individual. However, that doesn't mean you wouldn't hire him six months from now when a finance manager role becomes available.

This question may seem like it's primarily for the candidate's benefit. In reality, it's primarily for your benefit as the employer. The selfless nature of the question will always be well received, but you'll get to answer the critical questions that will ultimately make this candidate a strong fit: Is this individual thinking through his career options sufficiently, does he have the necessary longer-term career mentality that you're looking for, and will he remain around long enough for you to recoup your up-front investment in onboarding and training? If not, then asking the question now will save you lots of time and money by avoiding the turnover that certainly could happen six months from now, once the honeymoon is over and the individual realizes he was pursuing change for change's sake. (Note that this question works particularly well when you're interviewing someone who appears to be overqualified for a position.)

38

What was the most difficult ethical decision you've ever had to make in your career or during your education, and what was the outcome?

Why Ask This Question?

The millennials were affected by a number of historic events in their lifetimes: September 11, the Iraq War, the Columbine High School tragedy, and, in the workplace, the Sarbanes-Oxley Act of 2002. If that last one doesn't register quite as high as the first few mentioned, its effects are certainly felt in the office.

Millennials are known for being a "corrective" generation, committed to bettering the environment, strongly responding to sexual harassment in schools and at work, and ending corporate greed and corruption. The Sarbanes-Oxley Act of 2002, also known as "SOX," has mandated codes of conduct and workplace ethics statements in publicly traded companies that require ongoing training and certification as well as disclosure of potential conflicts of interest. And this workplace ethics standard has found its way into private and not-for-profit institutions as well, which makes this question a fair one for the younger generation.

Analyzing the Response

Some of the more astute candidates may have answers right off the bat to your initial inquiry, but others may need a little prompting, like this: "Ethics in the workplace has to do with sexual harassment, discrimination, and even potential violence in the workplace. Have you been involved in any of those types of events?" If you're still getting a clueless look back from the candidate, ask: "Has anyone ever asked you to speak off the record at work, and if so, have you granted that request?"

A typical answer may be, "Sure. People have asked me to talk off the record on more than one occasion. Is that an ethical issue?" And your response might be, "It certainly could be. We all respect others' privacy, but when it comes to maintaining workplace confidences, how do you know when it's best not to say anything versus when you have an obligation to disclose the information to your supervisor and to the company?"

This will generally trigger a conversation about workplace sensitivity levels, confidentiality, loyalty, and the like. Remembering that this generation has grown up sharing private information on personal web pages that grant access to "invited" friends, the conversation could easily turn toward matters of corporate confidentiality and nondisclosure as follows:

➡ "Mary, if someone asks you to talk off the record and you grant their request, what if they tell you that they're being harassed by their supervisor? Do you have an obligation to disclose that to the company or not?"

Similarly:

➡ "If someone makes an off-handed remark that they're feeling like they want to take one of their hunting rifles and 'do some justice' back in the office, how would you respond in terms of being torn between protecting their confidence and sharing that potential threat with management?"

➡ "Finally, what if a coworker said that he wanted to post internal company information to a corporate gossip blog because he was very dissatisfied with the way management handled a particular issue? Would you feel compelled to say something to management in advance, or would you simply let it be?"

These aren't meant to be easy questions, and younger candidates may often assume that you're looking for them to be more concerned about others' privacy rather than risk being seen as a disloyal snitch. However, younger workers, because of their tech-savviness and penchant for sharing personal feelings via electronic means, may indeed jeopardize your company's interests if they're not sensitized to these matters during the interview and during the initial onboarding process in orientation.

Before the candidate ponders these challenging questions too deeply, you have a good opportunity to jump in and outline your expectations:

➡ "Mary, I'm not asking you these questions to make you uncomfortable. However, I know that these very issues typically come up in the workplace as well as in corporate ethics training seminars and that most people have had some sort of experience with them, either firsthand or as an observer.

"I want to be clear about this as it's a very important workplace expectation here: In our company, we ask that employees do not engage in public blogging about confidential matters. In addition, if someone were feeling harassed or discriminated against, we would expect their fellow workers to help them by letting management know about the problem, under the assumption that people are sometimes afraid to get help for themselves for fear of retaliation. Simply stated, if we don't know about it, we can't fix it. Same thing with the gun example: We take potential threats, whether direct or veiled, very seriously and always want to provide our workers with a safe environment, even if that means meeting with an employee who made a flippant comment for a laugh.

"If you were to accept a position with our company, we'd want you to know in advance of your starting with us how strongly we feel about helping others and ensuring safety in the workplace. It's all about corporate responsibility and good citizenship. These values are simply too important for us not to address in the initial candidate screening process.

"Oh, by the way, the next time a coworker asks you to speak off the record about something at work, tell the individual, 'Maybe. As long as it doesn't have to do with harassment, discrimination, potential violence, or some other conflict of interest with the company, then you're free to talk away to your heart's content. Otherwise, I'm afraid I won't be able to keep it confidential.' See how it works now?"

And once again, you'll have provided candidates with quite a gift: workplace training and sensitivity to real-life situations they could encounter in the office. You'll have addressed your corporate expectations of honesty and confidentiality while demonstrating your commitment to ethics and corporate responsibility. Now that's a question geared toward the millennial generation's heart.

39

How would you describe "professional behavior" in the workplace?

Why Ask This Question?

Millennials generally define themselves as casual and laid back in terms of dress code and appearance. This is the generation of lip rings, tattoo sleeves, body art, and all sorts of self-expression. Whether you notice any of these items during your interview, addressing your expectations during the interview is probably a good idea, especially if you have a more conservative dress code.

Analyzing the Response

Candidates will typically address a question regarding professional behavior in terms of employee conduct, behaviors, and attitudes. And that's a good place to start. You might embellish your initial query by asking something along the lines of:

➡ "What constitutes exceptional customer service in your opinion? Give me an example of a time when you exceeded a customer's expectations."

➡ "Job security often comes in the form of customers and clients who find that they couldn't live without you. Have you ever had a customer write you a letter of recommendation or otherwise insinuate that you're the reason they keep coming back for more business?"

➡ "Have you ever experienced poor customer service either by a coworker or as a customer yourself? What did it look like, how did it make you feel, and what lesson did you take away from the experience?"

Next, your goal will be to move this question into the "appearance" direction. Remember that just because a candidate appears to interview in what you would consider appropriate dress doesn't mean that individual won't appear at work one day proudly demonstrating a new fashion decision.

Therefore, you might want to lead the conversation as follows:

➡ "Michael, you're dressed very appropriately for this interview, which is great, but I like to address the issue of appearance during meetings like this because it's an important aspect of who we are as a company.

"Let me start off by saying that I don't mean at all to dictate what people do in their personal lives and spare time. But I've got to ask you: Seeing that we're a bank and deal with high-net-worth individuals throughout the day, is there anything appearance-wise that you feel might be inappropriate to wear or sport in front of our clients?"

Understanding where you're going with this question, an astute candidate might answer, "Well, sure. I would expect every employee's attire to be neat and crisp at all times so as not to offend any clients and to be consistent with the image the bank represents."

This, in turn, would give you a grand opportunity to jump in with this natural follow-up query:

"Yes, I agree with you and feel the same way. Let me ask you one other question though. If you were in a management position here and noticed that one of your subordinates came to work sporting a lip ring or an eyebrow piercing or a huge neck tattoo, would you be comfortable asking that individual to remove the lip ring or cover the tattoo when dealing with the public so as not to alienate any of our clients?"

The value to this approach lies in its subtlety and reasonableness. Few companies have policies restricting facial hair on men or insisting that women wear dresses in the office. And even the Big 4 accounting firms' consultants now arrive at their assignments in more of a casual dress mode than in the blue suit and red tie combinations of the past. Still, body piercing and body art tend to result from revelations and epiphanies of what's cool, what's important in life, and what rights people believe they have over their own destinies. In short, it's not something to brush over lightly.

If your conversation leads to some kind of reasonable compromise where the candidate agrees that it would be reasonable to ask a subordinate to leave the hardware at home or to take it off whenever dealing with customers (if possible), then you'll have accomplished your goal. That's because if he would ask it of a subordinate, he would probably find it reasonable to do himself. Employees who feel they've been treated respectfully and not simply been told what to do will almost always agree to some kind of modification, which will please the company and also allow the employees to maintain their individuality. It's all about maintaining respect and dignity in the workplace, even in matters having to do with personal taste and self-expression.

40

I see you've had a tango or two at the Job Hoppers' Ball. How do you plan on rebuilding your résumé from a longevity standpoint?

Why Ask This Question?

One of the red flags frequently documented about this younger generation has to do with its flightiness—a commitment to "Me, Inc." rather than to a company. It poses a real challenge to the stability of your company operations and to their careers if it's not addressed and managed. Much like the baby boomers who saw their parents commit themselves to a company for lifetime employment only to be laid off and cast aside, the willingness to act as a free agent makes intuitive sense for a generation surrounded by new technologies and new opportunities.

That said, too much change may damage their candidacy, even if they don't realize it. Therefore, the interview once again provides a unique opportunity for getting inside individuals' heads in terms of how they see longer-term commitment while educating them about the importance of longevity in building their résumés and careers.

Analyzing the Response

We addressed issues surrounding career stability in Chapter 4, "Questions About Career Stability." However, with millennials, this takes on even greater importance. If you're recruiting for skilled professionals in a tight job market, you may be forced to engage job-hopper candidates with spotty employment histories and little apparent staying power or commitment to their prior companies. And because of market competition, you may not have the discretion to simply pass on individuals who have held four jobs in the last three years. Indeed, these individuals sometimes appear to be holding all the cards in terms of negotiating for signing bonuses and other perks once reserved for senior levels of management.

True, markets slow down, and a sense of normalcy gets restored from time to time. *Translation:* These career opportunists who pride themselves on being "recruiters' bait" waiting to jump at the next offer with an exponential increase in pay or perks may have the wind taken out of their sails. Indeed, prime jobs may actually return to those candidates who have been managing their careers correctly, according to more traditional norms: longevity with one company, progression through the ranks, and a broadening of responsibilities.

Still, the technical marketplace is morphing so quickly that identifying and retaining talent in areas such as IT, digital gaming, and biotech research remains exceptionally challenging for employers. Therefore, you may find that entertaining younger candidates with spotty résumés may become a mainstay of the recruiting landscape. The key to your interviewing strategy will lie in discussing the merits of longevity with the candidate.

Historically, that part of the equation was the candidate's responsibility. Employers didn't babysit and ask interviewing questions based on why joining the new company would make sense for the candidate from a career-progression standpoint. No more. The only real way to determine if candidates will provide you with a satisfactory return on investment for hiring them is to question their career-development and career-management goals. Once you understand if your job makes sense to them from a career-building standpoint, then you can estimate how long they'll remain with your company once the honeymoon phase is over.

Here's how you might kick off the questioning string:

➡ "Ashley, I see that you've held four full-time positions since you graduated from college three years ago. That's a fairly significant amount of movement. What would you say is a healthy amount of time to remain with a company—any company, not just ours?"

From there, you might want to reverse focus your question as follows:

➡ "Let me ask you this: If you were hiring someone for this position at your company, how important would prior longevity be to you in terms of a candidate's background, and how much would you expect to see?"

Finally, your closer would sound something like this:

➡ "Yeah, I agree. I think that one of the most important things that companies look for is longevity. In short, it's their ultimate return on investment, seeing that all the costs relating to recruitment, onboarding, and training can be very expensive. Every company wants to have stability in its ranks. But I'm sharing this with you not only to point out the benefits to the company but to you as well.

"You've been out of school long enough now that an employer like me would expect you to have kissed all the appropriate frogs and started to hone in on your prince. Whether it's with our organization or some other company, make sure that the next position you accept will be broad enough and have enough challenge so you could make a solid two- to three-year commitment. No one's expecting you to retire with your next company, but you'll want to build that longevity to strengthen your candidacy and build your résumé."

Now, that's a good response because it speaks directly to the candidates' career interests while once again emphasizing your expectations. Besides, if you don't shed some light on the damage they're doing to their career, who will? And by qualifying your response by saying, "Whether it's with our organization or some other company," your advice will be taken as objective and in the candidates' best interests.

41

Who is your typical reading audience when you're writing something, and what level of language do you use?

Why Ask This Question?

The evolving lexicon of instant-messaging has often been referred to as "e-illiteracy" and "IM-glish" in the sense that the writers have created their own jargon that may save them time and prove they're cool but may also alienate the non-IM generation. In fact, rules of grammar and syntax have in many cases fallen by the wayside in a world where kids grow up reading "ty ttyl" and understanding "Thank you. Talk to you later."

How much negative impact this Net lingo's lazy shorthand will have on the workplace is just now being seen, but it's certainly worth addressing in light of this younger generation's pride in expressing itself in its own unique way. Yes, to some it's just a creative twist on dialogue—a harmless version of teen slang. But to your workplace, new acronyms, abbreviations, run-on sentences, and emoticons (keyboard characters that resemble human gestures or expressions, like smiley faces) may leave some of your more mature workers feeling a bit isolated and unimpressed with this younger generation's grammatical shortcomings. Focusing your question on a so-called typical reading audience may help uncover applicants' penchants for expressing themselves appropriately in the workplace.

Analyzing the Response

One fairly common response to this question may be, "I live by IM and by email, and I'm comfortable addressing anyone within the company who needs my help or who could help me solve a problem."

That's a fair enough response, but it's also logical to take it to another level: "How would you define your overall writing style? And from the standpoint of traditional grammar, punctuation, and syntax, would you consider your writing abilities basic, intermediate, or advanced?"

Now, this is where the fun begins. Truth be told, this is a valid question for any job candidate—not just for millennials who may suffer from bad writing habits. But in the context of generational analysis, it certainly lends itself well to the preemployment screening process.

➡ "I feel my writing style is fairly informal but appropriate for a business audience, although English wasn't my favorite subject in school, and writing more than a few lines in an email isn't typically necessary to get your point across."

A logical follow-up might be:

➡ "Hmmm. Tell me about a longer and fairly complex document that you've had to put together recently. Who was your audience in that particular situation, and how did you tailor it to fit their needs?"

The candidate, a contract administrator, might respond like this:

➡ "Well, we had gotten approval to award an executive under contract with a 6 percent annual contractual increase. The merit range for people under contract was 4 to 6 percent, so this was within guidelines and didn't raise any eyebrows.

"However, once I got it approved, the supervisor came back to me and asked that we increase the 6 percent annual merit raise to 10 percent, which was out of guidelines and would require a number of additional approvals.

"As a result, I created an email string that first went to corporate compensation to ensure that, from an internal equity standpoint, we wouldn't be overpaying this executive relative to her peer group. With the written approval from our compensation group, I forwarded the email to our corporate finance person to ensure that there was money in the budget for the expense variance, which I confirmed. I was then able to send that entire email string to our COO, outlining again my case for the exceptional increase, along with compensation's and finance's approval. It was approved on the first shot because it had all the necessary blessings contained within the email thread. The supervisor was very appreciative of my turning things around so quickly."

And voilà. The response demonstrates the individual's problem-solving abilities in addition to the audience he's capable of writing for—in this case, human resources, the finance department, and the company's COO.

Combined with what you saw when you reviewed the individual's résumé and employment application, you probably have good reason to believe that even if this person grew up in and participates in the world of IM shorthand, he certainly can write for a corporate business audience.

However, what if this candidate had responded, "I don't write memos or narratives often, but I do rely on text messaging to my coworkers to get information on new and existing accounts"? In that case, it's a fair comeback on your part to address appropriate business writing skills and expectations in your workplace. For example, "Janet, when you write your coworkers using your company's IM system, do you write in what I would call 'Internet shorthand' or do you write in *English*?"

That should generate a chuckle. More important, it will get the candidate talking about when she feels that it is acceptable to use IM shorthand among workplace friends and peers and when that type of written communication might be inappropriate.

You might follow up with, "Are there times when you feel it could make others feel uncomfortable to use shorthand terms when writing to a broader audience?" or "When do you feel that 'IM speak' might even cast someone in a bad light from the standpoint of the individual not coming across as literate and well educated?"

Your close might then be: "I agree. I understand that, at times, IM shorthand and 'keyboard vernacular' may be appropriate in the workplace, but please understand our expectations that this would be an exception to internal written communication rules. Of course, if you have agreement with a friend at work to communicate that way, we would understand that. More often than not, though, coworkers, especially older coworkers, may find that type of written communication offensive because if they can't understand it, they may feel isolated or simply 'not cool.' Are you comfortable with that level of sensitivity in your writings and internal communications?"

Again, your educational interviewing style will make for a powerful communication session because you'll not only be assessing the candidate's qualifications but also sharing your wisdom and insights into success in corporate America—advice and counsel that works in the best interests of the candidate and, ultimately, your company.

And because there's such demand for more information about millennials, please see the two following bonus questions to help you round out your evaluations of these candidates.

BONUS QUESTION 8A: Where do you relate best: up one level, down one level, or with peers?

Why Ask This Question?

As a rule, the younger an employee, the more comfortable he or she will be dealing directly with peers. It will naturally be more of a challenge dealing with supervisors (up one level) or subordinates (down one level), because earlier-career workers are learning how to navigate the subtleties of interpersonal communication and corporate etiquette. Still, some candidates may surprise you in their responses, both in terms of their selections as well as their justifications.

Analyzing the Response

If a candidate responds, "I'm probably most comfortable dealing with peers at this point in my career," you might ask, "What is it about peer relationships that makes you more comfortable?" and "How would you intend to develop that same level of comfort with supervisors and subordinates?"

A typical candidate response might sound like:

→ "Well, I think it takes time to get to know people and to get them to trust you. People respect competence, and over time, I would hope that both my supervisors and subordinates would respect the work I do and develop a trust in my abilities so that they could feel as comfortable with me as I would feel with them."

Bravo. That's a very enlightened response.

Be a bit wary, however, of earlier-career candidates who respond that they're more comfortable relating to supervisors and/or subordinates, as there may be some gratuitous intentions in their response. First, keep in mind that a candidate who responds that he is most comfortable dealing with his supervisors (one level up) may indeed have a thoroughly good reason for doing so. "I tend to focus on my work when I'm in the office, and I don't do a lot of gabbing with my peers, so I've always seemed to have a stronger relationship with my boss than my coworkers" is a perfectly reasonable response.

Likewise, someone may answer, "I've always had the strongest bond to my subordinates—I love managing and leading others as I consider myself a natural-born teacher, and nothing gives me more satisfaction than putting their needs above mine while watching people thrive and grow." In this case, you may very well have a natural leader on your hands who feels protective of her staff and encourages their growth and development.

On the other hand, other responses may throw up red flags that require additional vetting via a reference check. For example, "My bosses have always loved me and said that they didn't know what they'd do without me" is an arrogant and self-aggrandizing response that smacks of brown-nosing. Similarly, "I enjoy supervising because I'm a leader, people love to follow me, and that's where the company gets the greatest value out of me" sounds a bit pretentious and bombastic. Someone with that high a level of self-esteem may get in the way of the teamwork and camaraderie that you're trying to build in your workplace.

Likewise, you might follow up on your initial question by discussing contemporary sociology in the workplace: "They say that millennials get along well with baby boomers but have a hard time with generation Xers. Have you read much about that or studied generational politics in the workplace? If so, I'd love to hear your thoughts about that."

In any case, asking how a candidate sees himself in light of those above, below, and beside him in a workplace context may reveal aspects of his business maturity, social well-being, and natural communication style. More important, your conversation may lead to insights in terms of how he sees himself creating harmony in the workplace and building strong interpersonal ties with those around and above him (people of different generations)—a critical link in the hiring process for a generation that is known to suffer from a lack of developed face-to-face communication skills.

> **BONUS QUESTION 8B:** How would you grade yourself in terms of face-to-face communication, especially in terms of negotiation or confrontation? Do you consider that a strength or an area for personal development?

Why Ask This Question?

Well, we always want to save the best and most compelling questions for last. In this chapter, we've addressed everything from IM illiteracy to workplace confidentiality to corporate ethics and the importance of professional workplace behavior. Still, the chapter wouldn't be complete without discussing the mother of all workplace issues having to do with millennials—holding their own when it comes to communication, negotiation, and disagreement.

From the time they were young, millennials had cell phones. And they called each other directly, avoiding the need to speak with parents who answered the home phone and engage in small talk like, "This is Sam Falcone. How are you, Mr. Cleaver? Is Theodore home?" Likewise, to the chagrin of many high school teachers, these students managed to plant an ear bud from their iPods into their ears, which ran from their hip, up their undershirt, over their collar, and under their hair to drown out any unwanted "noise" coming from the front of the classroom. And their response to any undesirable communication with former friends was simply to use a software solution to block all incoming messages from that ex-friend's screen name.

Now those youngsters have grown up. However, their ability to tune out and disconnect, which electronic tools make so easy, is a bit more limited when dealing with real people who won't go away just because you don't like them.

As they say, the path of least resistance is avoidance. And people will tend to avoid confrontation at all costs, if possible. So why would we hold these early-career members of the workforce to a higher standard than the generations that came before them? Because prior generations were at least tested in this area. The newer generation, for all its advantages and positive characteristics, has yet to reveal its true colors in this universally human realm.

Analyzing the Response

Don't be surprised to see candidates shy away from this question. "Well, negotiation isn't a typical part of my current job, and I guess no one really likes confrontation, so I guess I'd say this is more of an area for development than an area of strength for me."

With this open admission, you have *carte blanche* to launch into a discussion that truly sets the stage for a successful hire:

"Dennis, we hire a significant number of younger adults in our organization who would fall squarely under the millennial category—basically, people born after 1980 and now somewhere under age 40. And this younger generation has some unique talents and abilities, especially in terms of its tech savviness. However, some of the folks of my generation have had challenges with the generational politics that come along with working side by side with younger workers who have different ideals and expectations. Let me ask you this—"

At that point, ask one of the following questions using a behavioral interviewing format like this:

- ➡ "Have you ever disagreed with your boss? If so, how did you voice your opinion, or did you voice it at all?"

- ➡ "Can you give me an example of how you've handled confrontation with a workplace peer? What were the circumstances, and did you feel a need to escalate the issue to management?"

- ➡ "Did you ever find yourself in the midst of what I would call generational politics, meaning that typically an older worker had a harder time relating to you or agreeing with your recommendation? How did you handle it, and what would you do differently in retrospect?"

- ➡ "Have you ever had to supervise someone who was significantly older than you or who didn't take you seriously? What was your approach to strengthening that working relationship?"

- ➡ "Give me an example of a time when you received constructive criticism but disagreed with the feedback you were being given. Did you simply respectfully listen or did you voice your disagreement?"

➡ "Negotiation can be a win-win or it can be a war of attrition, with one side winning by simply wearing the other side down. What's your natural negotiating style, and how do you define compromise in light of tough negotiations?"

➡ "If someone accused you of focusing more on your lifestyle and friends than on blind careerism, would you consider that a compliment or be offended? What is it about you that makes you feel that way?"

You'll have opened Pandora's box and given the candidate the opportunity to self-assess in light of your biggest concerns. Of course, there's no right or wrong answer here, but you can expect to see candidates who either pride themselves on their association with their cool generation—"Yes, companies are going to have to conform to our generation's way of doing business because there are more of us than there are of them"—or who can objectively differentiate themselves in certain ways. For example, a candidate who responds "Yes, in many ways I can see what you're saying, but I've always been a hard worker; I've held at least a summer job since I was 14, and my parents taught me to respect my elders and prove my worth" will probably transition into your workplace with enough sensitivity to make for a very successful hire.

And there you have it: a strong enough relationship in the interview process to outline your core concerns about a younger generation and its ultimate fit into your organization. Of course, you'll be able to close a desirable candidate at this point by aligning his responses with your company's expectations.

"Dennis, I'm listening to your responses, and it sounds to me as if you have the proper perspective and business maturity to excel in our organization. I read all the literature about millennials, their workplace expectations, and their strengths and shortcomings because, as you know, we tend to hire a lot of earlier-career candidates in our firm. So it becomes important to me to vet all applicants and ensure that they have the business maturity and objectivity to assess themselves in light of generational differences in the workplace.

"I feel that you've got that maturity and objectivity, and I'd like you to seriously consider the opportunity of joining us. Think about this interview overnight, and if you've slept on it and are still excited about the opportunity in the morning, give me a call so I can line up additional meetings for you. You've built your résumé and career very impressively, and strong companies like ours are always looking for candidates who excel and who stand out as rarities among their peers. I very much believe you're one of those candidates, and I'm looking forward to hearing from you."

Now that's a close. And you'll certainly have addressed your key concerns so that you won't lay awake at night wondering if you really got into the candidate's head and truly learned what makes him tick.

Is this interviewing strategy for millennials too much to ask? If you go to this depth of interviewing just to see if the individual has the necessary business maturity and career introspection to excel in your company, will you be accused of coddling and coaching rather than bossing?

Maybe. On the other hand, it's possible that all job candidates—not just millennials—should come to expect this level of commitment from the stewards and guardians of the companies where they'd like to work. But the truth is, if you're not matching the individual's personality to your company's corporate culture during the interviewing process, you may end up having to fill that position again six months later.

Instead, think out loud and share your opinions up front. In a way, you'll be putting the candidate's needs before the company's, and that kind of goodwill goes a long way with all hires, not just with the idealistically young.

I know that it's so tempting to hire the individual and let him worry about his own career progression and fit factor. Truth be told, though, you want all the pieces of the puzzle to fit together for the company and the candidate. If this new hire reveals all the benefits of the millennial generation—hardworking, resourceful, and committed—and your position offers a learning curve, new skill sets, broader responsibilities, and appropriate compensation, then everyone will be happy and the hire will stick.

In essence, you'll not only have helped junior members of the workforce gain new insights into how they should be looking at their own careers but you'll also develop a reputation as a skillful and selfless leader and developer of people. You'll have shifted the employee-development paradigm to the preemployment stage. And maybe candidates deserve those few extra minutes of your time to benefit from your expertise. You may just find that a little short-term sacrifice and career counseling on your part will lead to greater stability in your staff and a lot of goodwill in your own career.

9.

The Sales Interview

Differentiating Among Top Producers, Rebel Producers, and Those Who Struggle to the Minimums

No doubt about it: The sales interview is one of the most challenging evaluations you'll encounter, with a hefty impact on your organization's bottom line. That's because top producers often march to their own drummers. Some focus on the quantity of transactions, while others build relationships over the long haul. Some consistently produce in the stratosphere, while others merely earn enough to get by. Some have more of a nine-to-five mindset than an entrepreneurial mentality and consequently rarely perform with distinction. Still others unfortunately define success not in terms of their accomplishments but by their peers' failures. Although such rebel producers often close the month at the top of the charts, they pull down the production of their team members in the process.

So how do you determine the potential of the stockbroker or loan officer or computer sales representative sitting in front of you? Equally important, how do you assess the impact this individual will have in terms of complementing your existing staff? Bear in mind that your task will be made fuzzier by the fact that salespeople are skilled at saying all the right things and landing on their feet in cold-call situations—which is exactly what your interview represents to them. In addition, many salespeople are criticized for selling their business better than doing their business, which means that many of them will sell themselves better than they'll actually perform on the job. So where does that leave you as the line manager with ultimate say over who gets to play on the team?

Because there are no clear-cut questions and answers that assess sales professionals consistently, you'll have to employ a series of questions that will help paint a picture of the individual's manner of doing business—a group of questions that, taken together, will address drive, energy, impulsiveness, discipline, and commitment. Patterns and inconsistencies will emerge only when these topics are addressed from several angles.

42

How do you rank competitively among other account executives in terms of your production?

Why Ask This Question?

Salespeople are typically bottom-line types who relish the chase of closing a deal and who measure themselves via their peer ranking. Opening your interview with a bottom-line question regarding the individual's production sets the tone for the rest of the meeting. Those with the most to offer will challenge you to provide them with even greater responsibilities. The opportunities they're looking for will come in the form of stronger commission payouts or long-term management opportunities.

In comparison, those who haven't been able to attain consistent sales often change jobs because they're not making enough money. Excuses and apologies drive candidates from company to company searching for illusory payout packages that will earn them higher wages. The reason why they're not more successful, however, is typically found in their inability to establish rapport, identify a prospect's needs, distinguish features from benefits, overcome objections, or, most important, close the deal. Your mission, consequently, will be to locate each individual's shortcomings.

Analyzing the Response

Good Answers. In response to this question, candidates often rank themselves according to percentages and quartiles:

➡ "I rank among the leading 10 percent of auto-sales executives in my region."

➡ "My numbers are typically in the top 25th percentile of stockbrokers in my firm."

127

➡ "I received a President's Club award for finishing last year as the number four producer companywide."

➡ "My production typically placed me in the lower 50th percentile in terms of sales, but that's because . . . ."

Obviously, those who enjoy the distinguished reputation of ranking at the top have no difficulty sharing those achievements with you. The sales field is all about competition, and those who perform with distinction relish their positions of power. In such cases, most of your interview will be spent discussing how the top producer got there, stays there, and plans to obtain the next rung on the success ladder.

 The last example, however, points to the problem producer. Salespeople who do not reach acceptable performance benchmarks immediately volunteer reasons why their numbers were not higher. Sometimes excuses are acceptable; other times, they have little credibility. Only you know what separates excellence from mediocrity in your field. However, your primary focus in dealing with individuals who rank themselves at the bottom of the heap lies in identifying the patterns for their excuses. Short-term tenures with similar types of companies usually spell inconsistent performance. In such instances, this interview question will immediately raise red flags in your mind. Proceed with caution, and measure the answers that follow in this light.

What are the two most common objections you face, and how do you deal with them?

Why Ask This Question?

Role-playing maintains a critical part in the sales interview. Because there are typically no more than two or three major objections that any account executive faces, it's important to hear how the candidate rebuts common rejections. This is an opportunity for the two of you to match wits. Therefore, this role-play will provide you with insights into the individual's sophistication and creativity as the two of you measure each other up.

Analyzing the Response

What are the most typical objections in your industry? Here are some common ones:

➡ "We don't have any need for your product."

➡ "We're happy with our current provider."

➡ "We've got a long list of vendors who have already sent in sales materials. If you'd like to add your public relations material to our list, then when we open up for bids next January, we'll consider your proposal."

 No matter what field of sales you're in, these stonewalling showstoppers typically throw salespeople off. So the first thing you want to observe is how confidently the candidate attacks the objection. Persuasion plays a big role, after all, in establishing rapport with new accounts. The second issue lies in the creativity of the individual's response. If her rebuttals sound like everyone else's in town, there's a chance she hasn't given much thought to what makes her product or service unique.

Therefore, beware of candidates who regurgitate hackneyed responses like, "Well, what would you do if you suddenly needed a . . . ," "I bet we could offer more competitive rates than your current provider," or "Change is good. I'm sure that's how you found your current vendor in the first place. Why not give me a chance to show you what I could do?" Such trite comebacks typically result in little new business.

Good Answers. Look for responses, instead, that reveal creative insights and go beyond the obvious. For example, a stockbroker who possesses a certified public accountant (CPA) license might respond to an objection like "I've been working with my current broker for fourteen years" with this rebuttal:

➡ "Nancy, I respect the relationship you have with your current provider. My only suggestion to you is that I might be able to provide you with financial advice under certain circumstances where your current broker can't. I'm a CPA, and my niche in the investment field is to help clients plan their portfolios with an eye toward the tax ramifications of fairly complex investment setups. I wouldn't

129

expect you to jettison a personal relationship that you have with a friend just because I happened to phone you today. But I'd like your permission to send you information about my practice since I go where most brokers fear to tread. A number of attorneys depend on me to provide them with timely tax and estate planning advice, and I've been successful at tying that back-end knowledge into front-end investing. Does that sound like something that could eventually benefit you?"

Similarly, a copier salesperson might respond to the objection "I have no plans to purchase new machinery" like this:

➡ "Doris, copiers and fax machines are only the products I sell, not the reason why I'm in business. I think that any vendor worth his salt will try to establish long-term relationships with as many companies as possible. The way I do that is by offering value-added service to people who need help when they're in a pinch. If your systems go down and your current provider is unavailable, call me. I'll be happy to personally walk you through the problem and find quick and practical solutions. Hopefully, if enough of a rapport is established over time, when you need to purchase new machinery, you'll naturally think of me. I know that doesn't sound like the way most copier salespeople develop business, but it's worked exceptionally well for me. I'd like to leave you my name and number in case I could ever be of service."

What's common to these responses? Creativity and uniqueness. People who leverage their backgrounds or education to a customer's advantage maintain an edge in the client-development arena. Similarly, those who put the customer before the sale build goodwill and credibility. After all, not many stockbrokers are CPAs. Most salespeople, as a matter of fact, do little to understand what their clients do. So when an executive recruiter, for example, gets a certificate in human resources management in order to learn his clients' business, he'll stand out. Look for such commitment to the industry being serviced.

Salespeople who present their services on a problem-to-solution level and who show patience and goodwill in the sales process turn prospects on. There's no sales pitch and, even more important, the salesperson shows a commitment to building long-term relationships. Sophisticated, relationship-driven salespeople will consistently outperform transaction-driven, buckshot types who see no farther than this month's billing log.

How to Get More Mileage out of the Question. Once you've gotten a rebuttal, pose a follow-up query as if you were the customer. Does the candidate respond to questions at face value, or does she try to close each response by setting an appointment? How many questions will she field before gaining some type of commitment from you? How does she respond to your requests for unreasonable discounts or service? On-the-spot role-plays, like pictures, paint a thousand words. Use them to gain valuable insights into the individual's style, character, and business savvy.

44

Role-play with me, if you will, presenting yourself to me over the phone as if you were a headhunter. Can you convince me that this "product" you're selling is worth my time?

Why Ask This Question?

No, this isn't only an exercise for hiring potential recruiters. Instead, it is an exercise to replace a hackneyed interviewing request used way too often in corporate America: "Sell me the pen." The problem with the "Sell me the pen" scenario is that it's so overused that candidates come to expect it. So they prepare themselves to sell pens better than they sell their actual products.

The reason this query has stood the test of time is because it forces job candidates to distinguish between the object's features and benefits; to overcome any objections that you, the pretend prospective buyer, could raise; and, most important, to close you on the purchase. However, Question 44 does all this much more effectively without being so predictable, so let's take a look at it.

Analyzing the Response

Asking candidates to sell themselves to you is challenging because they have to be totally objective about something very personal: themselves.

131

Distinguishing features from benefits isn't so easy when discussing their own strengths and limitations as well as what makes them stand out among their peers. Furthermore, because of the intimacy of the subject, most candidates are doubly challenged in providing role-play answers that mesh well with their interview responses. That extra dimension of accountability often adds some circumspection to candidates' otherwise bold responses and makes overcoming objections and closing you on the hire a tougher challenge.

How to Get More Mileage out of the Question. In evaluating candidates' responses, expect some initial discomfort on their part. After all, no matter how confident candidates are, this exercise does set them up to brag about themselves. (And most people on a job interview don't want to go overboard in that area.) Next, gauge the sales presentation. Does the individual start off timidly with a trite "How are you today?" or does the person get to the point right away? A creative presentation might sound like this:

➡ "Ms. Employer, I'm calling to tell you about a copier sales executive who's expressed an interest in meeting with your company because he's aware of your reputation, he works for a direct competitor, and he's thoroughly researched your organization. He ranks among the top 20 percent of producers in his company and has a proven track record of taking a poorly performing territory and increasing market share above the national average within two years. Would you consider talking to someone like that?"

Good Answers. It won't always sound this smooth, but the presentation should at least offer tangible results and future benefits. You're then free to lob some objections at the individual, including "I have no openings," "Tell me more about him," and "What's he looking for?" After presenting an objection like "We have no openings," look for such candidate rebuttals as "Well, you know, Ms. Employer, it's been my experience that strong companies would set up an office in a closet for someone who could immediately add to their top-line revenues. Perhaps you'd consider comparing his track record to some of your existing staff." Such heads-up rebuttals show a great deal of ingenuity, creativity, and wit.

Finally, the close in this scenario lies in setting up the interview. See how aggressively the individual overcomes your objections and gets you to commit to meeting with a top producer if only on an exploratory basis.

It's an exercise that will shed lots of light onto candidates' self-esteem levels and their abilities to present a product they're not naturally inclined to sell.

45

How do you define your closing style?

Why Ask This Question?

If there is one area in sales where people fail, it's their inability to persuade a prospect to take a recommended course of action. Some people just never seem to master this one technique regardless of the amount of training they've undergone. That's because closing skills really can't be taught; they stem from innate personality traits. As a result, people either (a) close prospects aggressively by repetitively asking for the sale and wearing the prospect down emotionally or (b) make a logical case for why customers would want the product and then induce customers to "close themselves."

Both styles work: There are too many fields of sales to isolate one closing style as *the* optimal manner for doing business. Although top producers usually fall into the aggressive closers group, many successful salespeople are gentle persuaders as well (especially when dealing with more sophisticated clientele). The brand of closer you want will ultimately depend on your product line and corporate culture.

Analyzing the Response

How to Get More Mileage out of the Question. Candidates typically respond that they're capable of adapting their style of closing to a prospect's needs. Such a wishy-washy response does little to get to the heart of the matter: closing abilities. Of course, you will already have experienced the candidate's real-life closing skills firsthand in the previous role-plays about overcoming common objections and headhunting. Still, this self-appraisal query completes the picture by allowing the candidates to explain why they consider themselves soft or hard closers.

Therefore, to encourage a more detailed response, ask candidates to grade their closing skills on a scale of one to ten (ten being very aggressive,

133

one being very benign). Such a weighted ranking exercise will result in responses like this:

➡ "I'd consider myself a four, meaning that I don't really believe that aggressive closing tactics work in the field of employee-benefits consulting. Clients expect their consultants to be excellent information and networking resources, so cold-call techniques and a transaction mentality simply won't work. Not that I can't make a strong recommendation to a client who's sitting on the fence regarding a certain issue. But you'll notice in my role-play of overcoming objections that I didn't push too hard on that first sales call. Building relationships takes time, and I'd rather nurture someone's business in small increments than aggressively push my way through the front door."

➡ "I consider myself a nine on a scale of ten. In auto sales, you have to strike while the prospect is sitting in front of you. At our branch, statistics bore out that once customers walked out the door, they had only a 7 percent chance of returning. So if you didn't close them on the spot, you lost the sale. If my role-play appeared to be overly aggressive, it's because anything less would result in failure."

In addition, you might choose the following behavioral question to aid the candidate in this self-appraisal exercise: "How do you define hard versus soft selling? Give me an example of how you've handled both situations." In this instance, you'll solicit real-life stories from an applicant's past that reveal an inclination either to educate and gently persuade a customer (that is, a problem-solving, rational approach) or to push reaction buttons that appeal more to a prospect's emotions and fears.

Other questions to determine an individual's closing style include:

➡ "Tell me about the last difficult sales negotiation you experienced. Could your sales manager have accused you of debating with customers rather than persuading them?"

➡ "When is the last time you chose to stick to your guns and lost a sale? How do you determine when it's prudent to walk away from a deal?"

➡ "Realistically assessing your style, do you find that you sometimes hesitate to ask for a sale? If so, what circumstances or kinds of people hold you back?"

46

**All salespeople need to find equilibrium between
(a) high-volume production numbers and (b) quality.
Which philosophy drives your sales style more?**

Why Ask This Question?

Most salespeople will tell you they're basically balanced in terms of harmonizing quality and quantity. Reality bears out a slightly different truth, however. Most people lean in one direction more than the other. Top producers are typically much more quantity driven. They close deals and don't look backward. If they're lucky, they have a great assistant to tie up the administrative loose ends. If not, they tie up their own loose ends when they get around to it, but not until all the deals that could possibly close that day or month are done.

Those who define themselves as more quality driven, in comparison, usually close fewer deals, but all the details are neatly accounted for. They take the time to follow up with customers to ensure their satisfaction. Their paperwork trails are logical and easy to follow. And they pride themselves on building a solid referral base to ensure future business. Yes, it takes longer to make the sale for these individuals, but does the smaller volume potential mean any less of a return on investment for your company over the long haul?

Analyzing the Response

How to Get More Mileage out of the Question. Only you can answer that question on the basis of your own sales style, corporate philosophy, and the amount of time you allow salespeople to show profitability. A smaller number of deals, however, doesn't necessarily equate with minimized revenues. If the profit-per-deal ratio is higher, then the number of deals closed becomes a secondary factor. Therefore, when employing this question, ask:

➡ "Please distinguish the *quantity* of sales from the *profitability* per sale."

➡ "Give me an example of your ability to structure high-point deals."

135

➡ "What's the size of your average sale, and how could you have gotten more mileage out of it by selling more add-on products or configuring your mark-up differently?"

For example, in the mortgage-lending business, subpar borrowers with poorer credit histories typically carry a greater risk that they won't repay their loans. To offset that additional risk, lending companies charge higher fees and percentage rates with variable payback terms. A loan officer who effectively structures higher-point deals—even though the volume of those transactions might be relatively low—ultimately rewards herself with higher commission earnings. A high-volume loan officer who structures fees below market, however, will typically earn little above her base salary.

Therefore, to further confirm your insights, distinguish between the candidate's monthly guarantee and gross monthly earnings. The difference will be the commission payout, and it should typically at least double the base salary.

47

Tell me about the last time you failed to meet quota. How many times did that happen over the past year, and what plan of action did you take to get back on track?

Why Ask This Question?

The quality-quantity debate will always generate definitive insights into a candidate's way of doing business. When push comes to shove, however, sales boils down to hard-core numbers. You'll always read on a candidate's résumé about quotas exceeded and top production awards. However, you won't find out about the hiccups in the individual's production unless you ask.

Analyzing the Response

Failing to meet quota is nothing to be ashamed of if you're a salesperson. It's happened to everyone—a lot. "Racehorses"—performance-driven, short-term-minded people—work in sprints. "Plow horses"—consistent billers—provide you with a consistent return but rarely win the Kentucky Derby. The brand of salesperson you desire is up to you.

If the candidate had four or five inadequate months in a twelve-month period, you should be concerned. Meeting quota 70 percent of the time is probably a realistic expectation (although this can vary from industry to industry). Even if the candidate bills well when he's hot, too many production gaps not only will lower aggregate annual production results but may also indicate problematic outside influences in the person's life, mood swings, and other inconsistencies that could negatively affect the team's performance.

How to Get More Mileage out of the Question. If the candidate responds that there were no problems making quota, follow up by asking, "How much does your production vary from month to month?" Learn about production changes that might indicate large rises and falls (even though the falls never went below the quota threshold). Finally, if a candidate provides only a vague response, ask, "Doris, we're very thorough in terms of reference checking prospective new hires. How would your past supervisor at XYZ Company grade the fluctuations in your production? What would she say we could do to give you added support in that area?" Remember, asking candidates to volunteer shortcomings will provide you with a blueprint for future direction and focus.

48

With no undue flattery, if you will, grade me on how well I'm conducting this interview: What can you tell me about my sales and management style on the basis of the questions I'm asking you?

Why Ask This Question?

People-reading skills are critical to any sales executive's success. Because perception skills can't be taught by training, each candidate needs to have a fairly well defined ability to recognize a stranger's personality and business style. Without that innate ability to adapt to another person's mode of communication, establishing rapport remains difficult, and sales opportunities will be missed. After all, prospects shouldn't have to adapt themselves to the salesperson's style: The salesperson is responsible for breaking through communication barriers and immediately establishing common ground.

Analyzing the Response

Testing an individual's people-reading skills should provide insights into how the candidate sizes up strangers. Since you're the only two people in the room, you might as well make yourself the focus of attention. This query will then reveal how accurately the candidate evaluates and bonds with newly introduced people on the spot.

How to Get More Mileage out of the Question. Since the candidate needs to gauge your values as a manager to answer this question, save this query until the second half of the interview. Note the kinds of words the interviewee uses to describe you: "You're a really nice guy and you like your job" is a cop-out response because it's so superficial. Push the candidate further by asking for specifics regarding your management and sales styles:

➡ "What would it be like working for me?"

➡ "Where do you think I'd have the least amount of patience?"

➡ "Tell me where I ranked as a salesperson when I was on the floor."

A candidate should be able to tell a lot about an interviewer by his attention to detail, his logical follow-up queries, and his questioning techniques. Similarly, a sloppy office with mounds of paperwork makes a different impression than a tidy office with neatly stacked files. These follow-up queries should consequently generate some firm responses from even the most gun-shy candidates. Their answers won't necessarily be correct, but there should be a logical basis for their responses.

Good Answers. A perceptive response might sound like this:

➡ "You're meticulous because everything is in order on your desk and on your bookshelf. You're taking lots of notes, so you obviously study applicants for later comparison and approach final decisions objectively once you've collected all the data. And just by asking this question, I see that you're not afraid of hearing rejections, so you obviously feel confident that you know your stuff. Finally, you listen intently to every word I say without finishing my sentences for me, so you've got excellent listening skills. I bet you expect the same kind of clean operation from your sales staff, so working with you would mean I'd have to dot my *i*'s and cross my *t*'s."

Don't be surprised, by the way, to hear some undue flattery. Do, however, watch out for candidates who shower you with insincere, unfounded compliments. That's a sales style in and of itself, but that approach went the way of the dinosaur once sophisticated consumers educated themselves and learned to avoid the Slick Eddies of this world.

49

How important is the base salary component to you? Would you prefer a straight commission if it offered you the potential for an additional 35 percent in aggregate earnings over the base salary?

Why Ask This Question?

Measuring candidates' risk factors says a lot about their sales mentality. Those who cling to high guarantees often come from conservative, risk-averse households where stability and steady income took precedence over risk-based earnings. These people have more of an I-work-to-live attitude, and they typically see their work as a means to an end—namely, putting bread on the table.

In comparison, entrepreneurs live to work, regardless of the amount of money they make. Their parents were most likely successful salespeople who opened their own businesses at fairly young ages and perhaps experienced a bankruptcy or two. The kids opened corner Kool-Aid stands once they turned five and have been bitten by the profit bug ever since. These are the people who never give up the helm of the ship even after they've made their millions. In short, they typically define themselves by the level of material success they generate.

Analyzing the Response

Distinguishing aggregate payout potential from guaranteed earnings could be telling. A salesperson with a husband, two children, and a mortgage may opt for a higher base pay with a lower payout potential because the timing in her life dictates conservatism over risk. If that's the reason this woman is sitting in your office for an interview (and you happen to offer the highest base pay program in town while all your competitors offer only straight commission), then you have lots to offer her. In this case, the problem that made her decide to leave her past company is solved by your organization.

If, on the other hand, you're interviewing someone who's fresh out of college, who considers himself a millionaire in the making, and who would opt for the $1,500-per-month base plus minimal bonus over the straight commission package, then beware: You're probably looking at another example of the classic risk-averse mentality mentioned previously. The moral of the story: Even if you don't offer a choice of earnings options (among base salary, commissions, and bonuses, for example), ask candidates how they'd ideally like to see their pay structured. Obviously, the higher the risk that candidates are willing to assume, the greater the reward for you and the aggregate payout for them.

Tell me about your quality ratios: How many prospects do you typically see before closing a sale?

Why Ask This Question?

Locking salespeople into a rhythm of activity dictates long-term success. Top producers focus on daily activity objectives rather than on monthly production dollars because daily activities are in their control and production results are not. Once the salesperson identifies the necessary daily activity numbers he needs to reach his production targets, you need to question his *quality ratios*. After all, the number of outbound phone calls and face-to-face sales presentations is limited. Tighter quality ratios, however, guarantee more results for the effort expended. Consequently, questioning an account executive regarding his activity level without balancing the equation from the perspective of quality ratios is the biggest mistake that sales interviewers make.

Analyzing the Response

Good Answers. The purpose of this exercise is to measure candidates' understanding of their own quality ratios and the activity numbers they need to make monthly production quotas. The most practical way to apply this question is to ask the candidate to reverse order the activities necessary to make a sale. For example, a pharmaceuticals salesperson who is expected to sell $10,000 in prosthetic devices per month might answer the question this way:

➡ "The cost of an average prosthetic device that we sell is $2,000 to $3,000. To meet my monthly quota, therefore, I need to sell four products a month, or one a week. My ratio of presentations to sales is about fifty to one, so I need to visit about ten medical offices a day in order to make fifty presentations per week and, in turn, close one sale. So, if my production ever drifts lower than it should, I make sure that I'm hitting my ten visits a day, and then I let my quality ratios take care of themselves."

 Beware candidates who have difficulty articulating their quality ratios. Without a thorough understanding of the average activities necessary to generate a sale, there's a great chance that the candidate hasn't given enough thought to the trade. If that's the case, challenge the person to calculate on the spot the numbers trail that leads to closed deals. Take notes on the out-loud calculations to ensure that the estimates (and numeric reasoning skills) are accurate.

How to Get More Mileage out of the Question. Finally, once those activity numbers are defined, query further:

➡ "If it takes fifty presentations to close one sale, what would you need to do to tighten your quality ratio to forty-five to one? How could I, as your prospective sales manager, strengthen your reward-to-effort ratio? How could you structure five more presentations per week to close more deals every year?"

Combined with the candidate's production numbers, quality ratios will help you determine whether the individual focuses on high-payoff activities and maximizes available time.

141

51

How much does production vary from desk to desk in your office?

Why Ask This Question?

Identifying huge discrepancies in per-desk production averages may point to a serious issue known as the rebel producer syndrome. Rebel producers are difficult to manage, and they destroy camaraderie and teamwork. Of course, determining how difficult an individual is to manage belongs in the reference-checking process. After all, previous managers will be much more forthcoming about a candidate's inclinations to undermine her peers than will the applicant herself. Still, allowing self-assessments in this critical area often points out problem situations that should be more fully explored in a background investigation.

Analyzing the Response

How do you know whether you have a potential rebel producer on your hands? There are two telltale signs of this syndrome: (1) a distorted ratio of per-desk billings and (2) a higher-than-expected turnover rate. For example, if you find out that the candidate in question produces 50 percent of her branch's revenues, your first reaction will be ecstatic: After all, you'll feel that you caught the goose that lays the golden egg. If a copier salesperson produces $600,000 of her branch's annual $1.2 million revenues, what could possibly be wrong with that?

After you think about it, though, you realize that this is a four-person office. If Kathy is generating $600,000 in revenues, then three other sales reps are producing only $600,000 among themselves: roughly $200,000 each. Since Kathy triples everyone else's production, ask her to account for the discrepancy. If all of her counterparts are trainees, then the disparity in billings certainly makes sense.

Kathy tells you, however, that everyone in the branch has similar tenure with the company. So why would the company keep all those underperformers who aren't making any money, you wonder, when Kathy is holding the bar so high? Perhaps it's because she's a rebel producer who indeed makes a lot of money but who, because of her insecurity, needs lots of "little failures" around her to convince her of her worth.

How to Get More Mileage out of the Question. If you find such a gross disparity in production among staff members, you should deftly probe for more information: "Kathy, what are the typical problems and grievances that plague your branch, and what has employee turnover been like over the past two years?" You learn from this follow-up query that branch turnover is greater than 100 percent per year—far exceeding what you consider acceptable. When questioned about this enigma, Kathy has no response: Apparently everyone else out there is having problems keeping up with her and can't take the pressure.

 These telltale signs point to a top producer with little empathy for the people around her. They also point to a management team paralyzed by the rebel's production because she's keeping the branch alive. Is Kathy the wrong person for your organization? It's too early to tell. Instruct Kathy, however, that in checking references, you believe in talking not only with supervisors but with peers and subordinates as well. They should be able to provide you with valuable insights into the individual's penchant for being a team player and maintaining a positive work environment.

Ending up with a high-needs superstar could ruin all that you've built in a particular unit. It will cause conflict and turnover and, more significantly, impede your ability to attract other top producers. In short, your branch will never earn much more than that one producer's billings because you'll never be able to build a staff on that foundation.

10.

Midlevel Managers, Professionals, Technicians, and Key Individual Contributors

Your Organization's Leadership Pipeline

As we discussed at the beginning of Chapter 8 on millennials, demographics is destiny. In our case, demographic shifts have forced companies to come to terms with succession planning as a key leadership imperative as we make our way further into the twenty-first century. Here's why: From 1946 until 1964, the baby boom generation in the United States witnessed the birth of seventy-seven million children, many of whom would eventually run corporate America. This was the largest cohort of newborns seen in the United States up to that time. It made sense to see a massive increase in family size during this period. World War II ended in 1945, and U.S. soldiers returned home to get married and start families. The demographic bubble continued until 1964, when the birth control pill was introduced. The baby boom quickly became the baby bust (a.k.a. generation X) with the introduction of the birth control pill, and the bubble of seventy-seven million newborns reverted to a cohort of forty-six million from 1964 to 1980 (after which time the millennials, or generation Y, came onto the scene).

That seventy-seven million new Americans drove consumer spending through the roof and impacted the trajectory of U.S. commerce and technology in exponential ways. This massive generation quietly began retiring in 2011 when the oldest ones turned sixty-five; the rest of the seventy-seven million people will retire for the next twelve years, through 2029. That represents ten thousand people per day for eighteen years leaving the U.S. workforce—a demographic challenge that requires U.S. employers to focus on succession planning and talent management to replace retirees at a staggering pace.

We typically think of C-level executives as the true leaders of organizations: CEOs, CFOs, and COOs run the executive, finance, and operational functions of organizations large and small. But many of those C-suite executives today are in their fifties and sixties. To replace them, wise companies are focusing more and more on the next generation of leaders and executives and rushing to provide them with the skills and knowledge to pick up where the soon-to-be retiring executives will leave off. The overall result will be a wave effect of retirements followed by promotions that hopefully won't skip a beat—organizations will hopefully continue to thrive as the baby boomers continue their transition into retirement.

That talent pool will likely come from those who make up the ranks of middle management today. Divisional vice presidents, department heads, and high-performing individual contributors hold the keys to becoming tomorrow's C-suite leaders. Where do you draw the line of distinction between senior executives and midlevel managers? Typically, at the vice president level: vice presidents, senior vice presidents, and executive vice presidents feed the chain of executive talent needed to run organizations at the C-suite level. That will leave an awful lot of holes in organizations at the VP and above level, however, so our focus in this chapter will be on assessing that next tier of talent: directors, managers, and key individual contributors who have the potential of skilling up to become VPs and department and division heads themselves.

This tier of middle management, from managers to directors, and in some cases to VPs, is any organization's true talent pipeline, its bench strength for meeting tomorrow's challenges and steering the course for their company's growth. Let's look at some key questions that will help us discern the talent potential at this critical level of the organization. After all, we'll remain in the hot zone of talent management and succession planning through 2029, so there's no better time to assess the talent potential that can drive our business and commercial growth into the middle of the twenty-first century.

BONUS QUESTION 10A: From a self-assessment standpoint, where might you be lacking in terms of being a perfect match for this position? What's your most critical self-assessment of your strengths and weaknesses for this position and in terms of your overall fit?

No job opportunity is a perfect match for a candidate, just like no candidate is an ideal fit for a company. It's all relative and depends on the circumstances, the players, and the timing involved. However, some candidates come a lot closer than others because of personal chemistry or some sort of "it" factor, and we all get excited about the possibility of hiring someone who can take our organization to the proverbial next level. But in truth, we're all human beings doing our best to fit in and make a positive contribution. We'll all make stronger contributions in certain areas of our jobs where we're more confident and more experienced.

Why Ask This Question?

Asking this question gives candidates permission to make themselves vulnerable in the hiring process, and as we've said elsewhere in the book, vulnerability can be a positive attribute because it begets trust. Giving candidates an opportunity to self-assess provides insights into their analytical skills and humility. Beware those who proclaim they can leap tall buildings in a single bound and have no weaknesses—they may be hiding behind delusions of grandeur or other insecurities. Likewise, they may just be snowing you. No one ever said that interviewing and hiring was going to be easy, and part of your job as the corporate gatekeeper lies in demonstrating a healthy sense of Sherlock Holmes–type curiosity and skepticism in evaluating prospective talent.

Analyzing the Response

Even if a candidate is an exceptionally strong overall match for a particular position based on a résumé or a peer's recommendation, it's still a matter of degree as to what particular aspects of the role will require more development over time. As a recruiter, I've never looked for perfection in the candidates I hired, only for a healthy combination of experience, achievement, and desire to learn and grow and contribute to the role. To look for anything more than that would be a fool's errand—human beings are complicated, and there are no guarantees. At best, you'll follow a strategy of making high-probability hires that maximize your chances of finding the right talent at the right time for the right assignment. Therefore, when asking this question and analyzing the response, look to see where the individual has hands-on experience to find the true comfort zones. For example, a vice president of human resources is responsible for a number of specialties within the HR spectrum:

Talent acquisition	Compensation design and administration
Benefits design and administration	Training and development
Employee and labor relations	HRIS administration
Payroll administration	Talent management and succession planning

Other specialties may include international HR, mergers and acquisitions due diligence and integration, safety training and administration, and metrics and analytics, and the like.

Even if an individual has a stellar reputation as an HR leader, she very likely won't have the same level of expertise and confidence in each of these very diverse areas. For example, if a candidate grew up in recruitment, employee relations, and training, then it stands to reason that those areas will be most comfortable for her in terms of providing direction, support, and structure to her team. So if she spent years or decades in those specialty areas, then payroll, compensation and benefits, and HR information systems (HRIS) will likely need to be more developed. Likewise, if she comes out of HRIS and spent years designing and defining the metrics and analytics that drive workforce change, then she may have less experience in some of the higher touch areas like recruitment and employee relations. There's nothing wrong with that; she simply hasn't had the time or opportunity to explore each discipline to the same degree. And let's face it: Some people enjoy the social aspects of their jobs, while others gravitate toward more introverted analytical work.

The key lies in hearing candidates tell you how they assess themselves and gauging how open they are to self-critical insight. Compare the following responses to determine whether you're more comfortable hiring Candidate A or B:

Candidate A: "Well, I've done HR in a startup environment before, so that appears to be an excellent overall match. I don't mean to say it's a been-there-done-that sort of thing, but I'm guessing there won't be much that I haven't already seen in one form or another. I've handled all the key areas of HR infrastructure setup, department design, team selection, and

147

budgeting, so I feel I'm very well qualified for this position. There really isn't much I haven't touched, so I'd imagine I'd be an up-and-running member of the team in no time."

Candidate B: "Well, I've done HR in a startup environment before, so this appears to be an excellent overall match. But there will certainly be challenges and a learning curve for me along the way. Every opportunity is different, and while I'm strong at setting up the department infrastructure and building a team, you'll see from my résumé that I don't have a ton of benefits or payroll experience. At my prior companies, payroll fell under finance rather than HR, so that's clearly an area where I can identify an opportunity for growth and development. And when it comes to benefits, with all due respect, I know they're important, but they've never really been my specialty or natural area of interest. That's just a broad assessment of my history and experiences, but I can certainly focus on the payroll and benefits piece to bring myself up to speed quickly."

There's no judgment here. In fact, you may prefer Candidate A because she doesn't show any weaknesses and assumes she'll perform equally as strong across the board from day one. Personally, though, I like the transparency of Candidate B; individuals who are willing to let their guard down and help you, the employer, come to a more informed decision are actually putting the good of the company ahead of their own needs. That's a great indicator of emotional intelligence and an exceptional benefit that indicates you'll always get a real answer—not just the juicy stuff that the individual thinks you want to hear.

How to Get More Mileage out of the Question. Regardless of the self-analysis provided, consider asking one follow-up question that will also lead to some interesting discussions: "On a scale of one to ten, ten being you're a perfect fit for the role, how would you define yourself at this point, based on your current understanding?" I wouldn't be surprised to hear Candidate A label herself a nine or a ten, while Candidate B might self-designate as a seven or an eight. Remember that these numerical rankings are arbitrary in and of themselves. What those numbers represent to the candidate as a point of comparison and self-evaluation is the point of this follow-up question because it helps filter the discussion even more finely: "Why would you say you're an eight, and what would make you a ten?" It could be interesting to see where each candidate goes with this. If the opening query requests a broad-brush overview in terms of a response, then this follow-up question requires an in-the-weeds answer. It might be interesting to see if Candidate A tamps down her qualifications in this second phase of the question, while Candidate B answers with a lot more confidence and conviction than you otherwise might have thought based on her response to your initial query.

Self-confidence is healthy, but overconfidence sometimes bespeaks insecurity. What you won't want, especially among more senior leaders or direct reports, is people telling you that they can do anything and then covering over any weaknesses or shortcomings that may make them appear to be less qualified in your eyes. Personally, I'll always side with the humbler candidate who demonstrates some level of self-deprecation in her response. Humbleness and selflessness go a long way in my book when it comes to finalist selection. Again, the choice is always yours, but this question may provide a gateway to an interesting and telling discussion about the individual's sense of self-worth and self-confidence levels.

BONUS QUESTION 10B: Tell me about your approach to goal setting. How do you measure progress and quantify your achievements?

Interview questions about goal setting and attainment can be healthy indicators of an individual's personal style and achievement mentality. Some organizations formalize goal setting as part of the annual performance review process: The review looks at the individual's historical performance over the prior review period (typically one year), and the goal-setting module focuses on future objectives, along with the measurable outcomes to demonstrate that objectives are achieved. If a candidate works for a company where formalized performance reviews and goal setting play an important role in performance assessment, simply discuss what last year's process looked like and how the individual delivered against her preset goals. On the other hand, if the candidate's prior company (or companies) didn't use formal performance evaluations or goal setting, it's just as safe to question how the individual goes about doing this independently, despite the lack of formal systems or processes at prior organizations where she's worked.

Why Ask This Question?

Goal setting and attainment are typically healthy signs of a productive worker with an achievement mentality. Committing to goals in writing and then completing them and celebrating successes speak to a healthy sense of accomplishment and focus. While many Americans set goals for themselves during the New Year, for example, some never make it past the end of the month of January before their annual goals fall by the wayside. On the other end of the spectrum, while some people don't necessarily commit to written goals as part of their performance profile, they consistently exceed expectations and perform like true superstars.

Therefore, the lack of goal setting shouldn't necessarily spell disqualification, but someone who can articulate their approach to goal setting and completion may help further their candidacy in your eyes, all else being equal. Even if they don't set goals or have a particular answer to your question, you can still adapt the query using a behavioral interview question like this:

➡ "It's okay that you've not had to submit goals at prior places where you've worked or even consider yourself much of a goal setter in your private life. Give me an example, though, of a time when you had to develop a blueprint for an extended list of activities and actions at work that were necessary to deliver a project by a particular deadline."

The value in this ancillary question is that it allows you to get to what you're really looking for: this individual's approach to completing what she starts, managing through time and resource constraints, and communicating progress and roadblocks.

Analyzing the Response

Think of it this way: If most organizational performance bell curves fall under a typical 70-20-10 spread, where 70 percent of workers meet expectations, 20 percent thrive, and 10 percent lag, you're asking this question to isolate the top 20 percent. Your top performers will always find new ways of standing out from the crowd, setting themselves apart from the competition, and holding themselves to higher standards of accountability than everyone else. When it typically comes time for performance review self-assessments, these are the chosen few who create detailed spreadsheets and charts with all the bells and whistles to point toward their achievements and quantify the results. While the 70 percent in the middle of the pack may provide feedback during the self-assessment process, their feedback will often be rote, repetitive, or otherwise without distinction. Ten percent of your lowest-performing employees may even refuse to engage in the self-assessment process, reasoning that it's their boss's job to evaluate their performance and that they want no part of the process.

But ah, that top 20 percent—they perform with distinction and pride themselves on their accomplishments. They take the bulleted achievements from their annual self-assessments and tie them to their résumés and LinkedIn profiles. The best performers will always be résumé builders, and it shouldn't come as a surprise that this subgroup typically sets and achieves goals. Further, they often measure themselves not necessarily in terms of meeting goals but by how much they exceed them percentage-wise. In other words, this question may give a top-performing candidate a chance to shine. In and of itself, it may help you attract those with a well-developed sense of achievement and inner competitiveness. Try asking this question to identify candidates that stand out as rarities among their peers; the results may surprise you when candidates sit up on the edges of their seats, their eyes light up, and they begin rattling off prior goals and accomplishments with pride.

BONUS QUESTION 10C: What's one thing about your career that's guaranteed to make you smile?

This may sound a bit too cutesy or too easy for a candidate to hit out of the park, but a light touch can go a long way in an interview, especially at the outset of the meeting. Remember, our goal is to get to know the real person behind all the interviewing hype, and to achieve that, you have to make it safe for candidates to make themselves somewhat vulnerable in a healthy sense during the meeting. Assuming that vulnerability builds trust, you'll want to figuratively reach across the table and extend open arms to get to know candidates more personally.

Why Ask This Question?

This interviewing query helps people smile. It gives them permission to ponder why they ever got into the field they've chosen, to reminisce about the old days when they were considering multiple career options, and to focus on what they continue to enjoy about the path they've chosen. It gives them a chance to lighten up and laugh: "I got into HR because I always wanted to work with people, but after the first few years I was ready to hang up my HR cleats and become an accountant." That's something that everyone can relate to, and it can become a lighthearted way to explain their career choices that led to the interview that you're holding with them today.

Analyzing the Response

There aren't many things that can go wrong in answering a question like this. Inviting people to talk about the positives in their career, their likes about the path they've chosen, and their preferences in doing their job faithfully day in and day out points to career satisfaction and enjoyment. Of course, there could be responses that sometimes throw up a red flag. If, for example, a candidate answers this question too seriously, has difficulty explaining his passion about his job, or fails to use words like *happy* and *smile* in his response, it could point to possible burnout. You would at least hope that someone could fake it in explaining what makes them smile about their jobs, but in extreme cases where they'd really prefer not to have to work another day in their lives (at least in their current field), this question could reveal some concerns about their level of motivation or engagement. A response like this from an emergency room nurse, for example, might make you think twice:

➡ "I love being a nurse because I can touch so many people's lives, but in truth, it sometimes infuriates me that people use emergency rooms as their go-to resource, full well knowing that they can't pay and not really caring that others with much more serious conditions or in real pain have to wait to be seen because these *repeat customers* appear at whim whenever they decide they need to see a doctor."

It's a fair enough response, of course, but you have to wonder why a bitter answer came out when a simple question like "What makes you smile about nursing?" was initially asked.

More often than not, however, this question leads to certain out-loud meanderings that can be telling about where certain candidates are at this point in their careers. In a different example, candidates may sometimes volunteer something like this:

➡ "I love being a nurse because I can touch so many people's lives, but in truth, it sometimes has me thinking about opening my own business or carving out some specific sector of the nursing function that can fill a specific niche in the market. I love touching people's lives, but I see too many young mothers struggling with the care that's available to their newborns. I often wonder how I can *keep smiling* but also provide more specific solutions to some of the broader challenges facing new moms in this day and age."

Likewise a fair enough response, but one that may beg for more information. Becoming an entrepreneur is a wonderful and exciting career opportunity for someone, especially if they can dedicate themselves to a segment of the healthcare market that they're passionate about. Unfortunately, that may not help you much if you're looking to stabilize your nursing team and want someone who's focused solely on general nursing administration at this point in their career.

If a question like this would get you talking openly and make you smile if you were on the receiving end of it, then consider adding it to your interview questioning lineup and see if it drives responses that add value to your meeting. Remember, interviewing doesn't have to be so formal. The best interviewers tend to be very comfortable with themselves, they know what they're looking for, and they're skilled at making candidates comfortable and building trust from the outset of the meeting. Asking questions about what makes you smile, along with a spattering of appropriate jokes here and there, can go a long way in making candidates feel at ease while highlighting your communication and leadership style.

BONUS QUESTION 10D: Are you satisfied with your career to date? What would you change if you could? Do you think you've had too many job changes or too few?

This could be an interesting discussion opener, especially in light of technology changes, corporate downsizings, mergers, acquisitions, divestitures, and subsequent integrations, outsourcing, offshoring, and the growth of robotics in corporate America. It's an amazing time for disruption and redefinition, and many U.S. workers have been displaced by tectonic shifts in the economy.

Why Ask This Question?

Many professionals and midlevel managers experienced excellent career stability through 2008, when the Great Recession hit, only to find their résumés looking like Swiss cheese afterward because of massive industry shifts and breakdowns. It may be interesting to open a discussion around this topic, especially if you notice short-term changes (e.g., less than two years per position over the past four to eight years) that vary from their historical patterns of tenure. HR, marketing, IT, communications, and others have had the rug pulled out from under them in many ways, finding it difficult to gain traction in an ever-changing economic landscape that's struggling to find a balance in a new economy. Of course, career changes that result from large-scale downsizings are not a candidate's fault, but it's interesting to hear candidates' accounting and reckoning of their careers in light of these current structural challenges.

Analyzing the Response

Frustration sometimes shows itself when candidates reflect on the unprecedented changes that have come their way in terms of managing their careers. It's interesting to see, however, whether individuals at the midpoint of their careers show anger and frustration or creativity and inspiration in negotiating the travails of career management at any given point in the economic cycle. For example, insightful candidates who look to make lemonade out of lemons may respond like this:

➡ "Yes, I've been challenged by constant changes in the organizations where I've worked over the past five years. I think that's mostly due, though, to the industry I've been working in. There's so much change in retail, and big box stores have been closing and consolidating aggressively, making it difficult to find opportunities in the first place and then enjoying some degree of job security and stability once you find one. I know that my résumé screams 'retail' based on the organizations where I've worked, but I recently learned about the Bureau of Labor Statistics' *Occupational Outlook Handbook*,[1] and I'm a firm believer at this point that the industry you choose is the most important factor in determining how much career success you'll enjoy.

"For example, I looked up 'HR Manager' to see where the growth would be, and while the typical HR role would grow at about the same rate as the average job in corporate America over the next ten years, HR roles in healthcare, medical technology and consulting, and home health will grow at triple that rate. That's why I'm so interested in shifting my career to this industry. My number one goal is to transition myself into a healthcare-related field because I feel that will provide me with additional job security for years to come, especially with the baby boom generation retiring at a rate of 10,000 people per day between 2011 and 2029.

"I looked up retail and saw that HR jobs in that field will continue to contract but not as bad as in the post office: HR roles in the post office will be down 28 percent over the next ten years, so I guess I don't have it that bad. But seriously, my main goal at this point is to transition from an HR career path in retail to HR in the healthcare sector. I think it's the smartest move I can make from a career-development standpoint, and that's why I'd be so interested in pursuing this role with your hospital."

Clearly, this is a candidate who's seen the light and done his home-work in terms of career research and introspection. Even if you don't hire him, you have to admire his ingenuity in researching the Bureau of Labor Statistics' *Occupational Outlook Handbook* and refocusing his career on where the jobs will be and where he'll have the greatest chances of career opportunities and stability. Not everyone will have the wherewithal to research their discipline and project future job growth, but the corporate futurists who demonstrate an inquisitiveness and curiosity about their career paths stand out among their peers.

The follow-up question "What would you change if you could?" is a fair one. It's interesting to hear how candidates conduct post mortems on their career choices. The invitation to look back and reevaluate the events in their education and career that have led them to this point can pro-vide healthy insights into how they assess themselves in light of what they know now. While there's no right or wrong answer, look to distinguish between candidates who constantly look for new opportunities versus those who see themselves as victims of circumstance.

Likewise for the follow-up question "Do you think you've had too many jobs or too few?" Asking middle management and professional/technical candidates to assess their job changes can lead to an insightful discussion as individuals evaluate their historical approach to career management. Responses here not only shed some light on their career-management

155

values and priorities but may point to their future career aspirations. Candidates who change companies too aggressively may appear to be chasing the almighty buck rather than thinking through their career development strategically. Those who stay put without assuming greater responsibilities or demonstrating some form of internal career progression may lack ambition.

The interpretation, of course, is up to you. What may appear like too much or too little change will always be subject to interpretation. But professional/technical individual contributors and middle managers at the VP, director, or manager levels represent the future of your company, the talent that may one day succeed you in leading a department or in joining the C-suite. Look carefully at their career assessments and gauge their goals, reasons for leaving, and criteria in selecting their next company. If their logic lines up and their goals can be achieved by joining your organization, you'll likely have the makings of a long-term successful hire.

BONUS QUESTION 10E: Would you classify yourself as a born leader, or is leadership something you've focused on and developed over time?

Leadership is a talent—an ability to influence others to follow you, trust you, and believe in you. As such, it's not a function of supervising others. To "manage" or "supervise" implies that others report to you and must follow your directives; to "lead," in comparison, requires no such reporting relationships. Anyone can be a great leader, whether they hold a management position within a company or they function as individual contributors. In fact, leadership ability isn't tied to rank and status—it stems from an individual's sense of otherness, of selflessness, and of assuming responsibility for results. Therefore, don't confuse leadership with management or supervision. First-time workers fresh out of high school applying for a position in a fast-food restaurant may have excellent leadership potential. Higher-level executives with decades of experience, in comparison, may not have a strong track record of exceptional leadership. It's important that you explore this particular talent in all candidates whom you interview—especially if they'll be supervising individuals at your organization or otherwise filling your talent pipeline.

Why Ask This Question?

For some, leadership is simply natural. Call it appeal, charm, or an innate ability to influence and persuade. Whatever it is, it comes to them as second nature. It's often combined with a healthy sense of internal competitiveness, ambition, and an inclination to want to stand out. That being said, leadership is like a muscle that can be developed. Not every great leader was born that way. A simple desire to become a stronger leader is sometimes all it takes for individuals to excel in this area and develop a reputation as a mover and shaker, a go-to person when times get difficult, or someone to rely on and trust in times of change and instability.

Not all leaders are extroverts, of course. Some of the greatest leaders are quiet, introverted, and somewhat shy. It's not so much what they do that makes them great leaders—it's who they are. They come more from "beingness" than from "doingness," meaning that people are attracted to them because of their character, their selflessness, and their trustworthiness. When asking this question and looking for healthy responses, focus on the candidate's approach to performance, communication, and teamwork. Look for an awareness of what leadership is—many won't really have given much thought to what it means to be an effective leader. Those who have given it ample thought have very likely reflected on their own strengths and weaknesses in terms of being someone's favorite boss, serving as a calming influence in times of crisis, or simply being someone who can retain confidences when others simply need to let their guard down and make themselves vulnerable. Healthy leadership can show itself in any of these varying ways.

Analyzing the Response

Some individuals respond to this particular question by focusing on active listening. They believe that effective leadership stems from selfless leadership, or as Robert Greenleaf called it in his 1970 essay of the same name, servant leadership.[2] People who ascribe to the Greenleaf philosophy put others' needs ahead of their own and expect them to respond in kind. They believe that we hear with our ears but listen with our eyes. They go out of their way to create an open and honest dialog, base their relationships on trust, and look at leadership as a process for self-discovery. They see themselves as effective advisers, not necessarily advice givers.

They're more about observation than they are about judgment, and this objectivity sets them apart. They set others up for success and then simply step out of the way. They commit themselves to helping others find their own way in an endless process of self-discovery.

Other individuals will respond to this question by distinguishing between management, leadership, and coaching. They may describe it along these lines:

➡ "Managing others is all about reporting, controlling, and pushing. Leadership is about modeling specific behaviors, inspiring, and pulling. Coaching is about selfless leadership, facilitating a process where others can learn in a safe environment, knowing that their boss has their backs, and feeling free to make healthy mistakes in an effort to learn, experiment, and innovate."

People who have this level of awareness often use terms like *engagement* and *motivation* in their responses. They strive to do their best work every day and encourage others to do the same. They demonstrate thankfulness and appreciation, which serve as a cornerstone not only for their work lives but for their personal lives as well. They even sometimes channel their responses through their personal experiences of being parented or being parents themselves, drawing out parallels for inspiring others in how they raised their children or how they were encouraged by their parents at a young age to want to change their behaviors for their own benefit.

Leaders are born, but they also can develop leadership muscle when it doesn't come naturally to them. That's why countless books, articles, and workshops are dedicated to growing this particular skill and ability. Look for candidates who respond to your question by making themselves somewhat vulnerable in their self-analysis: "I like to think of myself as a leader and constantly focus on helping others succeed in becoming their best, and I'm always looking for new ways to help others succeed" is a perfectly fine answer. It lends itself well to a behavior-based follow-up interview question like "Tell me about a time when you helped someone go inside themselves for an answer or when you helped someone challenge themselves to do something that they thought was above their ability. How did you convince them to take that step, and what is it about you that helps other trust you in those types of situations?"

Vulnerability begets trust. Selflessness begets confidence. After all, you can't give away something that you don't already have, so leaders who *give away* time, praise, and encouragement know that they themselves possess these gifts and can give them freely to others. You'll often find candidates who respond to this question by describing their favorite boss and how they strive to be that type of leader to others: "My favorite boss always made me feel included, she made me feel like my opinion counted, she challenged me to do things that I really didn't think I was capable of doing, and no matter what, she always made me feel like she had my back. That's the kind of leader I want to be, not only for the people I supervise but for my peers and boundary partners as well. I hope I can have one-tenth the influence on them that she's had on me. I was very fortunate to have a boss like her early on in my career."

These are all healthy responses to your initial question. Even if no examples come up like the ones above, however, it's often enough for candidates to discuss the courses they've taken or the books and articles they've read on effective leadership. Simply ask them to tell you about their favorite book or course and see what the main takeaway lessons were. You'll likely be able to see through any artificial or fictional responses pretty quickly. In short, if they don't have at least one pearl of wisdom, one takeaway from their books and courses that helped them redefine themselves, it's likely that they've not given much thought to their own leadership style or career development. In such cases, you might want to give the individual a second bite at the apple by asking a counterquestion this way:

"It's okay if you haven't given much thought to a question like this, but let me ask you another question in a different way: Bad bosses are important in our careers because they help us define who we're *not*. How do you think poor leaders diminish value in the workplace? In other words, what are some of the telltale signs when you're working around someone who doesn't practice effective leadership or who may not be aware of how he or she comes across to others? What might that look like from your past experience?"

No, this isn't meant to be a trick question. But if they can at least describe what ineffective leadership looks like—lack of respect, an overreactive grapevine, micromanagement, work-arounds rather than confronting problematic performance or conduct head-on—then they may be able to convince you that they at least have a distinguishing line in their minds that separates strong from weak leadership. As always, when in doubt about their commitment to effective leadership, communication, or teamwork, be sure to explore this key issue during reference checks with prior supervisors. There may not be a hardline, right-or-wrong response from a reference that convinces you to hire or pass on the individual. But combined with other aspects of the interview, testing, and the nature of the role in question, this one particular area may be enough to serve as a positive swing factor for a candidate or an ultimate knockout consideration.

> **BONUS QUESTION 10F:** Most jobs at your level require the ability to deal with ambiguity and shift gears quickly, even without having all the information. Give me an example of a time when you had to adjust for and lead through a sudden change in plans with no blueprint to guide you. What were the circumstances and how did you handle it?

I typically recommend using behavioral interview questions as follow-up questions rather than lead-in queries. In other words, if you ask candidates what they like least about their jobs and they say something like "terminating employees," you can immediately relate to that. Further, you'd naturally ask for an example of the last time that happened: what were the circumstances, the factors under consideration, the employee's response, and the like? Occasionally, however, you can open up with a question using a behavior-based format to invite candidates to jump right into an explanation of past actions that would be consistent with their level of responsibility at the time. Leading with a behavior-based query should create an opportunity for open and honest dialog about a real-life crisis or challenge.

Why Ask This Question?

The response you're looking for will measure the individual's agility, adaptability, and flexibility. Being able to make decisions and act on them while remaining calm in the face of the unexpected is a hallmark of a strong performer and leader. The ability to adjust and course correct when facing new and changing circumstances amid shifting priorities is critical to any organization's success, and you're basically looking for an individual's ability to bend without breaking.

Analyzing the Response

The inclination to act independently versus gain approval and sign-off from a superior may be a good thing or may be a fault; it depends on the circumstances, which is why diving deeply into this behavioral interview scenario may make sense for candidates for roles with the authority to make impactful decisions. Don't be surprised if you get a response that focuses on a rare or extreme event or exception—that's how many candidates may interpret a question like this. For example, a candidate for a director of international marketing role responded:

➡ "We were hosting an international film event at our Hollywood movie studio, and a whole contingent of buyers from China had just arrived at L.A. International Airport to visit the studios and prepare for their international purchases of movie rights and distribution deals. That very day, the Centers for Disease Control formally announced that visitors from China should be quarantined due to potential exposure to the bird flu. We were at our wits' end: We didn't want to risk alienating the visitors from China, our potentially largest global market, but we couldn't provide them unfettered access to the studio lot for fear of exposing our employees to the virus.

"We quickly reached out to the other major studios to find out what they were planning but soon learned we were on our own: Some were opening up their studio gates to the visitors, while others decided they would delay their sales and distributions exhibits and meetings for another time—even though the travelers had just stepped off a seventeen-hour flight to the United States. As the director of marketing, I didn't have final say to commit what our studio would do, but my voice was arguably the loudest, and our studio went with my recommendation: Create an off-site, smaller-scale exhibit area that would allow the meetings to continue but would not expose studio employees to potential safety risk. We had to move quickly and relocate our exhibits to the off-site facility within a few hours. We redirected the buses scheduled to arrive at our studio lot to the ancillary location not far away, and I was the first person to greet them, apologize for the change in plans, and explain the logic for our setup at the alternate facility.

"It was the highest stakes game I'd ever been involved in, but in the end, the Chinese contingent appreciated the fact that they could still complete their business with us during that trip. As it turned out, our Chinese visitors weren't infected with the SARS virus, and the CDC's preliminary cautions didn't pan out. Of course, we couldn't have known that at the time, so we felt our modified approach could still get the job done while protecting worker safety. I later learned that the studios that closed their doors to the Chinese visitors altogether because of the bird flu hazard had a very difficult time recapturing that lost business. It was considered a big win for us."

Risk and uncertainty are the costs of doing business; learning of the individual's immediate inclination and recommendations under the circumstances is invaluable. Composure is a hallmark of strong leaders faced with adversity; a calm voice and steady hand go a long way in furthering business interests when there are no rules to play by. Willingness to stand up and assume full responsibility for a situation gone wrong—especially where there's one with no blueprint to follow—tells you a lot about someone's self-confidence and willingness to take the bull by the horns. Likewise, an inclination to act independently versus sign off on someone else's directive isn't necessarily right or wrong—it's strictly a matter of how you see the individual's role as director of international marketing as opposed to that of the division president under those same circumstances.

In this case, the director-level candidate influenced the studio's decision, worked in concert with his boss, and lobbied for and ultimately gained approval to set a new direction for that event. The point is, employ a question like this when you're looking to learn more about an individual's decision-making abilities, willingness to take risks, and use of logic to proffer solutions that were reasonable, practical, and wise under the circumstances.

BONUS QUESTION 10G: How would you describe yourself in terms of your personal brand? How do you model the behaviors that you espouse?

This can be an interesting question. No, we wouldn't expect anyone to put themselves down, but it's interesting to see how candidates approach their response. Higher level individual contributors and middle managers who are often planning to increase their responsibilities in order to climb the corporate ladder approach the concepts of conduct and behavior quite differently. Some believe that productivity and results are all that count; how you get there is of secondary importance. Some come from a school of thought that fear begets respect and that being too nice may be a sign of weakness. Others will tell you that a healthy sense of humor and a spirit of fun and play are critical to the creativity and innovation processes. Still others will focus their responses on a lack of drama, always being in control of the message, and ensuring that they'll never have to ask for forgiveness because they'll always insist on gaining advance approval.

Why Ask This Question?

Much of how candidates see themselves stems from their philosophy of conduct relative to performance. Don't minimize its importance in the selection process because all employees—leaders and staff—are responsible for fulfilling both halves of the Performance-Conduct circle.

Figure 10-1. Performance-Conduct circle illustration.

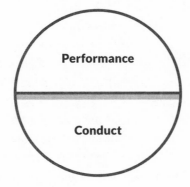

For example, when sales superstars or so-called rainmakers are difficult to deal with, demonstrate a poor attitude, or make others feel like they have to walk on eggshells around them, they fail the circle test: They may be performing exceptionally well in the top half of the circle, but they're failing in the bottom half. That only gives them an overall score of 50 percent—a failing grade in most employers' books. In fact, asking them to grade themselves in terms of their performance versus their behavior (a.k.a. conduct) may be an interesting conversation starter.

Analyzing the Response

What you're looking for clearly is someone who walks the walk of effective leadership and personal responsibility. Where do they see themselves relative to the concepts of communication, team building, accountability, and employee engagement? Do they pride themselves on modeling those behaviors, and if so, what do they do to proactively demonstrate their values? Does it find meaning in annual goal setting and quarterly update meetings with their direct reports where they focus on professional development and career planning? Do they ask their team members to assume responsibility for interim leadership roles or weekly staff meeting oversight? Do they support the idea of interim rotational assignments in other parts of the enterprise so that their team members gain a greater macro understanding of the business? Further, what three adjectives would they suppose others use in describing their leadership styles—direct reports, extended reports, and superiors?

Further, you may hear responses in which they describe their behaviors in terms of their own career growth and development. For example:

"One of my key values is to be viewed as a strategic thinker, but I don't know that people would have always thought of me that way. I realized that for a long time, I was working one pay grade below my job title. In other words, as a director I was more comfortable doing the hands-on things that I did when I was a manager. When I was promoted to VP, I again found myself working in the familiar and comfortable areas that made me successful as a director. I got good advice, though, from someone I trusted who told me that what got me here won't get me there, meaning I needed to change my approach to leadership when I became a VP. I acknowledged that I was overly busy and overly task focused and realized that I needed to slow down and not work above capacity, constantly focusing on doing more and executing on a lot of the smaller stuff.

"I had to keep asking myself whether I should be involved in certain activities and, if so, at what level. It took a good amount of discipline to pull myself back. I finally realized that at the VP level, there's a shift in the success equation: Busyness and capacity work against you at some point in your career, and at the VP level I really needed to give more thought to impacting the organization and especially my department and pulling back from actually doing many of the activities myself (unless someone was absent or the situation became critical, for example). At this point, I think it's fair to say that others would grade me well in terms of being a bit more strategic in my thinking and less tactical, but it didn't come easy, and it's still something I have to force myself to focus on."

Whether candidates respond to this question in terms of workplace values like respect, work ethic, and accountability or approach the question from a standpoint of personal leadership development, strategic thinking, or change leadership, look for evidence in the form of behavior-based interviewing follow-ups like these:

➡ "Give me an example of the before and after, and how your most respected critic would grade you in this area."

➡ "Tell me about the last time you got to apply this new skill called *strategic thinking* or *change leadership*, what the circumstances were, and how you approached the matter."

➡ "Knowing now what it takes to feel more confident in making the leap to strategic leadership that you're finding at the VP level, how would you prepare one of your director-level subordinates to make this same transition? What would your coaching focus on?"

➡ "I agree that accountability is key in developing strong teams. How do you deal with someone who demonstrates an entitlement mentality, complains that there are never enough resources, or assigns blame to others?"

➡ "Can you share any times in the last year or so where you weren't proud of the behaviors that you demonstrated? It's okay for all of us to get frustrated at times and show angst, but what's an example that you wish you could erase and start over again with?"

Inviting middle managers to assess their own strengths and weaknesses in the critical areas of behavior and conduct often makes for good conversation. Look not only to the philosophy behind their answers but also to the concrete examples they provide in response to your behavioral interviewing question. Do their style of communication and their expectations surrounding employee performance and achievement appear to match yours? Whatever their response, this question lends itself well to examining with prior supervisors during a reference check. After all, hiring someone at this level can catapult your organization to new heights—or drag it down dramatically—depending on their approach to dealing with others and holding themselves accountable to the bottom half of the Performance-Conduct circle.

BONUS QUESTION 10H: What career advice would you give someone getting into the field right now?

Why Ask This Question?

Responses to this invitation to critique career possibilities and limitations can be insightful. First, you want to gauge the individual's global awareness of industry trends and patterns so you can compare notes and gain insights about things you might not otherwise be aware of. After all, when candidates are on the job market, they become astutely aware of who's hiring, who's laying off, and who's merging, divesting, outsourcing, offshoring, automating, and the like. Busily employed professionals like yourself may miss some of the newer trends going on out there, so picking candidates' brains provides you with a good opportunity to catch up on some of the broader trends in your field. Further, you want to ensure that this individual possesses a healthy dose of career introspection and can articulate some of those broader trends and patterns that she should be aware of. Finally, you'll want to ensure that there's still excitement in her voice, that she's still motivated about what she's doing, and that she's not coming across as burned out or as a "downer" who clearly sees her better days behind her or is otherwise questioning why she entered this career path in the first place.

Analyzing the Response

Industries, companies, and roles are morphing at an incredible pace. We're seeing significant downsizing in print media but booming additions to digital media. Retail closures are on an epic rise, while distribution centers can't find qualified people to fill fulfillment roles. Organizations that were hot just a few years ago may be holding on for dear life right now, while some of the underperforming organizations from years past may find themselves at the top of their industries. See where candidates take your invitation to pass judgment on the state of your industry or professional field. In addition, see how many contacts you have in common. It's interesting to learn where your paths may have crossed in the past, whether through educational contacts, professional networking groups, or shared conferences and events.

For example, a marketing executive might focus on the significant growth in social and digital media relative to traditional roles in advertising and public relations. Other candidates might focus more on metrics and predictive measures available through Google Analytics relative to more traditional data-gathering techniques. Here's what the response might sound like if an HR professional responded to this question:

➡ "By far the biggest need in HR today is for organizational-development skills. If I could have focused more on talent development, retention, and succession planning when I was working on my MBA, I'd be probably be further ahead in my career today. It seems like everyone hiring HR leaders wants someone who can take the organization to the next level, and that typically comes from defining a strategy for leadership-pipeline development, addressing organizational design issues, and combining effective talent-acquisition strategies with performance-management and leadership development to strengthen the muscle of an organization's front-line leadership team. Strong front leadership lines should typically spike employee engagement, and as all the current literature will tell you, organizations with a high degree of employee engagement will benefit from greater revenue and profit generation, lower turnover, and higher productivity per employee."

Bravo—a realistic assessment tied to current organizational-development trends in the field, relative to more traditional HR subdisciplines like recruitment, employee relations, and compensation and benefits. But what about a candidate who responds this way:

➡ "It's just not like it's used to be, and it feels like you need a surfboard to stay afloat amid the constant changes and downsizings that are hitting our company and our competitors right now. Truth be told, I was surprised to see you were hiring, and I'm guessing you've got hundreds of applications for this job, but being the only company in town that's hiring, I'm sure you'll have your choice of talent for this position."

In fairness, pessimistic responses shouldn't be held too harshly against candidates. After all, mergers and automation have hit certain industries, companies, and roles particularly hard. Technology changes are eliminating the need for human beings to perform certain jobs, and permanent position eliminations are very scary. Still, only you can determine what's an appropriate response versus a depressing, cynical reaction. Gauging candidates' overall advice to new entrants into the field, considerations for alternative career planning, or overall willingness to get back on the horse after they've been thrown off can tell you a lot about the person's character and innate self-motivation.

BONUS QUESTION 101: Tell me about the difference between leadership and management. Is it necessary to supervise someone to establish your reputation as a leader?

One of the key elements of career success lies in appreciating the differences between leadership and management and between supervising and coaching. The truth is that at some point in a leader's career—typically at the juncture between director and vice president—a fundamental shift occurs in terms of how success is defined. As the saying goes, "What got you here won't get you there," and one of the most common reasons why midlevel managers don't get promoted to the senior leadership ranks can be found in their lack of people skills.

If an individual demonstrates subpar leadership skills, it may likely stem from an inability to gain buy-in and trust, bond normally conflictive groups, or create trust and loyalty among peers and team members. Any of these scenarios can be career limiters. The question is always, where is this individual now in terms of his ability to forge individual bonds, grow teams, and turn around situations where employees will be expected to perform at a heightened level?

Why Ask This Question?

The clearest answer often reveals itself in terms of the candidate's ability to distinguish among management, leadership, and coaching. Candidates who can paint a picture with words of how they differentiate these three concepts will often distinguish themselves during the interview and selection process. That's because posing an answer will stem from practical experience rather than book knowledge, from personal belief and self-identity rather than from theory.

Proven leaders or those with innate leadership abilities will often describe themselves in terms of how their actions have touched others—how they've helped others through challenges, encouraged others to get ahead, and supported others' growth and development. They see themselves above the trenches in terms of their impact on those around them: Their answers are broader and describe group and team impact rather than how matters only affected them, and they are quick to give praise and recognition for other people's contributions. While this question may appear to lend itself to a hypothetical response, it typically draws out the real core of the person in terms of how he sees himself via the relationships to those around him.

Analyzing the Response

Here's what a solid answer might sound like:

➡ "First, I would say that you don't need to supervise anyone to be a great leader. The Boy Scouts and Girl Scouts teach leadership essentials at a fairly young age, and that has nothing to do with being in a certain position on the corporate totem pole. Great leaders can be individual contributors whom others rely on and trust.

"Management is all about giving directives and pushing work out. Leadership is about motivating and developing your people so that they want to give the discretionary effort to support you and follow you into battle. It's about pulling people into the work, engaging them, and motivating them to do their best work every day. That's because selfless leadership creates trust, and trust is based on respect and appreciation. So leadership in my mind is a whole different animal than management and is at a much higher level because of the emotional commitment involved.

"Coaching is a way of demonstrating excellent leadership. I've always seen my role as a coach in terms of helping others challenge themselves, look inward for answers, and get comfortable relying on themselves for solutions. For example, when someone on my team comes up to me and asks what she should do, my typical response is, 'Well, what do you think you should do?' They typically respond with something like, 'I don't know—that's why I came to you for help.' And my response is always something like, 'I know you don't know, *but if you did know*, what would your recommendation be?'

"They typically roll their eyes and giggle at that point, but they know what I'm getting at. The answers are in them already, and my goal is to tease those answers out. I want them to think things through and get comfortable with the idea that they can do this without me. Nine times out of ten, they hit the nail on the head in terms of providing the right answer. And when they're sometimes off by a bit, I could ask coaching questions to get them back on track so that the final answer is still theirs. It's a fun technique, but after a few times doing this, they know they'd better have some answers in hand when they come to me with their questions."

169

And there you have it: an excellent response that demonstrates wisdom and selflessness. When interpreting candidate responses to this question, look for individuals who pride themselves on building relationships based on trust, tapping into a person's or a team's potential, and developing a vision of the future with real strategic clarity and the detailed tactical plan to get there.

They will likely describe themselves doing this by listening carefully, asking insightful questions, and fully committing themselves to helping others succeed in terms of their personal and career growth. In short, this question is a dividing line. Not every successful leader who's geared for progression in their career will be able to articulate this as carefully as I've outlined above in the sample response. But as the interviewer, you'll want to listen to their response with your eyes and heart. Are they motivated about leading and influencing others? Can they share personal wins where others were positively impacted by their actions? Have they helped staff members create individual development plans around what was most significant to them at that point in their careers? Can they pass the selfless-leadership test in terms of positively influencing those around them and helping them grow and develop according to their own priorities?

How to Get More Mileage out of the Question. A natural follow-up to this question might be, "I like what you're telling me, but let me ask you this: Would you like to work for you? What would be some of the positives and challenges about reporting to you?" Ah, now *that's* an interesting question. You'll definitely get a smile initially as they ponder your question, but it's a fair one. Why not ask them to assess how others might see them as leaders? Invite them to identify their style further, differentiating between practical strengths and areas for development. Are the areas they're looking to develop something you can help them with? Will you be able to mentor them to help them progress further in their career at this point?

This question works well with candidates at the middle-management and professional/technical stages of their careers. It gives you a chance to discuss philosophy, book knowledge, practical experience, and personal inclination. It lends itself well to behavior-based follow-up questions where you can discuss examples of how they've impacted others, learned from mistakes, and reinvented themselves over time. Consider making this a staple question for high-level individual contributors and midlevel managers who represent your organization's natural-talent pipeline.

11.

Senior Management Evaluations

Leaders, Mentors, and Effective Decision Makers

Senior managerial candidates come in all shapes and sizes. Some want ultimate responsibility for their operations and insist on making all the decisions themselves. Others define themselves as fiercely loyal to their people and pride themselves on the teams they build by promoting their direct reports. Some march to their own drummers without necessarily linking their agendas to the company's bottom line. Still others are more comfortable not making waves and look for sign-off from above before implementing any new programs. These are all very human inclinations, but because senior managers maintain such a high profile in corporate America, their work habits and business philosophies warrant much closer scrutiny. Few people, after all, will be able to influence your corporate culture and increase top-line revenues more than your senior management team.

Only you know how to determine profitability for your particular line of business. This chapter will consequently focus not on the nuts and bolts of revenue generation but on the people issues surrounding candidates' actions. The challenge in any senior managerial interview is to create and maintain a balance between the macro business issues and the daily operational activities encountered by each candidate. That's because translating strategic issues into tactical objectives is the measuring rod against which managerial effectiveness is gauged. As a result, your interview questioning techniques should typically look for concrete examples of candidates' people strategies and their track records for influencing an organization's corporate culture.

171

52

Can you give me an example of your ability to facilitate progressive change within your organization?

Why Ask This Question?

Progressive change may certainly be evidenced by technological innovations in the workplace. That's especially the case when evaluating senior IT candidates who focus their solutions on developing client servers, implementing predictive dialing units to increase outbound call volume exponentially, or automating manual systems to expand the organization's capacity for output.

Most senior managers outside of the data-processing realm, however, will define their achievements by facilitating change according to productivity—not technological—issues. But before productivity changes can be determined, production measurements need to be established and then ratcheted up according to the talents of the workforce. Therefore, real productivity change is often tied to new expectations being established for the staff. Your focal point in assessing a candidate's response will consequently target *how* the individual achieved buy-in for the new programs and established more of a performance culture.

Analyzing the Response

Good Answers. How do senior executives implement change management? One way is by making information available to everyone and creating an entrepreneurial mentality where workers assume ownership of their projects as if they were outside consultants bidding for the company's business. Another way is to give everyone a piece of the action and tie compensation to group performance as opposed to individual productivity. Similarly, look for executives who make organizational commitments to lifelong learning and a continuous improvement ethos by encouraging their staff members to further their own professional educations and, in turn, offer the company more creativity and innovation.

How to Get More Mileage out of the Question. For example, let's assume you're interviewing a plant manager for your liquid and powder detergent manufacturing plant to streamline production procedures and increase plant productivity. The candidate has a track record for running a productive operation at a competitor firm—a plant that was close to extinction before she came aboard. Your interviewing mission will be to learn how she diagnosed and solved production problems through people. You might ask:

➡ "How did you gain a firm understanding of what was working and what wasn't when you first took over the plant?"

➡ "How hands-on were you in working the production line and sitting in on planning meetings with the engineers?"

➡ "How were the ideas for streamlining production developed: Did you encourage team suggestions or have a mandate from headquarters to artificially impose new production standards?"

➡ "What kind of resistance did you encounter from your existing staff?"

➡ "What were the criteria you used in hiring new staff?"

➡ "How did you improve the baseline? Without thought to how the plant was currently processing soap products, what did you need to do to make the process better?"

➡ "What kinds of cost factors did you consider to meet the organization's redefined needs?"

➡ "How did you negotiate with corporate to attain the necessary improvements?"

➡ "And finally, how effective were you at negotiating costs with vendors?"

This is an ideal setting, by the way, to use behavioral questioning techniques:

➡ "Tell me about your biggest obstacle—was it with people, budgets, or a stubborn and unyielding corporate culture? Give me an example of a reluctant compromise you had to make in order to reach your goal. How would the executive vice president to whom you reported grade your accomplishments in that plant's transition? Give me an example of something you would do differently if you had the chance to do it all over again."

Does this seem like a lot to ask a candidate? Absolutely. But facilitating change is a lengthy process that defines itself by planned benchmarks and the attainment of preestablished goals. The people factor is critical at every step of the process, and this type of query allows you a window through which to measure the candidate's dealings with subordinates, superiors, and vendors. In short, it provides a prism through which you can see the future.

53

Tell me about the last time you inherited a problem unit— one suffering from poor productivity or low morale. What was the scope of the problem, and how were your direct reports affected?

Why Ask This Question?

Every senior manager has a problem unit all the time. Even if things are going fairly well overall, then the unit with the least amount of output relative to its peers is a de facto problem unit. Dealing with a unit's problems might entail increasing employee morale, determining a unit's policies and procedures to provide clearer direction to staff and to avoid redundancies in job functions, reexamining the budgeting process to cost-justify ongoing programs, or revamping equipment and systems to bring a product more swiftly to market. Again, the focus in this issue will remain how managers accomplished their agendas through their people.

Analyzing the Response

Candidates typically have no problem painting a picture for you of a particular problem unit that they successfully turned around. Those bragging rights are often one of the first things candidates volunteer during an interview, and it's not uncommon to find them detailed on a résumé as well. Still, problem units more often than not stem from problem employees— ineffective middle managers who (1) don't believe in or don't understand the corporate mission statement, (2) doubt their ability to effectuate positive change in the organization, or (3) adhere more to an entitlement mentality and feel they're owed a paycheck simply for showing up at work. These are all common scenarios that beg for effective management intervention.

Changing people's attitudes about work sometimes takes a carrot and sometimes takes a stick. Whatever motivational means senior managers use to change others' feelings about work, altering subordinates' behaviors and attitudes is one of the most challenging aspects facing management today. To complicate the problem even further, weak farm systems make it difficult for executives to weed out subpar performers aggressively.

How to Get More Mileage out of the Question. A senior managerial candidate responsible for repairing a problem unit will always need to remove middle managers with incurable weaknesses. Therefore, this query often leads to situations where staff had to be cut. How those people were let go will tell you a lot about this individual's style of dealing with subordinates.

Some managers, for example, lop off heads. They're the Bloody Marys of corporate America who draw blood first and ask questions later. Others view the progressive discipline process as an opportunity to salvage subordinates via training (as opposed to a tool for getting rid of people). Whatever the case, question candidates about their opinions of how the terminations occurred:

➡ "How did your direct reports respond to your programs for changing production standards, motivating staff, and disposing of those who couldn't make the cut?"

➡ "How did you determine who should stay and who should go? What criteria did you use in the final analysis?"

➡ "What kinds of training programs did you install to help your existing staff to meet your new performance initiatives?"

➡ "Tell me about your most difficult termination: What made it so hard, and how did you handle it?"

➡ "What kind of time-frame benchmarks did you set for yourself, and how successful were you at reaching them?"

It's also logical for you to look for contrary evidence and ask for an example of a situation where the candidate wasn't successful at solving the problems that made a particular unit lag. No one can fix everything all the time, and it's interesting to hear about the times when the candidate was unable to manage the problem. Note what obstacles got in the individual's way, and examine them against your organization's current barriers.

54

**Did you create a culture of open information sharing
and increased accountability by giving responsibility to
your subordinates, or did you focus more on establishing their
parameters and controlling the decision-making process?**

Why Ask This Question?

Senior managers affect your organization's corporate culture because they make an impact on the way people communicate with one another and feed information across departmental boundaries. On a broad behavioral spectrum, executives usually fall between two extremes: They either manage by consensus building and participative input from their subordinates, or they autocratically decide what is to be done and then force their mandates down on their staffs.

Of course, no one style is necessarily correct. And daily business life necessitates that a successful employee will be able to wield both styles of management depending on the situation. Still, most people are inclined toward one way of supervising more than the other, and hiring the wrong style could create rifts in your senior management team. If, for example, you're used to running your company close to the vest and employing a trickle-down theory of decision making, then the new hire who prides himself on empowering his direct reports and allowing them to operate autonomously may build resentment from other department heads. The centralized decision maker, conversely, in an open, enlightened environment may stir feelings of animosity in his direct reports, who feel as if they have chains around their necks.

Analyzing the Response

How to Get More Mileage out of the Question. This query is fairly simple and practical to apply. As a self-appraisal query, ask the candidate:

"On a scale of one to ten—one being that you have a totally autocratic style, ten being that you make almost all your decisions by consulting with your staff and gaining their buy-in—how would you grade your decision-making style?"

Once the candidate admits to being a six or a four (most people will give a middle-of-the-road response unless they know that you're specifically in the market for, say, a Bloody Mary type), ask, "What makes you a four? If I were to check references with some of your direct reports, how would they grade you?"

Additionally, you might ask:

"If you're a four and naturally lean toward a more paternalistic, controlling style, what would make you a one? In other words, what would drive you to the extreme of becoming a total autocrat? Give me an example of how that's played itself out in real life."

Reciprocally, you might ask, "What could make you swing in the other direction and become a six? When have you chosen to not follow your natural inclination in supervising others, and how did that work for you?" Finally, ask, "What should I expect if we were to bring you aboard? You've been a four in the past; do you continue to see yourself that way, or is that natural inclination something you're seeking to change?" Forcing the numbers issue can be an effective way to assess candidates because it allows them to critically evaluate themselves and volunteer shortcomings.

How do you typically stay in the information loop and monitor your staff's performance?

Why Ask This Question?

Senior executives can't be everywhere all the time. Therefore, many of them adopt a policy of hiring good managers beneath them and letting them manage. That's because the strength of the senior manager's directives is only as viable as the chain of command ordained to carry out those orders. Granted, insulation is a factor in any senior manager's life because there necessarily must be a distance between operative employees and key strategic decision makers. Time constraints ensure that. Still, no one should operate in total isolation. Therefore, mechanisms have to be put in place to feed information back to the source.

Analyzing the Response

Will a senior management candidate readily admit that she's too hands-off and doesn't have a total grasp on what's going on underneath her?

177

Never—nor should she. Still, the way information gets fed back can be telling. The key to diagnosing the candidate's response is often found in the person's communications philosophy.

You've no doubt heard of MBWA, or management by walking around. That can be a viable style if the individual knows what she's looking for, has well-developed intuitive skills, and has a knack for standing over people's shoulders and observing direct performance. Otherwise, it can merely be a façade with little value to the observer or those being observed. After all, how much can anyone glean while casually walking through a department? Sure, this slice-of-life technique places the general among the infantry, but it's often the case that little more than a superficial observation is gained, and observers perceive the show of involvement as insincere.

What about managers who hold lots of meetings? Meetings can be positive in that they allow staff members to share ideas, vent frustrations, and creatively brainstorm to customize solutions for the organization's changing needs. Meetings mandate communication, and there's typically not enough open information sharing in most organizations. On the other hand, meetings held too often can serve as superficial mechanisms that delay action and lead to analysis paralysis.

How to Get More Mileage out of the Question. Therefore, question the perennial meeting holder like this:

"John, what triggers your need for a staff meeting? Give me an example of the last meeting you held and who attended. What issues were tabled and what conclusions were reached? Tell me about a time when necessary action was postponed because you needed staff feedback before proceeding. How would your peers and superiors rate the value of your meetings?"

Managers who have the inclination and time to work side by side with their troops make no bones about it. When senior vice presidents of loan service sit down next to collections agents and crank out collections calls, those executives typically pride themselves on being in the trenches fighting alongside their troops. They feel that it builds loyalty among the ranks and keeps them close to the grassroots of their business. Is that the optimum management style? Again, that depends on your point of view and your particular line of business. Question the candidate as follows:

➡ "How was your call to action perceived by your troops?"

➡ "Do you train people when you sit next to them and listen to them as well, or do you typically pick up the phone and do all the talking?"

➡ "What's the goal of this sit-in: Are you trying to instill a sense of camaraderie by working among the ranks, or is it more of a 'If I can do it, you can too' type of message you're sending?"

➡ "How do your peers regard your hands-on management style with your people?"

➡ "Can you give me an example of a time when a subordinate was embarrassed or otherwise uncomfortable with your actions when you were cranking out collections calls?"

You can gain a lot of insight into candidates by gauging how they keep themselves in the daily communications flow and manage feedback. That's how corporate cultures are made and broken.

56

How do you typically confront subordinates when results are unacceptable?

Why Ask This Question?

Confronting problem employees is daunting for even the most confident managers. Some take a direct, unequivocal approach in delivering constructive criticism. Others provide a light and tactful touch and couch criticism in a context of warranted praise for work well done. Whatever your particular style, remember that many subordinates don't do what you *expect* but what you *inspect*. Therefore, imposing discipline on underperformers, setting well-defined objectives, and then policing the plan is a necessary part of everyday executive business life. The consequences of inaction, after all, could be perilous.

Analyzing the Response

The ability to distinguish sound supervisory approaches from ineffective ones reveals itself best through a behavioral questioning format. Bear in mind, however, that whatever response you get will call for a follow-up confirmation via a reference check. No one, after all, will describe his primary weakness as an avoidance of confrontation—that shows no backbone. On the other hand, candidates won't reveal their hotheaded tendencies lest they be perceived as undisciplined, reckless, and tactless. Outside third-party references will consequently offer more-balanced insights into this touchy yet critical issue.

How to Get More Mileage out of the Question. During your interview with the candidate, you might ask:

➤ "Can you tell me about a time when you had to be a strict disciplinarian?"

➤ "How swiftly will you resort to written documentation when a performance problem occurs?"

➤ "Have you ever had to fire someone on the spot?"

➤ "Would your boss ever describe you as a person who was more inclined to maintain smooth and amicable relations at the expense of avoiding confrontation at all costs?"

➤ "Could a subordinate accuse you of being too heavy-handed and intent on pushing your agenda through with little regard for others' feelings?"

➤ "Have you ever been accused of making unduly optimistic assumptions about your direct reports?"

➤ "If you had to grade yourself on a scale of one to five (one being you're a strict disciplinarian, five being you avoid confrontation at all costs), where would you fall on the spectrum?

➤ "What is it about you that makes you a three? Tell me about the last time you had to show your teeth and turn into a one."

There are obviously multiple ways to uncover a candidate's inclination to confront problem issues and stand up and fight. The key lies in allowing the individual to paint a picture of the circumstances and explain the necessity for taking such a strong course of action.

BONUS QUESTION 11A: What kinds of organizational transformations have you led? What lasting value have you created for your organization?

Most senior leaders in corporate America have been involved at some level in significant change that impacted their companies. Companies have been transitioning and transforming at a record pace in light of new technologies and the effects of globalization. The local impact of such macroeconomic, tectonic shifts includes large-scale downsizing, mergers and integrations, outsourcing and consolidation, and organizational redesign in light of changes due to customer purchasing patterns, newly developing digital distribution models, and head-count restrictions and budget pressures.

Just look at the massive changes in retail due to online commerce. People see large-scale layoffs at retail stores like Macy's, JC Penney, and RadioShack and assume the industry is unwinding. In reality, while brick-and-mortar stores continue to close at an alarming rate, the retail industry as a whole is gaining far more jobs than it is losing. According to the Progressive Policy Institute in Washington, D.C., 51,000 retail jobs were lost between 2007 and 2016, while 355,000 jobs were created in online shopping and warehousing operations during that same period.[1] It turns out that the retail industry has been gaining far more jobs than it has been losing. But it doesn't feel that way if you're amid the downsizing crisis. The challenge, of course, is that retail workers don't possess the same skills, talents, and interests as those who work in distribution centers, and there you have the all-too-common challenge: Companies are laying off with the left hand (retail stores) while having tremendous difficulty hiring with the right (distribution centers) for lack of qualified talent.

Does the candidate possess the wisdom and broad overview to explain these massive shifts to you—not just how he's affected, but how the industry is changing? Can he see beyond the immediacy of the current situation and explain both sides of the story? Can he explain the matter objectively even if he's personally impacted? Senior leaders at the VP level and above should possess the knowledge and wisdom to view changes in the business environment dispassionately, regardless of how it impacts them and their staff members personally. Look for that level of distinction in assessing candidates' responses.

Why Ask This Question?

Your organization may not be going through what some are calling a retail apocalypse like that industry is experiencing. But organizations large and small are still attempting to come to terms with e-commerce disruptions to their business model and the idea of monetizing the Internet. If you're a head of human resources and experiencing the downsizing of your field HR generalists as your organization moves to an HR call-center model based out of an office three thousand miles away, you know the pain of large-scale transformation. If your sports agency recently merged with a competitor to focus only on the video side of the business, laying off your entire team of sports writers and social media coordinators, then you know how these massive global changes are impacting your local community. Or maybe you've just had four bosses in the last two years—in which case, you're all too familiar with organizational transformation, albeit on a smaller scale.

Then again, maybe you're challenged by the positive impacts of change. Growing a small but booming business by scaling up from 50 to 120 employees in the next six months will certainly keep you awake at night. Going back to those retail distribution warehouses in our example above, maybe you're facing the need to institute a large-scale training program to teach new hires a new trade. As another example, you may be a corporate leader who's experienced excessive turnover that was damaging your ability to deliver consistent quality and service to your customers. You built a turnaround model that reinvented your organization's entire approach to retention and saved the day. Whatever the experience— positive or negative, in your control or out of it—few business leaders today have been shielded from these massive changes. Even public-sector governmental organizations and universities—two areas that have historically been somewhat shielded from the vagaries of the markets—are under tremendous pressure to meet budget-cutting targets.

Analyzing the Response

When posing questions about organizational transformations and value creation, look first to see how the candidate approaches the topic. Happy stories about creative ways of scaling up to meet staffing needs are very different than examples where large-scale layoffs had to take place. Mergers and integrations don't always start smoothly, but some executives excel at bonding normally conflicting groups and developing creative ways of aligning new teams by spiking their communication and team-building efforts to establish a greater sense of trust and support within the group. What aspect of the picture does the candidate choose to share? Do you get a sense of bold leadership or victimization?

In all cases, focus on the people impact of their actions. Does the individual know her employees? Does she pride herself on remaining available, accessible, and responsive? Does she discuss the importance of sharing negative news in a constructive manner and recognizing and rewarding employees who are enduring significant change—even with some who know it may ultimately result in their own job loss? Does she believe in change *leadership* (rather than change management) to spearhead company efforts at arriving at change with as much buy-in and support from the front line as possible? If talent is any organization's primary profit lever and most critical asset in a knowledge-based economy, does this candidate focus her response on the impact of those organizational challenges on the people she led who were impacted most?

Today more than at any time in recent memory, candidates will likely respond in terms of operational changes that needed to be made and that negatively impacted workers. As a result, this question can open a window into the individual's emotional intelligence: her awareness of her own and other's emotions, her selflessness and natural level of empathy, her ability to handle interpersonal relationships during stressful times, and other intangibles that point to how people lead through change. The response to this question can come in many shapes and sizes, but one thing is for sure: Lasting value often comes from how leaders touch others' lives, so steer the response toward the people impact in addition to the operational and financial results that were involved.

How to Get More Mileage out of the Question. In fact, depending on the feedback you get from the example shared, you might further ask:

➡ "How would you predict the company will be different in two years, and how do you see yourself shaping that change?"

➡ "A lot of what you're describing speaks to a leader's emotional intelligence. How would you generally describe and then grade yourself in terms of your emotional intelligence?"

➡ "How did you share your vision with the rank and file, and how did you intend to stay connected with those working in the trenches at the time?"

A candidate's involvement in large-scale change initiatives and transformations is a critical aspect of how they identify and define themselves. Consider making this question a staple in your senior management selection criteria.

BONUS QUESTION 11B: Tell me about your approach to strategic change management. How do you approach change yourself, and how do you get your people's buy-in?

So much seems to be changing nowadays—all at once and at a very fast pace. The pressure on organizations to adapt to changes in technology, coupled with global competition, the Internet's burgeoning commercial capacities, social media, legislation, regulation, compliance, and other factors are driving evolutionary change at revolutionary speed. How senior executives drive change, view their roles, and describe stubborn resistance to change in their current or prior organizations is therefore not only a fair question—it's a critical one. Look for responses that address both their personal philosophy about change and the real-life results from a practical example as you explore this issue with them.

Why Ask This Question?

When you hear about executive recruitment firms conducting a search for a senior leader and ask about the most critical selection criterion being sought, the typical response you'll get from the headhunter nowadays is "the ability to take the organization to the next level." What does that mean exactly? Well, it all depends on what the organization's priorities happen to be. In general, though, it's probably safe to assume that the company looking to fill the position needs to hire someone with stronger skills and experience than incumbents have held in the past, someone with a greater capacity for leadership communication and change, a strategic thinker who can look past structural or procedural barriers and reinvent the way business gets conducted. Change management—better named change leadership—is the Holy Grail of executive impact. It distinguishes and sets apart those who can build and lead into the future versus those who will likely administer and continue the status quo. Look for hard evidence in candidates' responses, therefore, both in terms of their philosophy about change and its hardcore impact on a real workplace situation.

Analyzing the Response

Following is an example of a well-thought-out response. Let's follow along with the candidate's logic and then parse his response in more detail:

➡ "I think effective change management stems from strategic thinking and a willingness to explore alternatives that may not be considered traditional. It emanates from how someone is cut: If executives are highly certain of complex problems and know all the answers in advance, it's likely that they're more comfortable relying on the past rather than seeking new alternatives. The more certain they are, the fewer the options they tend to see. The answer to effective change leadership relies less on replicating the past and more on integrating different pieces of information and points of view. The ideal framework for addressing change lies in having the widest range of choices, but that also means that you have to be willing to recognize that you'll be wrong sometimes and then will have to course-adjust accordingly.

"I believe that your job as a strategic leader is to help your team slow down and create space for new possibilities and then use the appropriate tools to frame and structure the situation. Asking so-called strategic questions is uncomfortable by nature because strategic questions don't have clear answers. People don't like feeling vulnerable by raising issues that are unanswerable because it may require them to prove themselves wrong. That being said, as the saying goes, 'If I trust your methods, I'll trust your outcome.' Clarity and transparency are therefore critical to effective change leadership, and everyone's got to have skin in the game and be part of the solution.

"As I think about it, you've got to emphasize with your team the importance of getting away from convergent or corollary thinking (like they teach in school) and moving more toward divergent thinking—breaking your business model before someone else does that for you and eats your lunch. Personally, I've always used a star visual on the board and mapped out the five points of the star as strategy, structure, systems, skills, and shareholder value.

"Creating that kind of visual as a starting point gives the team members the free reign to approach the change-management challenges from different perspectives and at different levels. That's how I've always fostered clear and innovative thinking through new challenges and obstacles. Your goal at that point as a strategic leader is to help people choose the best processes and methods that will move us forward.

"Next, I think it's fair to say that workplace change causes predictable things to happen. There's always fear around large-scale

185

change events, and you can expect that there will be a loss of confidence when people realize that what you were doing before is no longer working and you have to learn something new. As they say, people don't resist change as much as they resist *being changed*, so you've got to get everyone on board with a sense of urgency and make sure they understand the 'why' early on.

"Your pessimists will be the first to jump in, outlining all the reasons why something new won't work. Next, your mavens counter the resistance of the pessimists: They're the credible, charismatic types who were the cool kids in high school who serve as your social connectors to support your vision. Third, the early adopters will step up and be the first to try and implement the change, kick the tires, and see what works and what doesn't work. They'll help convert the pessimists. What's key, though, is that you assume a concentric-circles approach to drive the change initiative, repeating the key points in different ways so it makes sense to different people at the various stages of the rollout.

"Whatever else you do, make sure you keep communicating. It's not how many times or how often you communicate, it's how effectively your message gets through. Understand that people hear things differently, depending on their comfort level with a proposed change—especially something that could negatively impact their job security. So always err on the side of overcommunicating and ensuring that they understand the 'why' of it all and the urgency in getting through the transition. If they still aren't getting it, reframe their resistance in your communications, recognizing that enabling resistance and making passive resistance active and open is all about transparency and honesty in your working relationships.

"In short, you create the framework for the change initiative by making it safe for group input and the possibility of being wrong. Expect resistance and negativity. Overcommunicate the vision and the 'why,' encourage different points of view by being superinclusive, and then model the behaviors that drive acceptance and engagement. As the senior leader, you're responsible for creating the vision, developing the road to strategic thinking, and making it a safe environment where team members know you have their backs. Realize that people don't change because they want to—they change because they have to. Create that space for innovative thinking and problem solving, and then get out of the way. Your executive leaders will typically be the best ones to solve organizational and operational challenges that stem from change and disruption."

What do you think? Personally, I love that response. It maps out many of the key drivers of successful organizational change: expected resistance to change; making it safe to think outside of the box and drive divergent thinking; the importance of inclusion, urgency, and overcommunicating; and even the star diagram as a tool to visualize the key change elements under consideration to kick off the conversations. As an interviewer, you can parse the various parts of the individual's response above, or you can move to asking for a real-life example that demonstrates how this theory all comes together in practice. Following is a senior HR executive's response that might make sense in terms of adding meat to the bones of the initial, more philosophical response above:

➡ "When I joined my last company, I recognized that the structure of the HR team didn't match the employee life cycle. We had longer-term staff members who didn't exactly welcome change, but the traditional pockets of recruitment, training, compensation and benefits, payroll, HRIS, and employee relations were too structured as silos, and there was little cross functional reach. I've always believed that HR structures should be built around the horizontal employee life cycle, so we had to tweak certain functional areas while making wholesale changes to others.

"For example, recruiters were traditionally responsible for hiring candidates and getting them to day one when new-hire orientation took place. That's where their involvement ended. That vision needed to change: Recruiters should be responsible for hiring and onboarding through day ninety. In other words, if recruiters were responsible for the entire onboarding experience, in conjunction with a new hire's immediate supervisor, then they would have more skin in the game and be better invested in a new hire's success.

"I took it a step further in that I wanted recruiters to also be responsible for employee relations. That combined function gave them much broader responsibility for a new hire's overall success. On a more practical basis, if there were performance or conduct problems, they were responsible for addressing them—or else disciplining and ultimately terminating the employee and then finding the replacement. Talent acquisition became much broader, recruiters expanded their skills and responsibilities, and their

187

relationship to front-line hiring managers became much stronger. It was no longer a one-and-done mentality—they were vested with the responsibility of hiring right the first time or having to fix their mistakes, which increased their hiring abilities as well.

"Was there resistance to this change? Of course. But with time and repetition of the vision and an understanding of the "why," they came to realize this was better for their own career development and better for the organization. Once they saw that their relationships with hiring managers extended beyond day one, they built stronger bonds and realized they had a greater influence on their line-manager peers than they originally thought. Sure, it took some getting used to, but it was a win-win-win for the recruiters, the hiring managers, and the organization as a whole, so it was a worthwhile change initiative that better aligned our department's structure with the company's needs."

And there you have it: the theory made real, the philosophy enacted in real-life terms. Not all candidates will demonstrate such clarity in leadership philosophy and offer such comprehensive examples of successful change interventions, but you get the idea. Look to see if ample thought has been given to this critical skill called *change leadership*, understand that candidates' philosophies toward change management often stem from their comfort with being vulnerable and permitting themselves to be proven wrong, and look for hard evidence of change leadership in action. This type of questioning focuses on both knowledge and wisdom, with the latter receiving greater emphasis: wisdom is knowledge applied, and you're looking to see just how wise a leader this individual may be relative to the ever-present challenge of a changing workplace landscape.

BONUS QUESTION 11C: Have you ever considered starting your own business?

Depending on the type of position you're hiring for, this can be an exceptionally insightful question. For example, it's probably safe to assume that most salespeople have given some thought to opening their own firms. That's because salespeople are responsible for bringing in new business, and that's the lifeblood of any organization in any industry. Reasons why salespeople typically opt not to open their own firms have to do with enjoying the social elements of working on a team, preferring corporate to solo healthcare and other benefits, or working with a product line that benefits tremendously from the name of the organization distributing it (i.e., where solo players may have significant disadvantages). But it's a fair question for anyone in sales or development, and you shouldn't be surprised to hear that they've at least given it some thought at one point in their career or another. Ditto for senior executives, especially those in the C-suite (e.g., CEOs, CFOs, and COOs). It's not uncommon for senior level executives to consider shucking off the chains of corporate America and going it alone, especially if finances are no longer much of an issue because of earlier career successes.

Why Ask This Question?

So much of an interview focuses on where a candidate's head is. There are often no right or wrong answers to questions like these, but they certainly can allow for interesting insights into what's important at this point in the individual's career. Should you be concerned about someone who tells you openly that they'd love nothing more than to open their own business right now if they could? Possibly—it depends on the nature of the job you're looking to fill. For example, when it comes to hiring salespeople, some organizations won't hire anyone who's owned their own firm before. Their concern is that the individual will likely get frustrated in a more structured sales environment and at some point bolt out the door with your company's customer list in hand. As far as hiring senior executives who share that they'd consider going solo, there might be concern as well that they'll make the break with corporate America once they're in your role long enough to realize that the honeymoon is over, life is too short, and the endless hours and hard work are simply not worth all the drama. Again, there's no judgment here; it's a matter of lining up your company's longer-term needs with the candidate's inclinations and preferences, and timing will always play a significant role in every hire you make.

Analyzing the Response

When candidates state that they've considered going solo before or may even be considering it now as an alternative to full-time corporate employment, it's important that you explore their responses in more detail to gauge how serious they are (or were) about the possibility of joining the gig economy and hanging out their own shingle. Gently press the conversation further by asking them to tell you more about the time and energy they invested in opening their own business. Some of the telltale signs of a serious entrepreneur in the making may show themselves, depending on how candidates answer the following questions:

➡ "When you were considering opening your own business, what steps did you take or consider to launch the business formally and get it off the ground? In other words, was it more of a wish or something that you investigated seriously?"

➡ "Did you ever get to the stage where you registered your company with the secretary of state?"

➡ "Did you have a chance to name the organization formally, and did you share that with people in your network?"

➡ "Were you planning on remaining a sole proprietorship or filing as an LLC or an S-corporation?"

➡ "Did you go through the steps of obtaining a seller's permit or applying for a federal employer ID number?"

➡ "Did you create your own website?"

Any one of these questions could point to a serious entrepreneur in the making, so it's never a bad idea to gain a more realistic understanding of how far the candidate took the concept. Obtaining a federal employer ID number only takes a few minutes, but filing for an LLC (limited liability corporation) can be costly and time intensive. In any event, it may be worth exploring this possibility, especially for senior executives and sales professionals, just to see where their heads and hearts are. Entrepreneurism is a fine and noble career path, and corporate types have been transitioning into the gig economy in record numbers since the Great Recession of 2008 reared its ugly head. Use this question whenever candidates have been in business for themselves for considerable periods of time or may be prone to breaking with the corporate lifestyle. It may be worth asking in order to avoid a surprise resignation in the not-too-distant future.

12.

Pressure Cooker Interview Questions

Assessing Grace Under Fire

One of the more common methods of measuring candidates' abilities to land on their feet is to challenge their assumptions and beliefs during the interview. Stressful interview questions can intimidate candidates, squelch spontaneity, and consequently allow for little bonding and few shared insights. Asking a candidate "Why shouldn't I hire you?" "Why aren't you making more money at this point in your career?" and "Why, with this résumé, would you see yourself as remotely qualified for this job?" only makes the person defensive and more inclined not to give you real answers. Besides, the candidate reasons, if the interview seems like such a challenging obstacle, then imagine what the real job will be like. In such circumstances, the carrot-and-stick routine will do little in the way of making the position or your company appear especially attractive.

So, why have this section in our book? First, because many employers still apply this methodology, it is important to evaluate and reexamine some of the more sophisticated pressure queries. Second, and more important, note that there is a big difference between *stress interviews* and *stress interview questions*. Every interviewer should be able to apply a pressure question when the need arises. That's especially the case when the position you're filling has lots of high-maintenance customers to tend to or if it historically suffers from high turnover. In such circumstances, a number of questions to test an individual's mettle might come in handy. Furthermore, if you sense that a candidate is a little too cocky, then a skillfully placed pressure question could help humble the individual somewhat. **191**

Following are some of the more effective stress queries that force individuals to volunteer self-critical insights. Remember again that an entire interview composed of such challenging questions will only cause ill will on the part of the candidate. So use them sparingly, but be prepared to pull one or two of these out of your hat when the situation arises.

57

Tell me about your last performance appraisal. In which area were you most disappointed?

Why Ask This Question?

Remember that it is perfectly acceptable for you to request a candidate's most recent performance appraisal in the preemployment process. Many companies nowadays insert signature waivers in employment applications granting the company permission to check the candidate's past references. (Such releases are meant to remove, or at least minimize, the hiring company's exposure to claims of invasion of privacy or misuse of confidential information.) Similarly, a short paragraph in such a handout requesting a recent performance evaluation could go a long way in scaring off mediocre performers. Handed out at the beginning of the interviewing process, that written notice will tie in well to this particular interviewing query because candidates realize that their interview responses will be substantiated when they turn their actual evaluations over to you at a later date.

Of course, no employee is perfect, so don't expect to find a halo above anyone's head. Still, some of the most graceful and polished interviewees may have committed some pretty egregious faux pas that will be reflected on paper. Knowing that they will have to present a recent performance evaluation as a condition of employment will go a long way in encouraging those candidates to speak openly about even the most uncomfortable performance situations.

Analyzing the Response

Performance appraisals historically addressed traits or work characteristics regarding an individual's cooperation, production, supervisory skills, and ability to get along with others. More progressive companies nowadays focus less on traits and features and more on specific performance goals. For example, they may encourage employees to evaluate themselves in terms of areas where they have made the most impact on the company over the past year, areas where they need additional support from management, and quarterly or annual goals that they wish to achieve with their managers' aid over the next evaluation period.

Whatever the appraisal methodology, it is important to evaluate candidates' measurement yardsticks in their responses. When candidates come from companies that use traditional performance appraisals focusing on worker characteristics (like loyalty, dependability, and cooperation), then candidates' areas of disappointment will usually focus on disagreements they have with their *bosses'* perceptions. For example, you will hear the individual speak about frustration at having received only a "good" instead of an "excellent" mark in one particular area.

When companies use more self-directed performance-appraisal techniques, inviting workers to identify their own performance goals and measurements, then candidates will often discuss their own *personal* disappointment at not meeting individually set objectives. The difference is worth noting because it will indicate the type of corporate culture the candidate comes from. Those from self-directed environments who were expected to set their own agendas and act autonomously are much more apt to assume responsibility for things gone wrong. They typically work with less supervision and structure because they are accustomed to higher individual and group performance expectations.

Good Answers. Whatever the orientation of the prior company's performance-appraisal techniques, look for areas of performance weakness that are really overstrengths, or virtues driven to an extreme. For example, someone censured for not delegating work appropriately or occasionally forging too far ahead of projects requires only mild tempering of his or her ambitions. In essence, those so-called weaknesses hold a lot more future value than they do downside risk. In contrast, beware of the candidate who provides information regarding lackadaisical performance standards, low tolerance for adversity, or reliability problems. These problems typically reveal themselves when candidates blame others for their own shortcomings.

Again, because candidates realize that they will have to provide an actual performance evaluation some time before you make them an offer, they will typically feel much more obliged to come clean regarding past indiscretions and failures.

58

In hindsight, how could you have improved your performance at your last position?

Why Ask This Question?

Even candidates with stellar performance evaluations would opt to rewrite history in light of their 20/20 hindsight. Improving performance is sometimes a factor of increased personal involvement. Sometimes it's a matter of wishing to change organizational limitations. Whatever the case, look for solutions in the candidate's response that show creativity and ingenuity in reframing problem issues and their outcomes.

Analyzing the Response

High-performance job candidates do their jobs exceptionally well but continuously try to increase the impact of their results. Newly opened sales territories could be larger; reductions in departmental operating budgets could be deeper; new program launchings could have had greater market penetration. Accordingly, the hallmark of high achievers' productivity is the desire to cut themselves in half to capitalize on their accomplishments.

In addition, when a candidate provides you with a specific shortcoming in the previous query regarding performance-appraisal disappointments, this natural follow-up demands (a) specific actions that reveal how the weaker performance could have been strengthened and (b) the candidate's willingness to accept responsibility for things gone wrong. For example, you might say, "Tell me, Dorothy, about your last performance appraisal. In which area were you most disappointed?" Dorothy, a human resources manager, responds that her greatest disappointment was in not reaching the goal she set for herself of lowering the company's cost per hire from $1,500 to $1,100. She instituted an internal referral program that she assumed would account for a 20 percent increase in staffing.

Because of market conditions and less-than-ideal marketing of her plan to coworkers, the program never really took off.

How to Get More Mileage out of the Question. Your follow-up sounds like this: "So tell me then, in hindsight, how could you have improved the results of that program?" Dorothy then explains:

➡ "I still believe that the internal referral program could have been successful. I was told when I first proposed instituting the plan that it had been tried before and failed miserably. I wanted to prove them wrong because it had worked so well for me at my previous company. Still, my fate was somewhat sealed from the start in that my own boss predicted failure from the get-go. The marketing folks never seemed to get my ad copy into the monthly newsletter, and I consequently let the program drift. Still, I can't blame anyone else for the program's failure—it was my responsibility.

"If I had to do it all again, I wouldn't have given credence to all those naysayers. I would have found ways to publicize the program myself via email, the lunchroom bulletin board, and management-training seminars. I learned that I shouldn't sit back and wait for others to do my bidding, especially when those folks aren't initially enthused about the prospects of the program. I got the okay to go ahead with it, and I accept responsibility for not having reached the program's goals."

The two key areas to look for in candidate responses focus on (1) what the candidate learned from the incident and (2) how willing the person was to accept responsibility for her actions. Both are earmarks of business maturity and reflect well on a candidate's objective self-evaluation skills.

59

Where do you disagree with your boss most often? How did you handle the last time she or he was wrong and you were right?

Differences of opinion are inevitable; conflict is optional. Still, there are times when conflict is forced on you, and you have no option but to defend yourself. It's certainly difficult evaluating candidates' responses when it

195

comes to addressing disagreements with their bosses. After all, you want someone who can stand up for himself. But you don't want someone who's too eager to draw lines in the sand and prepare for battle. As with all other responses that surface in a typical interview situation, if your gut tells you that you're getting less than the whole story, mark down your concerns in your notes so you can address the issue from the other party's perspective via a reference check.

Candidates obviously feel challenged by such queries because they are forced to defend their actions unilaterally and pit themselves against the people to whom they should be most loyal: their bosses. Still, your question will surface extreme issues at the margin of that person's work history, namely disagreement and disharmony with an immediate supervisor. Although you hope that such conflict is rare, it will inevitably face you one day if you hire this person, so it is useful to find out how the candidate deals with it.

Analyzing the Response

Like many of our queries in this book, the two-pronged questioning pattern forces the candidate being interviewed to logically connect multiple facets of the issue at hand. Your first quest in gauging someone's response is to find out what kinds of issues trip the argument threshold. Next, you want to see how the respondent relates to the supervisor when differences of opinion or outright discord occur. The best way to bring this issue to the surface is to specify situations where the candidate was probably right and the supervisor wrong. That's because such situations will more clearly reveal the candidate's inclination to avoid confrontation, be humble about winning, or rub the boss's nose in it.

Disagreements usually occur for several reasons. Perhaps the candidate disagrees with the boss's opinions on how to best reach a predetermined business goal. Such dissension is usually technical in nature. More often, an emotional disparity ignites the struggle. Such interpersonal conflict surfaces when a boss perceives a subordinate as overstepping his or her bounds, when a subordinate senses that a boss is not carrying an appropriate share of the workload, or when personal issues carry over into the work environment and staff members feel resentful of special exceptions made for certain people. Whatever the case, you should note whether there are technical or emotional lightning rods that bring about crisis in the candidate's work life.

Next, you need to examine how the candidate handles the boss's feelings after the conflict resolution. Responses like "It turned out I was right after all. I had to be. It was obvious to me that she wasn't thinking the whole thing through" might leave you feeling a little ill at ease with the candidate's gloating. After all, even the best boss can't be right all the time. And you certainly don't want someone who's going to remind you of the times when you called the shots incorrectly.

Good Answers. If the true nature of the superior-subordinate relationship lies in complementing each other's strengths and supporting each other's weaknesses, then you'll want to find a subordinate who wants to keep the peace and who is able to maintain an objective perspective even in light of an all-out victory. In such cases, candidates' responses will sound much more conciliatory because they see the bigger picture of their actions:

➡ "Oh, I know that my boss would say that my decision, in retrospect, was more appropriate. But that's just because I dealt with that matter more often than she did, and I was better able to project the impact of that decision. But who's right and who's wrong is irrelevant; the point is, we made it through a difficult issue that was building pressure for quite a while. I think we both learned to respect each other's abilities a little more because of that conflict, and our relations since then have become a lot stronger."

Hiring a peacemaker makes a lot of sense when your goal is to maintain positive interpersonal relations with your staff. People who are at ease with themselves and keep an objective distance from the action will offer you a rational sounding board even when emotions are high. In the final analysis, it's not who's right or wrong—it's how the inevitable conflict gets resolved. The fewer emotional battles and histrionics that occur, the better. After all, you have a business to run.

Is this necessarily a make-or-break interview question? Probably not. Just be aware that you should be prepared to develop and cultivate a greater sense of objectivity in the candidate who's too focused on winning the battle. Because this person tends to focus more on *who* is right rather than *what* is right, he may have a tendency to divide rather than heal. Forewarned is forearmed, and the insight you gain from this question puts you in a better position for damage control.

197

How would your supervisor grade your ability to cope with last-minute change without breaking stride?

Why Ask This Question?

One of the greatest attributes of any employee at any level of the organization is the person's ability to multitask and adapt quickly to new circumstances. Certain people thrive in an environment of last-minute change, whereas others resent having the rug pulled out from under them as they attempt to accomplish a particular goal. If your environment necessitates quickly changing priorities and you hire the one-track, one-speed candidate, you might encounter resentment as the new hire interprets your shifting priorities as a poor, reactive management style. In such cases, you will probably end up spending more time counteracting the new hire's need for control, structure, and defined parameters than you would normally deem acceptable.

Analyzing the Response

This query could unnerve candidates who mentally operate on a more linear playing field and who dislike the lateral thinking involved with changing priorities. It's difficult for candidates to proffer an encouraging answer when their inner conscience tells them that they need to avoid such situations. Therefore, you'll probably notice some discomfort in their responses and have your question immediately challenged:

➡ "Oh, does this position require a lot of jumping around from task to task? Not that I mind; it's just that I prefer to complete one task before going on to another."

Careful now. If the candidate feels so strongly about this issue, it probably suggests that she worked before in an environment of quickly changing priorities where she was in over her head. Your query simply sparked feelings of gross discomfort and sent up a signal flare in this individual's memory.

Your follow-up query will naturally attempt to probe for details using a behavioral questioning format:

➡ "Tell me about the last time you felt as if you were in over your head. Was it the changing priorities at work that made you uncomfortable, or was there some other reason?"

➡ "How many balls in the air do you have at any given time, and how hectic a pace are you used to working at?"

➡ "Do you prefer to tie together all the loose ends of project A and then move on to project B, or do you typically jump from project A to M, onto Z, and then back to A if time permits? Tell me how a situation like that actually played itself out in the past."

In these cases, the behavioral interviewing format demands that the candidate weave a tale of dealing with pressure and setting priorities when few structural systems are in place. As with all series of behavioral questions, inconsistencies may surface in the responses if candidates weave a tall tale with little basis in fact. Furthermore, if you sense in the person's response a low tolerance for dealing with changing priorities, then add this query to your reference-checking activities to gain objective, third-party insights into the matter.

Interviews should be challenging meetings focused on discovering the real person behind the résumé. A little discomfort is not necessarily a bad thing. The strategy is to balance your investigation so candidates feel welcome to share insights with you freely while you gather authentic data about their strengths, weaknesses, inclinations, and dislikes.

13.

Generic Interview Questions Known to Challenge Candidates in the Final Rounds of Hire

Sometimes the most enlightening queries are the simplest. The purpose of this book is to look at various types of questioning techniques to meet the specific demands of particular hiring situations. And although these specific interviewing insights help you define and refine your choices from the broad spectrum of available candidates, it remains critical to balance your approach with some good old-fashioned horse sense queries.

The following questions are the ones that register more in a candidate's stomach than head. That's because they're so broad that they're usually difficult for candidates to put their hands around. Therefore, they make candidates feel a little awkward. After all, when an individual is totally geared up for a big interview, has studied your annual report, and has prepared detailed responses regarding career-management successes and failures, it could get a little cumbersome to answer something as seemingly mundane as "Why do you want to work here?"

The purpose of the question is not to unnerve the candidate. It is, instead, meant to evaluate the individual's gut responses to seemingly obvious issues. Consequently, no interview preparation book is complete without a look at these generic questioning challenges. These are, after all, the old hard-core interviewing questions that have been used for years by staunch businesspeople who want immediate bottom-line responses. One caveat, though: These questions work best in the final rounds of hire. Only after job candidates have met with a number of potential coworkers and heard several versions of the organization's challenges and focus will they be in a position to address the following broad-based queries.

Why do you want to work here?

Why Ask This Question?

Have you ever heard someone say something along the lines of, "Well, I really need a job so that I don't lose my house, and you're the closest I've gotten to being hired in the last thirty-seven interviews"? Perhaps you might admire the person's honesty, but you know that such a candid response isn't going to catapult this individual's career to new heights. As a matter of fact, anyone who hints that he just can't seem to find work throws up a red flag in even the most empathetic interviewer's mind. After all, if no other employers out there seem to find this person worthy of hire, maybe they're all seeing something that you're not, right?

And desperation to pay bills is never a valid reason for a candidate to accept a job, because once the immediacy of the acute financial pain subsides, that candidate will be off again wanting to get back on the fast track—most likely outside of your company. So what should you be listening for in a solid response?

Analyzing the Response

Good Answers. By the time the candidate's gotten through four rounds of meetings with your staff, she'd better have some clear insights into why she wants to come to work for you and what she can contribute. Candidates will typically link their desire to join a particular company to one of three things:

1. *The Company*—its reputation as a quality employer; its high-profile, brand-name recognition; or the fact that the organization is growing rapidly and perhaps offers a ground-floor opportunity to help the company grow.
2. *The Position*—its variety, pace, reporting relationships, technical orientation, or scope of authority.
3. *The People*—a personality match revealed via a feeling of acceptance and the fact that the candidate believes she'll fit in and her contributions will be recognized.

201

Look to see which of these three aspects of the opportunity makes most sense for the individual. Their response will indicate where their heart and passion lie.

On the other hand, you may hear some responses that scare you off from an otherwise successful interview. Candidates should typically articulate what they could do for the company, not what the company could do for them. (Forgive the twist on John F. Kennedy's words.) Consequently, individuals who strictly limit their answers to what *they* want to get out of the relationship weaken their cases. For example, people who say they want to come to work for you because your benefits are outstanding, you pay higher than your competitors, or because you're known for aggressively promoting from within create a selfish perception about themselves and offer your organization little initial goodwill.

After all, benefits packages change. Similarly, if a candidate is solely motivated by money, he may end up as recruiter's bait, staying only until a higher-paying position surfaces elsewhere. And if a candidate appears overly interested in being promoted to a higher position before even being hired for the job at hand, then he may have premature assumptions about moving up the ladder after only six months of employment—long before you'll have had the chance to gain some stability and continuity in that position you filled.

There is nothing more irritating than having a recent new hire constantly reminding you that he needs more challenge from a higher position within the company. You'll reason that he shouldn't have accepted your position in the first place if his real intention was to seek higher levels of responsibility. In short, his real reason for leaving his present company will most likely recur at your organization over the long haul.

Note as well that this issue typically surfaces when a prospective hire prepares to take a significant salary cut by joining your firm ("significant," in this case, means greater than 20 percent). Let's say an office manager lost her $45,000-a-year job with a Big 4 CPA firm eight months ago and has had a difficult time finding work because everyone tells her that she's overqualified and that organizations aren't creating a lot of middle-management, administrative supervisory roles. Well, she doesn't feel she's overqualified at all. And she certainly doesn't think anyone else should be attempting to crawl inside her brain to make decisions about her based on what *they* think she's thinking.

Still, offering this candidate a $30,000-a-year executive secretarial position should throw up some red flags for you. First, although she is probably being honest and open with herself and you about wanting to get back to work even if it means accepting a position with less money, glamour, and responsibility, human nature predicts that she'll eventually want to get back to her previous salary range and status. But salary and status are only symptoms of the real malady: You could end up hiring someone who has matured (in a business sense) beyond those lesser responsibilities. That's the real problem.

Let's say, for instance, that this candidate was promoted into office management five years ago, leaving behind the tasks associated with hands-on secretarial assignments. If that's the case, she may have stretched her mental rubber band to a salary range, status, and level of responsibility and challenge that your secretarial position simply cannot fulfill. Your job will in essence only provide her with a backup to put bread on the table. Therefore, her accepting your position may be nothing more than a been-there-done-that proposition to tide her over for a while. There's definitely not a lot of potential for a long-term successful relationship here.

You may argue that such an otherwise successful worker deserves another chance at building her career again. After all, just because corporate America lost a lot of its midsection in the aftermath of the dot-com bust and September 11 doesn't mean that people like this office manager should be disenfranchised. Indeed, she may be more motivated than most to roll up her sleeves and find new ways of contributing to her next company. These are all valid issues, and you have to let your conscience be your guide when hiring people whose positions were eliminated through no fault of their own. But such hires deserve extra special consideration lest you become victim of a candidate wanting to park her wagon in your lot while she explores options with greater career potential outside your company.

62

What do you know about our company?

Why Ask This Question?

Oh, that's an easy one. I've heard candidates respond with answers from "You're a bank" to "I researched your organization thoroughly, and I read that you were founded in 1913 under a thrift charter, went public in 1919 at a share price of $8, and then went on to benefit from the post–World War I lending climate by . . . ."

Okay, I'm being facetious—it's not really an easy query. If the candidate's answer is too generic, and he is unable to paint a picture of the organization's place in its market, its uniqueness, its corporate mission and culture, then that individual may lack the critical global reasoning and research skills necessary to provide solutions to your problems. On the other hand, if the candidate goes into too much detail about issues that have little bearing on the organization's challenges today, then you might reason that he's a pedant who lays undue emphasis on less-than-critical issues. Either way, the candidate loses.

Analyzing the Response

Good Answers. What should you expect in a well-balanced response? A well-informed candidate should be able to rattle off the demographics fairly quickly and then get to the meat of the issue: what your organization does differently from its competitors and what challenges you face in your changing market. As a quick checklist to the first issue, any finalist candidate at the middle-management level or in the sales arena should be able to identify the following issues about your organization:

- Year founded
- Headquarters location
- Number of employees
- Revenues, assets under management, size of government grant
- Primary and secondary product markets and lines
- Computer systems
- Exchanges where the company's stock is traded
- Even administrative support staff and clerical candidates should have developed an overall understanding of your company's particular line of business by the final round of interviews. It's not unrealistic on your part to expect a stock or mailroom clerk to be able to articulate such issues, especially if your first-line interviewers provide handouts about the firm. Note that the depth of

their understanding of these broader issues is not what is at question here. Instead, it is their interest in the job and their desire to impress you that matters most.

- The second issue is a little bit more challenging. *Line managers* who are directly responsible for increasing your organization's top-line revenues must clearly understand and be able to articulate where your industry is in its development, where your organization fits within that industry, and what new areas of market penetration need to be exploited and developed to maintain profitability. Line managers, therefore, must be challenged to articulate what solutions they can provide on the basis of their experiences working for your competitors. Because they are insiders, they should be much more forthcoming in terms of mapping out specific directions and plans to guide your company's growth.

- In contrast, *staff managers,* like those found in accounting, IT, and human resources—the noncore segments of a business—will typically have less of an understanding of your company's or industry's current state of affairs. In return, however, they will bring with them a particular specialty that supports your organization's core business activities. Expect staffers to focus more on the demographic information mentioned earlier; material that can be researched in the library should suffice to convince you that the candidate values your time and is serious about the opportunity.

63

Can you tell me about your understanding of the job you're applying for?

Why Ask This Question?

Similar to the preceding question, trying to answer this query in thirty seconds or less can be harrowing for any candidate. Attempting to regurgitate everything the person has learned through library research and four previous rounds of interviews can make even the most organized applicant gulp. What counts, after all, is the individual's ability to synthesize mounds of information on the spot and prioritize key issues quickly. Since this kind of question is often used to open up a final round of interviews, there will be a little more pressure on the individual to make the right impression on you. So don't hold it against finalists who sweat while articulating their responses. They just want to make a favorable impression.

Analyzing the Response

Good Answers. What should you expect in a well-balanced response this time? A well-informed candidate should be able to rattle off the following issues clearly:

- The position's title
- Its reporting relationship upward on both a straight- and dotted-line (indirect) basis
- Its reporting relationship downward (the numbers and titles of direct and extended reports)
- The position's primary duties
- Its secondary responsibilities
- The reason the position is open
- Its key challenges within the first ninety days or one year
- The problem the company is trying to solve by hiring someone new

Obviously, the information flows from the specific and concrete (the position's title and reporting relationships) to the broader implications of providing a solution to the organization's needs. Here's how it sounds in real life from a candidate for an IT position:

→ "Dennis, I understand that this is a newly created position for a computer operations manager to report directly to you, the IT director. Apparently, you've decided to create this new job to prepare for a systems conversion from your HP3000 platform to a UNIX client server environment. Therefore, you're looking for someone skilled in that target software area.

"I also came to learn that you feel that creating a new operations managership will relieve the workloads of three people—you, the VP of information technologies, and the current operations manager, whose background lies more along the programming lines than along traditional operations lines.

"Anyway, you've got a staff of forty people who almost all come from HP3000 backgrounds. Your biggest challenge in addition to preparing for the conversion to UNIX lies in simply keeping up with the workload as your organization opens its first operations in Canada and Mexico. And the person you hire will have to be a high-output production person who's sensitive to the current strain on the organization due to both the company's growth spurt and the introduction of a new software system.

"I'd like to think, Dennis, that I'm prepared to meet those challenges and offer solutions to your key needs."

Bravo. A well-rounded yet specific rendition of identifying the organization's wound, so to speak, and then preparing to provide a particular solution to heal the wound.

64

What can you do for us if we hire you, and when should we expect to see concrete results?

Why Ask This Question?

The first three questions in this chapter probe for an individual's ability to comprehend the overall picture and then point out areas of focus and concern for you, the hiring manager. This query presents a practical follow-up technique to bring closure to those previous queries. For example, now that you know why the individual wants to join your team and what he has learned about your company and the position via research and previous rounds of interviews, you need to see how he will specifically solve your problems. In gauging this answer, you'll also gain critical insights into why accepting this position would make sense for him from a career management standpoint.

Analyzing the Response

The first rule in assessing this critical response is to look beyond the perfect-match syndrome. Many hiring managers mistakenly look for a 100 percent match between a candidate's experiences and skills and their company's immediate needs. Yes, it would be great to bring in someone who could come aboard immediately as an up-and-running problem solver. But that role should be reserved for outside consultants. Instead,

207

you should be looking for a 70 to 80 percent fit so that the individual has room to grow within your firm. Only then will you be offering the candidate a chance to develop greater skills and build a stronger inventory of achievements—which is the glue that binds people to any company.

 The second rule in evaluating candidates' responses focuses on the amount of concrete information provided. Look for candidates who are willing to show you their cards in terms of how they'll attempt to address particular issues. People who shy away from sharing with you their approaches for improving your work environment reveal little goodwill in the preemployment process. Yes, the candidate runs the risk of having one of his ideas stolen—especially if you don't hire him. And yes, there is a chance that what he sees as a potential solution might not be exactly what you had in mind. But those risks are more than offset by his refusal to accept your invitation to brainstorm and problem solve.

In the case of the computer operations manager discussed previously, it is critical that this individual accepts your invitation to spell out potential solutions for your firm's needs. After all, he did an excellent job gathering the data necessary to complete the picture of why this newly created position has developed. He pointed out the department's discomfort with the UNIX software-conversion process since most of the staff members were HP3000 specialists. He readily identified the stress and strain felt by everyone as the company grew rapidly on the IT group's back. And he pinpointed the fact that this new position could relieve the workloads of three coworkers. These are all excellent insights, but it's obviously the third issue that begs for more clarification. So here's how the candidate continued:

➡ "Dennis, the VP of the IT group is clearly more concerned with the strategic issues of determining the organization's changing needs as you move into the international arena. You, as the director, have worked on a UNIX client server platform, but as the only key player in the organization to do that, you'll need someone to relieve you of that sole burden. And your current operations manager comes out of the programming and analysis environment more than a traditional operations school, so we would complement each other well.

"My first area of focus would be on clearing a path for data conversion. I've got a solid UNIX client server background, and I'd suggest possibly holding weekly meetings with the staff for the first quarter to keep a tight handle on problems that surface.

"Next, I'm more than willing to lend an extra hand in any areas where the workload is overwhelming. I have no problems sitting down and coding all day, and even though that's something I've long since outgrown from a career standpoint, it sounds as if now you need someone to fill in the gaps.

"Finally, I believe that within ninety days we'll have laid the groundwork to begin the data-conversion process, and the entire program could be managed within six to eight months. Again, I want to be a part of an organization with national expansion plans, and overseeing a software conversion of this size would be the ultimate challenge to me."

Obviously, you may not have the same plans for this candidate. As a matter of fact, your priorities may lie in a totally different direction. But his willingness to share his expertise and point out priorities that *he* feels you'd want most is the ultimate in goodwill and open information sharing. The key issue is not necessarily that you both agree on what gets done and when—that can be decided once the new hire comes aboard. The critical nature of this response has to do with the fact that this person will risk being wrong to help you make an open and honest assessment of him. Such candid offerings typically have positive results over the long term. Therefore, putting a candidate in the position to share some of his expertise and project target-completion dates may reveal a lot about the individual's style, communication skills, and organizational forecasting ability.

PART 2

SELECTING CANDIDATES AND MAKING THE OFFER

14.

Reference-Checking Scenarios

Administrative Support Staff

Administrative support reference questions focus primarily on superior-subordinate relationships in terms of how candidates follow instructions, work independently, respond to constructive criticism, and feed information back to you. The career opportunities for secretaries, administrative assistants, and other members of the administrative support ranks offer more variety, reward, and independent decision making than ever. Consequently, the talent emerging from their ranks is nothing less than astounding. As a result, you'll need to sharpen your referencing skills to separate excellence from mediocrity. These questions for candidates' former supervisors will be an excellent place to start.

65

How structured an environment would you say this individual needs to reach her maximum potential?

Why Ask This Question?

This supervisory issue is always brought up first in the reference-checking process because it gets former employers talking freely. Since it requires an objective response with no right or wrong answers, an employer won't initially feel as if he's playing God with the former employee's future by having to immediately address weaknesses and shortcomings. (Those issues will follow shortly.) More important, this query provides future advice on how to bring out the best in the individual. You'll have a lot more success getting people to speak about future guidance issues rather than past performance problems because it places past employers in a mentoring role capable of adding valuable career advice.

Analyzing the Response

Some people require fairly structured direction with lots of feedback and ongoing open communication. Others work much more efficiently when their bosses simply set the parameters for a project and leave them alone to complete their work independently. Again, this is a matter of style, so there is no right or wrong answer. Many managers feel that option two—total independence—is the ideal response. That's because most people want some kind of assurance that they won't have to babysit a demanding new employee.

Although that's generally true, the best answer simply hinges on your personal management style. If you like working fairly independently without a lot of interaction with your staff, then such a response would be great. On the other hand, if you have trouble totally letting go of projects under your control, you'll probably want your subordinates to keep you in the progress loop as if you were still in control. Therefore, you'd probably prefer working with a subordinate who enjoys ongoing direction and feedback because it keeps you tuned in to what's happening.

Remember that the purpose of the reference check is not solely to determine a candidate's hireability vis-à-vis past-performance issues. The best references, in contrast, provide insights and future direction for giving the new hire added support from day one. This way, no one has to reinvent the wheel in terms of meshing personal styles with business cultures.

How to Get More Mileage out of the Question. There is a variation on this theme that you might favor as a first question in the reference-checking process:

➡ "John, you're Doug's past boss, and if all goes well, I'll be his next supervisor. My management style is to be fairly laissez-faire in the sense that I really cherish my time and independence. Some people might consider that a weakness of mine, but I don't want to provide a lot of structure and direction to my staff. I guess I value their independence as much as I cherish my own, and I expect them to complete their projects all by themselves. How would Doug fare under my type of management style?"

If you use no other reference-check question in the preemployment hiring process, use this one because it will provide you with some very important information about the optimal management style for a prospective new hire.

66

Does this individual typically adhere strictly to job duties, or does he assume responsibilities beyond the basic written job description?

Why Ask This Question?

As a second question out of the starting gate, this one should again prompt the past supervisor to talk openly about the candidate's work ethic. The entitlement mentality of "I'm owed a job" and "I don't do windows" is totally out of sync with today's high-demand jobs. Indeed, for the first time in U.S. business history, large companies forced to downsize are looking more at performance than at tenure in deciding who makes the final cut. And in a radical and aggressive business environment that defines itself as streamlined, lean and mean, responsive to change, and globally competitive, increasing productivity per employee has become the key mechanism for companies to maintain a competitive edge.

Analyzing the Response

Good Answers. This is an appropriate query for gauging administrative support candidates because it paints an immediate picture of an individual's values. One of the best pieces of feedback you'll generate will sound like this:

➡ "The clock never stops for this guy. He's always looking for more things to do when things slow down in his area. More important, he has a sense of urgency and immediacy that gets things happening.

215

It's the pace and commitment to results that make him a natural at customer service both with internal and external clients."

Other times, you will find that *everyone* at a particular company is so overloaded that assuming additional responsibilities is really a nonissue. Because of understaffing, people are working through their lunches, committing themselves to unlimited overtime on last-minute notice, and barely keeping pace with the existing workload. Still, when a past employer provides that kind of description of the business environment, it's fairly safe to assume that the candidate will have little problem keeping up with you if your organization moves at a fast clip.

On the other hand, you will sometimes receive responses that politely brush around the issue:

➡ "Well, I can't say I really expected him to do anything above and beyond the call of duty. He does his job, and he does it well, and I expect all my staff members to strictly adhere to their basic job duties. But I wouldn't expect him to go looking for more just because it gets slow in the office all of a sudden. I don't expect my people to go out of the box and get creative on me in terms of doing others' work for them, since that could create confusion and drama. So my answer to your question is no."

Would you hire this person or keep looking for someone else? The answer, again, is simple—it depends. Although this book focuses on identifying high-performance individuals who are top producers in their respective disciplines, not every job requires a hero. Some positions simply need worker bees, the types of folks who never seem to tire of highly repetitive tasks. And if that's your mandate for the next opening you need to fill, then don't be turned off by a response that provides little enthusiasm for a track record of assuming greater responsibilities. Workers who do their jobs and go home, after all, have a place in many companies. Just be sure you're matching the right type of individual to that kind of job.

67

Can you comment on this person's ability to accept constructive criticism?

Why Ask This Question?

This is another showstopper that will gather data pertinent to your future management of this individual. First, identify your own style of providing constructive criticism right now. And be honest—it might not be constructive at all. If you have difficulty communicating with people because you have a short fuse when things go wrong, then emphasize in your interviews and reference checks that you don't have lots of patience and need someone who's fairly thick-skinned and who doesn't take things personally. In contrast, if you've been in situations where you felt that your subordinates took advantage of your good nature, then ask about the candidate's inclination to shortcut the system when the boss isn't around.

Analyzing the Response

How to Get More Mileage out of the Question. It is not uncommon to weigh this issue against all else in the selection process. Oversensitivity in a subordinate is the last thing many managers want. For example, you might approach the whole issue of discipline during your interview this way:

➡ "Jim, if you're not thick-skinned and can't take it right between the eyes, then I'm not the right boss for you. I don't have a lot of time to coddle my staff, and I won't worry about hurting your feelings if anything hits the fan. This is business, and I want results, not excuses."

Similarly, you could explain your supervisory approach to a former employer during a reference check:

➡ "I'll be candid with you regarding one of my key concerns in adding a new member to my support staff. I'm fairly short-tempered, and I don't always say thank you. I don't want to have to mince words or worry about others' feelings being hurt. I've left out the issue of oversensitivity when hiring in the past and found out the hard way that I had to walk on eggshells around the new hire for the duration of that person's tenure. Can I get right to the point with Jim when there's a problem, or would he have problems working for someone as demanding and direct as I am?"

At the administrative support level, hurt feelings and a sense of being put down and underappreciated are some of the most common reasons

217

why employees leave companies in pursuit of greener pastures. By all means, don't leave this issue in the "wait and see" column of your hiring checklist. Identify the candidate's capacity for taking it on the chin before you say "I do" to a new employment arrangement.

On the other hand, if you recognize too much tolerance in your own management style and fear being taken advantage of, ask:

➡ "I'm not an overly aggressive manager, and I've been somewhat taken advantage of in the past. I don't particularly like confronting problem employees, so I try to hire very independent types who don't rely on my being present to get work done. How independently will Jim work? How inclined is he to take advantage of another person or situation when the opportunity arises?"

When your concerns are openly shared this way, you'll generate straightforward responses that provide optimal insights into managing this person.

How much do outside influences play a role in this individual's job performance?

Why Ask This Question?

This query works well with administrative support workers who are often younger, less experienced, and less balanced in their lives and careers than their more senior counterparts. Just because immaturity is a part of growing up doesn't mean you have to bear the burden of the individual's coming of age. Work is a significant rite of passage in a person's life, but that empathetic notion aside, you don't want to be caught in the middle when someone is in the process of deciding what role work should play relative to personal life.

You've no doubt heard of an otherwise successful hire being derailed by boyfriend or girlfriend problems. Or maybe everything's going great, but 9:00 a.m. seems to be too early for a new hire to start because of other nightly social activities. If your company's hiring strategy is to employ early career people who have minimal experience and salary requirements, then grab onto this query and employ it religiously.

Analyzing the Response

How honest will past employers be regarding a subordinate's extracurricular activities? It depends on the past supervisor and the nature of the problems vis-à-vis their impact on job performance. And that's very important to keep in mind. Just as in an interview, you don't want to know about personal problems outside the office that have no bearing on the individual's job performance. That's an invasion of privacy and may well end up compromising mechanisms for employee protection contained in the Americans with Disabilities Act, the Family Medical Leave Act, and other employee rights safeguards. Make no bones about sharing with a reference contact that you want only job-related information. If unrelated information is unintentionally volunteered, keep it in perspective and, by all means, don't write it down.

One final point here: Historical problems are not necessarily clear indicators of an individual's future work performance. People change by learning from their mistakes. So the individual with the tardy problem because of late-night soirees might have graduated from school or relocated away from old friends. The man who couldn't seem to locate stable housing and consistently needed to leave work early to apartment hunt might have finally established some roots. And the woman who was preoccupied with incoming calls all day from her mother who was having serious troubles with the Internal Revenue Service may have resolved those issues by now.

In all fairness to yourself and the candidate, therefore, delve more deeply into the resolution of any problems. Ask past employers whether they're aware of the problem being resolved. In some cases, you might even want to call the candidate yourself and ask about the status of those issues. In that case, you'll be establishing a relationship based on open communications and simultaneously setting your future performance expectations in one fell swoop.

Would you consider this individual more of a task-oriented or a project-oriented worker?

Why Ask This Question?

Task orientation lends itself more to the clerical-level job opening, where work instructions are dictated from above and followed rigidly. Project orientation involves much more freedom, independent decision making, and discretion to reach targeted goals. The work mode that you desire simply depends on the amount of autonomy you want the individual to exercise in the overall decision-making process.

Analyzing the Response

Past bosses typically respond to this question subjectively. If the worker exercised a fair amount of discretion on the job and was capable of moving from point A to point C while delegating someone else to tie up the loose ends at point B, he will be categorized as a project-oriented individual. Note, however, that even if the person holds the title of executive secretary or administrative assistant (titles you would expect to be more project oriented), he may be categorized as a task-oriented worker by his previous employer. Why? Because titles don't necessarily depict assertiveness, independence, or project-management orientation. Don't forget that this is a highly subjective definition.

Some administrative support employees come from environments that strongly discourage independent decision making. Thus, they are conditioned to obtain waves of sign-offs from their supervisors before venturing into even common activities. When this is the case—even though the employee is acting according to company mandates—this individual will still be described as task oriented. This doesn't mean she couldn't handle project work independently; it's simply that she wasn't given the opportunity to exercise much discretion.

Why is this significant? If you feel you've interviewed someone whose title should correspond with more of a project orientation and the supervisor classifies this candidate as task oriented, it's probably worth your while to question the employer about her company's expectations and how *she* defines task versus project orientation. The extra clarification could explain the former supervisor's subjective interpretation.

70

How does the candidate handle interruptions, breaks in routine, and last-minute changes?

Why Ask This Question?

This is the foundation of the administrative support worker in corporate America: flexibility, adaptability, and an ability to deal with last-minute change. Any kind of superior-subordinate relationship requires the subordination of one party's needs to the other's—especially in an intimate working relationship with a personal or administrative assistant. Of course, staff accountants need to subordinate their needs to the demands of the accounting manager. But such relationships are typically less dependent on each other and allow for greater flexibility in response time. So use this question when evaluating workers whose schedules and priorities will need to mirror yours rather closely.

Analyzing the Response

There are two basic ways that people coordinate the activities on their desks. Some need to complete one project and tie up all the loose ends before moving on to another task. Others pride themselves on their ability to juggle multiple tasks and keep a number of balls in the air simultaneously. Obviously, those who fit the second profile typically respond to last-minute changes more effectively than those who innately need to complete one task before moving on to another.

How to Get More Mileage out of the Question. You might also ask the former supervisor a question along the lines of:

➡ "Maggie, my needs change on a dime, and I really would be a challenging boss if I hired someone who got flustered under pressure. How does a break in the routine throw George off? What's the worst scenario you could think of where he really became unwound by a last-minute change?"

This question adds a behavioral element to your reference check in that you ask for concrete, historical evidence of how the candidate performed on the job. Behavioral formats work well in reference checks, just as they do in interviews, so apply this technique for your most important issues.

How would you grade the candidate's commitment to project completion?

Why Ask This Question?

Administrative support workers may be task oriented or they may be project oriented. They may assume a strict interpretation of their job responsibilities or demonstrate a mentality for going outside of the box. They may require a structured environment with lots of feedback and direction or a hands-off management style to succeed. But the bottom line is that projects must be completed on time and accurately. There is simply no excuse for mediocre work product.

Analyzing the Response

Project completion means follow-through. You've probably supervised people who walked around the office with legal pads jotting down anything and everything that needed to be done as ideas came to them. You've most likely also supervised people who had the best intentions of seeing a project through to completion but tried to keep everything in their heads no matter how quickly you threw new information their way.

Most managers are big fans of daily planners and to-do lists because they represent physical proof that new information is being stored for future action. Of course, people have different capacities for staying on top of their work. However, you'll most likely have more empathy for the employee who writes something down and doesn't get to it than for the worker who simply forgets details of particular assignments. If detailed follow-through is a critical skill that will separate winners from losers in your business, then ask this question to see what results you get.

How to Get More Mileage out of the Question. If a past employer says the individual's follow-through could be better, ask:

➡ "Give me an example of the types of assignments she falls down on. Are they immediate tasks that don't get done, or does Mary Jo have difficulty completing longer-term projects?"

➡ "Does Mary Jo write her planned activities down on a to-do list, and if not, would that kind of time-management tool help?"

➡ "How fixable is the problem? Is it a matter of her not understanding what's expected of her? Does she have problems comprehending the work in general? Or does she simply forget?"

➡ "How committed is she to developing better follow-through skills?"

By using these kinds of qualifying questions, you should be better prepared to dissect responses that beg for more clarity.

15.

Reference-Checking Scenarios

Professional/Technical Candidates

The reference-checking questions that follow will allow you to continue in your quest to gain third-party, objective information regarding an individual's ability to excel in your company. Bear in mind, though, that critical queries for professional and technical candidates go beyond what's below. These queries are useful and practical in terms of gauging candidates' historical work patterns and providing future insights regarding optimal management techniques. However, they necessarily lack the specific details unique to your industry or discipline. Only you can develop adequate questions to measure a candidate's specific performance in a number of given areas.

For example, if you are checking references on a residential real estate appraiser, you'll probably want to address these position-specific issues:

➡ "What were the daily production standards at your firm in terms of full-blown, Fannie Mae appraisals versus limited, drive-by appraisals?"

➡ "How would you grade this candidate's narrative skills?"

➡ "How consistent was this candidate at selecting adequate comps for a given property?"

➡ "How willing was the individual to handle appraisals in dilapidated structures or generally go beyond the call of duty?"

Similarly, if you're staffing openings for insurance claims adjusters, you might ask:

➡ "What was the size of the typical caseload assigned to this individual?"

➡ "How aggressive was this adjustor at auditing medical bills and setting adequate reserves for a given claim?"

➡ "Would you consider this candidate a soft negotiator who backed down from a confrontation with an aggressive attorney, or did this person show a stubborn resistance toward settling beyond a predetermined limit?"

The specific nature of these questions depends on your particular business and industry. The key to developing such queries lies in assessing the skills that your most successful staff members have in common as well as the knockout factors that have historically made people fail at the job. The development of such a skill-based or performance-based inventory is a simple and straightforward exercise, and such questions will definitely complement the queries that follow.

72

How would you grade this candidate's capacity for analytical thinking and problem solving?

Why Ask This Question?

It's probably uncomfortable for you to just come out and ask how smart somebody is. You also don't want to lob a query like "Does Jane have a good head on her shoulders?" because people are predisposed to say yes to such general issues. After all, a former employer who says no to that kind of question would not only be guaranteeing that Jane loses out on your company's job offer, but he would also insult his own management skills for having hired Jane in the first place.

Still, you have a right to know whether someone is predisposed to react with emotions instead of reason. You might learn that the individual has a restless nature and is easily sidetracked, distracted, or bored. Perhaps the candidate is opinionated and argumentative, and such an inclination impedes her ability to solve problems analytically and objectively. Additionally, you may hear that the individual is overly optimistic about how

225

quickly and easily things can be made to happen; therefore, she spreads herself too thin and makes unduly optimistic assumptions about her subordinates' abilities without developing contingency plans.

Analyzing the Response

In essence, this query demands a response to "How well does this person know her business?" You're not necessarily gauging IQs or natural propensities for genius. In contrast, this is a hands-on question regarding the candidate's ability to distinguish sound decisions from ineffective ones. And expertise in decision making is more a function of exposure and experience than of natural intelligence. After all, no senior manager will have risen through the ranks of middle management without having had his nose bloodied somewhat. And we all learn more from our mistakes than from our successes anyway.

Still, analytical thinking demands business maturity, solid listening skills, and a propensity to project the consequences of one's actions. It stems from self-confidence and awareness of personal limitations. Therefore, when interpreting the feedback you get, look out for problematic responses that point to an irrational, shoot-from-the-hip mentality. The problematic feedback you get might sound like this:

➡ "Oh, Dave is a very good underwriter, but he sometimes overcommits himself because he wears rose-colored glasses and is overly optimistic as to what can be accomplished in a given day."

➡ "Rachel makes a fine corporate attorney, but it's only been two years since she graduated from law school, and I think she's still contemplating where she can make the biggest impact in the legal field in general. Her calling may be outside the corporate world, such as working for a nonprofit organization, and the fact that she grapples with a higher cause in all her actions can blur her ability to make effective and sound decisions."

➡ "I've addressed this issue with Sharon before, and I feel that although she's very smart, her lack of organization puts her in a position to put out fires all the time rather than work proactively at staying ahead of problems before they surface. She doesn't always structure her plans for working through a project. That's impeded her ability to solve problems as effectively as she otherwise could, so that's an area where you'd definitely want to give her added support and structure."

Such feedback will merit closer scrutiny as you speak with other references.

73

Does this individual need close supervision to excel, or does she take more of an autonomous, independent approach to her work?

Why Ask This Question?

Some people naturally like to work in groups, or pods, side by side with their peers. They crave recognition for a job well done, and they enjoy ongoing social interaction. For them, work is all about deriving a psychic income from developing other people's skills and abilities as they move through corporate America fulfilling their own life's agenda. These people will keep their managers in the loop regarding the status on a given project because they feel that their managers have a right to know. This way, those managers don't have to worry about the individual's performance, and there's ample reason for social interaction.

On the other side of the spectrum, you'll find the loners—the folks with a fierce level of independence who cherish the freedom to get work done their way above all else. If you oversupervise such employees, you will be accused of being a micromanager and being distrustful of them. Why else, goes their reasoning, would you need to be on top of them so much? "If you trusted me and my work, you would allow me to come to you when I had a problem." Interaction above that level is simply uncalled for.

Analyzing the Response

Not to overgeneralize the categories of workers out there, but you'll often be able to distinguish between *affiliative* and *analytical* types of people. Affiliative types always focus on the people factor in business situations. Their primary concerns revolve around their coworker relationships:

227

personal disappointments and surprises, feelings regarding people's perceptions about their work, and an interest in others' career and personal development. These are the folks who immediately identify themselves as people persons and who place fellow workers' needs above profits or other business concerns.

Analytical types, in comparison, value their own freedom and the ability to work independently. They often see little need to get too close to coworkers. Accountants, architects, and computer programmers who sit in front of PCs all day creating solutions to complex problems are usually analytical kinds of people. These types of independent thinkers are usually the ones with the greatest need for autonomy and freedom.

The feedback you'll get regarding analytical types during a reference check will sound like this:

➡ "He works best in an environment where you're not looking over his shoulder. He's not a yes-man by any stretch of the imagination. He'll creatively get things done, he'll reinvent the wheel if need be, and he'll constantly network and develop new alliances. But he's got to have the latitude to reach his goals. If you oversupervise him, you'll squelch the enthusiasm and creativity that makes him happy and keeps him producing."

It is ultimately your choice to hire either kind of person. Be especially aware, however, of hiring analytical types if you prefer to provide lots of structure, direction, and feedback on a day-to-day basis. Your natural style of management and goodwill may be perceived as burdensome to the solo flyer. In that case, recognize your own need to control situations and your preference for keeping your people on a short leash, and hire accordingly.

How global a perspective does this candidate have? Do you see him eventually making the transition from a tactical and operational career path to the strategic level necessary for a career in senior management?

Why Ask This Question?

The ability to see beyond the immediate areas of impact and scope of responsibility helps middle managers move up through the ranks within their departments. It also prepares department heads to climb successfully to higher realms of corporate accountability. Consequently, it becomes important in evaluating professional and technical candidates to measure how much the Peter principle has played a role in their careers. The concept behind this principle is that some people have simply risen in the organization to a level where they are incompetent, and this precludes their climbing any further.

Analyzing the Response

There's nothing wrong with reaching such a plateau in anyone's career. After all, most people aren't cut out to be CEOs of Fortune 500 companies. As a matter of fact, you may view the Peter principle as a practical necessity of business life that ensures continuity in the positions you're filling. After all, if you need a controller to head up a section of your accounting department, you might not really want a candidate who sees herself becoming your organization's next CFO. Not that becoming a CFO isn't a noble aspiration; it's just that it can become uncomfortable trying to placate someone who wants too much too fast. And there are few managers out there who haven't had to face that leapfrog syndrome before.

Of course, others hope to reach their first chief financial officership via a steady and planned progression through the ranks. They realize that it could take ten years in a company to reach that goal and are willing to build a list of credentials that ultimately qualifies them for such responsibility. More important, they are realistic about the time and energy commitment necessary to achieve their plan. You certainly can't take away from someone the fact that the person is realistically building a foundation for greater responsibilities.

How to Get More Mileage out of the Question. But what about those candidates who see themselves reaching grand career achievements but who lack the requisite talent or commitment to make that happen? That's what you want to find out via this reference-checking question. Follow up your initial query with a qualifying one like:

➡ "Eileen, could someone argue that Diane may have reached her maximum ability to make an impact on your company as a controller, or do you see her as an up and comer with a lot more potential to take on more global responsibilities?"

If Eileen responds that Diane is an up and comer, you could qualify that response with the follow-up:

➡ "That's great, but I don't want to hire someone who's itching to move through the ranks prematurely. Is she prepared to spend three more years as a controller, or do you sense that she's more aggressive in wanting to reach certain goals in a shorter time frame?"

That generic add-on query should suffice to provide you with an insight into the individual's career expectations and ability to stick it out with your company over the long haul.

How would you grade this candidate's listening skills?

Why Ask This Question?

The difference between *hearing* and *listening* is that hearing simply entails sound waves bouncing off a person's eardrum and then resonating through the cranial bones a little bit. Listening, on the other hand, is a much more mentally engaging activity, demanding that an individual make an effort to internalize those sound waves and interpret the message sent to the brain in order to make some kind of decision. Listening is therefore an active process that requires energy and willingness on the part of the receiver.

There are some humans out there who hear but refuse to listen to what you're saying. That's because they typically choose to do things their way and selectively listen to what is most convenient. I assume you can think of at least one such specimen in your life. The question is, how do you identify these selective listeners via a reference check?

Analyzing the Response

When asking this question, beware the respondent who goes overboard at impressing upon you the need to be clear in your dealings with the candidate. For example, you might get a response like this:

➡ "Paul, David has to have a blueprint of your needs or else he'll go off and make all the decisions himself. What worked best for me was repeating, 'This is what we agreed to,' and, 'Let's go back over this to make sure it's clear,' and, 'I want to make sure that there's no ambiguity here: Tell me again your understanding of what I want.'"

Wow. Are you getting the message? This past employer is painting a picture of throttling this guy who's obviously burned that employer on occasion by not following instructions. To be fair in my treatment of this particular case, the employer continued his response by stating:

➡ "Without such specific directions on your part, he'll make all the calls himself the way he sees fit. Not that he's a poor decision maker—on the contrary, he's very capable and competent. Still, you just can't expect him to follow your directions for arriving at the finish line unless you're absolutely clear from the beginning."

Obviously, that qualifier redeemed the candidate somewhat. But this response points out that there may be mental tugs of war with a selective listener bent on manipulating the rules to his own liking. Is this a matter of poor listening skills or a determined desire to carry out one's own agenda? You'll never know. Just remember that you're not questioning whether the person needs a hearing aid. Instead, you're delicately probing to find out how strong-willed the person is and how insistent he might be to circumvent your authority.

76

How effective is the candidate at delivering bad news? Will the person typically assume responsibility for things gone wrong?

Why Ask This Question?

Thank goodness most people fall into the middle of the spectrum when it comes to assuming responsibility for mistakes. At the far end of the spectrum lie the martyrs—the people who take blame for everything even when they have little control or direct responsibility over the outcome. At the other extreme are the Teflon managers who are never at fault for anything; it's their supervisors, leads, technicians, and secretaries who blow it all the time.

Hmmm. Which one bothers you more? You'd probably prefer the martyr to the Teflon manager. That's because the majority of business-people would agree that nothing is more reprehensible than failure to assume appropriate responsibility for things gone wrong. Locating this tragic flaw in the reference-checking process is difficult. But since it's pretty much impossible to get such information during an interview and because personality tests typically can't judge this particular issue, the reference-checking process is the only medium available in which to generate candid feedback.

Analyzing the Response

How to Get More Mileage out of the Question. You might choose to let the question stand on its own. The silence following your question, after all, can be a powerful tool that demands an honest response. On the other hand, you could employ a situational questioning style that throws the past employer into a scenario like this:

➡ "Michelle, Charlotte is your lead heating, ventilation, and air-conditioning engineer. If the machines on the assembly line run a little too hot and the filled liquid containers coming out the other side end up with uneven distributions, does Charlotte turn into a martyr who accepts total responsibility for the whole team, or is she inclined to become a Teflon engineer who has a tendency to find fault with others?"

A tepid and apologetic response such as "Well, I don't want to say that she lays all the blame on everyone else, but she does have some difficulty accepting total responsibility for her team's output" is a red flag that begs for more explanation. Press further:

➡ "What would her subordinates say about that? Is it a matter of an overly inflated ego, or would you say that it's a fear of loss that dictates her response? Has she ever had occasion to throw a subordinate under the bus to free herself of responsibility?"

Again, remember that this is a difficult issue for employers to address. It's an ugly characteristic of what may otherwise be a successful management candidate. Still, if your previous employee had a tendency to undercut his staff's loyalty by hedging his involvement in his unit's short-comings, then you'll want to cover this issue in checking the backgrounds of all finalist candidates.

Note that if one supervisor tips you off that this serious problem may exist, you'll want to speak with other past superiors regarding the issue. In addition, it would make sense to conduct subordinate references, which seek to gauge the candidate's management style from the bottom up. Subordinates will typically be a lot more forthcoming in sharing information regarding a manager who places blame disproportionately on the more helpless members of the staff.

Please grade the individual's capacity for initiative and taking action. Does this person have a tendency to get bogged down in "analysis paralysis"?

Why Ask This Question?

It is not uncommon for specialists in analytical disciplines to demonstrate substantial resistance to predicting final outcomes. After all, business is a practiced art of weighing risks and rewards by maximizing growth opportunities and hedging downside uncertainties. And with so much information available from computer databases and the Internet, making the final call can become rather difficult as mounds of contradictory evidence pile up for and against certain options. Place this information-overload formula into a business environment that demands a consistent track record for making the right choices, and you'll end up with pressured and stressed-out executives who are gun-shy about making final determinations.

Still, right or wrong isn't always the primary issue: The consequences of inaction could lead to an even more significant erosion of confidence in your organization's credibility and viability. So like it or not, analysis paralysis isn't an option even if you're the most caring and empathetic employer in the world.

Analyzing the Response

This scenario is the opposite of when candidates shoot from the hip. Just as you want to avoid those folks who play fast and loose with the facts and shoot first, ask questions later, you need to avoid those who never shoot the gun at all. The problem with the hip-shooters is that they don't thoroughly measure the consequences of their actions before making a decision. The problem with the procrastinators is that they dissect the possible outcomes of their decisions to a point where they get frozen like deer in an oncoming car's headlights. Not always, of course, but in enough situations (or in one critical instance) to make the former supervisor label the individual as gun-shy when the heat is on.

How to Get More Mileage out of the Question. An excellent way to play this issue out in the reference-checking process is to force a comparison (rather than ask for a cut-and-dried, one-way-or-the-other outcome). Here's an alternative way to ask the question or follow up when the employer is having difficulty interpreting what you want to find out:

➡ "Larry, every employer in the world wants to find that perfect balance of decision makers: folks who don't shoot from the hip without measuring the consequences of their actions and people who don't lack self-confidence when it comes time to make the tough calls. Still, most people lean toward one extreme more than the other. Would you say that Heidi is more of a hip-shooter or perhaps someone who gets bogged down in the details and has difficulty making a final decision?"

If you receive a benign response stating that Heidi never shoots without aiming and equally has no problem making the tough calls, then conclude that this issue will not adversely affect the candidate's performance. If, on the other hand, the past employer raises serious issues regarding the candidate's tendency to leap without looking or to freeze up from the pressures of taking definitive action after analyzing complex information, then reexamine the individual's candidacy. If your style will temper the individual's approach toward decision making, then your being forewarned will put you in a better position to provide added support immediately. If not, realize that your decision-making styles are incompatible and move on to your next candidate.

16.

Reference-Checking Scenarios

Senior Management Candidates

How difficult is it to gather critical background data on senior management candidates in the reference-checking process? Well, it's not as difficult as you'd think, considering that most high-level executives are wise enough to realize that providing reference feedback for a peer is nothing short of career insurance. After all, a quirky twist of fate may have that past supervisor depending on his subordinate for career opportunities in the future.

Combine this with the fact that senior managers don't get the same drill from human resources departments regarding the legal pitfalls and judicial exposure associated with providing reference feedback (HR's dictates, after all, won't always carry all the way to the executive suite), and you'll see why many senior managers are willing to share their opinions freely and help out peers and subordinates who are in a career transition. It's simply in everyone's best interests to say good things about a fellow executive who—"There but for the grace of God go I"—has the misfortune of being terminated because of political upheaval, management change, or lackluster stock performance.

However, even though senior managers are willing to talk, they can sometimes sugarcoat their responses. Again, what goes around comes around in the inner sanctum of the executive suite, and competitors today may be allies tomorrow. Consequently, you may end up with an overly optimistic picture of a candidate's performance because of this unspoken gentleman's agreement to aid others in transition. Therefore, it becomes critical that you fine-tune your questions in the reference-checking process to highlight performance and style issues that otherwise might be covered up with a polite and safe "Oh, Ralph is great, and he'll do a wonderful job for you" response.

78

Is this candidate's management style more autocratic and paternalistic or is it geared toward a more participative and consensus-building approach?

Why Ask This Question?

We know that individuals influence corporate cultures. We also know that senior managers, more so than anyone else in the organization, set the formal tone within their divisions for internal communications, problem solving, performance expectations, sign-off procedures, and accountability. Employ this query first in the reference-checking process to get straight to the people-skills issue. The response you generate will set the tone for all the answers to follow. (After all, if you find out that the candidate takes a my-way-or-the-highway approach to problem solving, that will most likely color the rest of the responses you get.) This is also a question that typically gets employers talking freely because it commands a very subjective and fairly safe response.

Analyzing the Response

How to Get More Mileage out of the Question. Let's assume you get an answer that sounds noncommittal: "Peggy can be an autocrat when she needs to achieve a definitive goal in a short amount of time, but she also encourages her subordinates to chip in when the situation calls for it."

The fact that this past supervisor points out Peggy's flexibility is a good sign that her management style isn't too autocratic or too laissez-faire. To encourage more-specific feedback, however, focus the employer on the number of meetings the candidate holds on a regular basis. In general, senior managers who hold few if any meetings with their direct or extended reports tend to govern a little bit more unilaterally than most. After all, if participative input isn't called for, there will be little opportunity to benefit from others' suggestions.

In contrast, senior managers who strive to orchestrate the combined activities of direct reports by holding lots of meetings, cross-training their teams, or job swapping lower-level staff members so that workers more clearly understand their internal clients' needs obviously depend more on consensus building and buy-in at the grassroots level. Again, there's no right or wrong answer here. It's simply a matter of encouraging the respondent to be more descriptive in interpreting your question.

In terms of this individual's energy level, how would you grade his capacity for hustle?

Why Ask This Question?

A capacity for hustle relates to the abundant reserves of energy that an individual has to draw on. Increased speed in daily activities doesn't necessarily equate to higher-quality output or more-effective decision making. Indeed, the most effective decision makers may be the most reluctant to commit to a final resolution. Still, this query may raise two issues that are critical to you in the selection process. First, you are looking for compatibility issues when bringing someone new aboard: compatible decision-making styles, communication approaches, mentoring philosophies, and speed in processing information. Second, you might find out via this reference-checking query that an individual suffers somewhat from analysis paralysis, meaning he has a tendency to get bogged down in minute details rather than look at the big picture.

Is either issue a deal breaker? Of course not. If you happen to move quickly and you find out that this vice president who will report to you is much slower to come to a decision, you might appreciate the fact that he will most likely temper your inclination to move too rapidly or to make overly optimistic assumptions about the market or your staff's ability to reach a predetermined goal. Similarly, if you could be accused of bordering on the more cautious side, then a sidekick who is quicker to the draw might add an extra level of oomph to your own management style.

The bottom line remains the same: These background investigations you're carrying out serve as objective evidence that should convince you

237

that a particular candidate's needs will not exceed available corporate resources (like your time and patience).

Analyzing the Response

How to Get More Mileage out of the Question. We've helped interviewees respond to this question by delineating three speeds from which to choose: (1) a moderate, controllable, and predictable environment, (2) a faster-paced atmosphere driven by occasional deadline pressures, or (3) a hyperspace, crisis mode, as you'd expect to find on the floor of a stock exchange. These same choices may be shared with the individual who's providing you with reference feedback about a senior management candidate. After all, they certainly help to paint a vivid picture of what "hustle" means to you, and that clarity of definition might come in handy in assisting the other party to interpret your question.

Remember as well that capacity for hustle speaks to going above and beyond the call of duty on last-minute notice. Such actions represent nothing less than an individual's pride in work and commitment to a job well done. Consequently, a response along the lines of "She's not going to move too fast for you—that's just the way she is" might call into question the candidate's enthusiasm for her chosen career path or her resilience in coping with adversity. In such a case, the response you receive could very well reveal that an applicant is unmotivated, tired, bored, or otherwise burned out.

80

How does this individual approach taking action without getting prior approval?

Why Ask This Question?

Who was it who said, "Never ask for permission, just ask for forgiveness"? Well, whoever it was, it's a good thing he or she never worked for your company, right? Actually, taking unilateral action is called for practically on a daily basis. No senior manager could have risen through the ranks without the ability to call the shots independently on occasion, and without a track record for calling the *right* shots the majority of the time. Still, there are rebels. These folks pride themselves on doing things their own way. They are entrepreneurs in every sense of the word—they may work for you and be on your payroll, but they run that company as if it were their own. And that fierce defiance sometimes looks for opportunities to express itself.

Whether you want that brand of self-reliance and autonomy depends on what you need to achieve by bringing the new hire aboard. This one particular aspect, however, could have terrible ramifications if a new hire is marching out of step with the rest of your management team. Feelings of anger, jealousy, and favoritism will inevitably develop among peers, and lines of demarcation will be drawn that force your team to form camps of allies. Your culture will have been violated, and you will be immediately forced either to censure this new rebel or to give the person a lot of backing and support—much to the chagrin of your existing staff, who have been playing by the rules the whole time. Such issues guarantee one swift result: lower employee morale.

Analyzing the Response

How to Get More Mileage out of the Question. As with many of our interviewing and reference-checking questions, it is often best to employ behavioral interviewing techniques in gauging responses. In this instance, you should explain your concerns first and then invite the past superior to comment on the candidate's ability to meet your needs. For example, you might say to Acme Corporation's chief financial officer:

➡ "Nina, I need a vice president of finance who obviously has the ability to make effective decisions independently, but I can't have a rebel who looks for opportunities to take action without getting my prior approval. I've suffered from that rebel syndrome before, and it just goes against my style of running a business. Would you give me an example of a time when Sam could've gotten prior approval from you and didn't? Was it inappropriate, and should he have known better?"

By clearly articulating your needs and asking for a concrete historical issue to demonstrate the candidate's inclination to shoot from the hip and bypass the proper channels of communication, you'll not only gauge whether the candidate would inappropriately jump the gun but how flagrant an incident was. Again, because of the critical impact this one issue could have on your organization's performance, it is worth the time

239

employing a behavioral questioning format to more clearly understand the ramifications of the candidate's past actions.

81

Is it this person's natural inclination to report to someone else for sign-off, or does the candidate operate better with independent responsibility and authority?

Why Ask This Question?

This is a natural follow-up query to the previous question if you want even more objective feedback to measure the individual's inclination to follow all the rules or occasionally strike out on his or her own by making new rules.

Analyzing the Response

How to Get More Mileage out of the Question. Here's how it works. Let's say you've asked the first query in this two-question string like this: "Nina, how does Sam approach the issue of taking action without getting prior approval?" Nina responds, "He's an effective decision maker, and he won't go out of his way to step out of line. He's got a healthy ego, but it's not so big that he needs to prove his authority by circumventing your procedures."

Your natural follow-up would be:

➡ "Great, Nina, I'm glad to hear that. Let me ask you this: In terms of giving him the proper managerial support from day one, should I expect him to come to me for sign-off because he feels protected by doing that, or is Sam better off if I simply give him as much responsibility and authority as possible right up front?"

And voilà—you should generate an honest and open answer regarding Sam's feelings toward being supervised. After all, your questions show nothing but concern for getting this new hire off on the right foot. Therefore, you'll gain reliable third-party data with which you can also make a more effective hiring decision.

82

**After so many years in the business, is this candidate still on a
career track for which she can sustain enthusiasm?**

Why Ask This Question?

Our introduction into this query—"After so many years in the business"—is a function of senior management in general. You simply don't
get to the top unless you've spent years learning your business inside
and out. The latter part of the question—"is this candidate still on a
career track for which she can sustain enthusiasm"—is a euphemism for
"Is this candidate burned out on the business?" It's a practical question
that's worded nicely.

The point is that there are lots of mentally unemployed folks out there.
They're still generating paychecks for themselves. They might even be
looking for greener pastures by coming to you on an exploratory basis.
However, they may be looking because their ticket is about to be punched
at their current company, and they simply can't afford to be laid off for too
long. There's nothing else they can do to earn the kind of money they're
earning, but their hearts just aren't in it anymore.

Analyzing the Response

Interestingly enough, while other questions in the reference-checking
process may run smoothly along, this one particular query often throws
respondents into a quasi-confession mode. That's because it usually hits
the nail on the head by making the former supervisor admit that the
real problem lies in the individual's staying power. There's just not a
lot of fight left in this person, because plastics manufacturing has just
gotten too predictable. The challenge is gone, so the fun has long since
passed. The person is at a career juncture and either has to get off the
train and adjust to a much more modest lifestyle (because of severely
reduced earnings) or smile, suck it up, and get back aboard for another
trip around the tracks.

How to Get More Mileage out of the Question. When you sense the hes-
itation in the past supervisor's voice, ask:

241

➡ "I know that Chuck's sole focus in his career up to now has been in general management at plastics plants. Would he rather be doing something else? I mean besides lying on the beach in Hawaii, does he live for his outside interests? Has he fallen out of love with the business?"

Of course, such prodding could lead to some candid insights that go beyond strictly work-related issues. Still, work never exists in a vacuum—it's only one element of the total person. Note as well that this issue has little to do with a candidate's age. Spending eighteen years in plastics manufacturing could be a very long time for a thirty-six-year-old.

Gathering this information is critical because you inject a serious element of risk into the picture when the candidate needs to work but doesn't really want to. Not to get too philosophical here, but you may be doing such individuals a favor by not hiring them so they can put that terminable career issue to rest and be free to begin the first day of the rest of their lives. No one, after all, lives to work and forgoes all other outside interests.

But when candidates have an overwhelming need to find satisfaction totally beyond the workplace, they may have difficulties making a break with their careers because of guilt or social pressures. Still, similar to early career job hoppers, they have to kiss some frogs before they find their prince. You don't have to be one of those frogs. In this case, although the candidate may have mentally made the break with that career (which is now earning her $125,000 a year), she is not going to tell you that. An objective third-party reference, however, may be more forthcoming.

83

How effective is this person at orchestrating a corporate ensemble of functional areas?

Why Ask This Question?

Higher-level managers often oversee multiple functional areas. The lines of supervision may be direct or indirect, but the bottom line is that the organizational chart can point to only one ultimate source of responsibility. Line (revenue-producing) and staff (noncore, operational, and supportive) functions work together just like woodwinds, brass, and strings in a symphony. But what can separate a sleepy little company from a lean performer poised for growth is often a management team's shared understanding and appreciation of what it takes to run the company from a more global perspective. Senior managers must consequently see to it that their direct reports understand the financial end of the business and comprehend the way their departments connect to the rest of the company.

Analyzing the Response

This query is probably the loftiest of all the questions put forth in this book. After all, if the person isn't successful at coordinating an ensemble of functional areas—in other words, *managing multiple departments or divisions*—then he or she should be in a different line of business. The application of this question, however, isn't as grand and lofty as you might think. A simple focus may be, for example, to identify a senior management candidate's inclination toward open financials and economic advocacy—that is, the individual's willingness to share profit-and-loss information and company-performance status with the rest of the management team.

It is not uncommon in small, privately held companies for owners to guard the books rigidly. "Employees don't need to know how the company is doing—they just need to do their jobs" is the hard line taken toward information sharing. Publicly traded companies, on the other hand, legally have to make financial performance data available. That includes documenting the number of shares of common stock the CEO has outstanding as well as the makeup of key executives' compensation packages. Still, even if the information is public, that doesn't mean that an organization will purposely disclose such data to employees. After all, if employees don't know to look at 10-K, 10-Q, and proxy statement filings, then they're none the worse for wear, right?

Although it's not uncommon for companies to maintain a veil of secrecy around corporate performance, cutting-edge organizations with enlightened management teams voluntarily involve their managers in global performance issues. The logic goes that if all the employees see which way the ship is sailing, they'll have a greater understanding of how their masts should be strung. And should the ship suddenly change course, they will be able to adapt more quickly to the captain's new needs if they're aware of the overall goal.

243

How to Get More Mileage out of the Question. Therefore, to make this seemingly lofty query a practical tool in the reference-checking process, ask a past supervisor:

➡ "As CFO, Dave was overseeing human resources, the IT group, accounting, and administrative services. How did he encourage the heads of those departments to advertise their services to other parts of the company?"

➡ "Did he hold ongoing meetings with his direct reports to encourage them to work together, or did he discourage that kind of intermingling?"

➡ "Did he involve his people in the financials of the organization at all and expect them to take on an ownership mentality, or was that strictly his domain?"

➡ "Should I expect him to be very proactive at coordinating the activities of the various departments he'll oversee at this firm if I bring him aboard, or will he keep the functional areas fairly separate?"

With answers to questions like these factoring into your employment decision, you should be feeling much more confident about the kind of human being you're considering and his projected impact on your existing staff.

84

Can you address the candidate's ability to cope with the significant pressures associated with senior management?

Why Ask This Question?

Some people have tendencies toward self-doubt as pressure increases. Others are more likely to overreact to relatively minor setbacks, irritants, and disappointments. Still others are inclined to be run ragged and get burned out when the heat is on. Determining whether candidates are capable of coping with the pressures and rejection involved in senior management tasks necessarily belongs in the reference-checking realm.

After all, no candidate will reveal such self-admitted shortcomings in a face-to-face interview.

Analyzing the Response

How to Get More Mileage out of the Question. This question is broad enough to allow for liberal interpretations. Therefore, you could simply employ this direct query and then allow the former supervisor to fill in the silence and respond. On the other hand, you might want to employ some trailer queries to provide the respondent with more concrete choices. Here are some options to follow up the initial question in your reference-checking conversation:

➡ "Would you say that Laura has tendencies toward self-doubt as the pressure increases and the heat's on?"

➡ "Could Laura be accused of being likely to overreact to relatively minor setbacks, irritants, and disappointments?"

➡ "Is she inclined to be run ragged by demanding customers? Similarly, could she be accused of carrying the virtue of a service-minded, helpful attitude past the point of diminishing returns?"

These follow-up questions will allow you to articulate the nature of your concerns and help the respondent answer your question more accurately.

Does this person ever delay the inevitable in terms of disciplining or dismissing employees?

Why Ask This Question?

Some people just aren't natural-born disciplinarians. As a matter of fact, they'll avoid confrontation whenever possible. Of course, few managers (as opposed to boxers) enjoy interpersonal conflict. Still, occasionally nipping at the heels of underperforming staff members remains a necessary managerial skill. As a matter of fact, it is often said that a CEO's ability to instill fear in subordinates is one of the most critical elements of executive management. Employing this query as a litmus test of the individual's willingness to set and enforce competitive standards should reveal an important aspect of the candidate's interpersonal and communication skills.

Analyzing the Response

How to Get More Mileage out of the Question. The previous employer's response must be qualified during the reference check to address under what circumstances the candidate will formally discipline or terminate a direct report. In addition to determining what triggers the candidate's call to action, you also have to uncover whether the candidate confronts subordinates in a constructive or negative fashion.

A practical way to generate details regarding the candidate's natural inclination to discipline underperformers is to apply a fictitious comparison—in other words, you would state what problems the last manager had (which may be exaggerated for the purpose of amplifying this issue) and then ask the former employer to measure the candidate against this fictitious manager's performance. For example, you might say:

➡ "Mary, let me share a little background. Our last vice president of sales probably failed to discipline underperformers as she should have, and too many branches weren't reaching their potential because a number of the branch managers took advantage of her good nature and her unwillingness to address problems."

➡ "What kinds of turnover patterns did you notice when Peter was at the helm of national sales in your company?"

➡ "What typically triggered his need to formally discipline or terminate someone?"

➡ "When he needed to be a disciplinarian, did you find his approach to be open and constructive or aggressive and caustic?"

➡ "What was the most common cause of termination during his tenure?"

➡ "Could he ever be accused of being so reluctant to engage in a confrontation that his managerial effectiveness suffered?"

246

Again, painting a picture of a nonassertive supervisor against which the candidate can be measured will help you clarify the candidate's past performance in one of the most challenging areas of interpersonal communications: direct discipline.

86

Is this individual inclined to maintain smooth and amicable relations at all costs, or is she more likely to show her teeth when faced with adversity?

Why Ask This Question?

On a broader basis, this query continues the theme of the previous one. Unlike the former question, however, it addresses the candidate's dealings with peers and superiors as opposed to subordinates. If you're not comfortable with the answer you got in the last question and want more evidence of this individual's ability to manage problem situations aggressively and gear up for interpersonal conflict, then pose this follow-up query to develop the issue further.

Analyzing the Response

Simply put, if this query reveals someone incapable of or unwilling to meet a challenging coworker head-on, then this issue could very well function as a negative swing factor in the final selection process. Few hires require the talents of a strict disciplinarian, but a nonengaging communication style coupled with an unstructured supervisory approach could leave subordinates without a proper sense of direction or a desired level of accountability. Such individual shortcomings could lead to a swift breakdown in productivity.

87

Does the candidate stay open to all sides of an argument before reaching a decision, or does he get personally involved in conflicts?

247

Why Ask This Question?

What if the preceding question generates a response showing that the candidate may be all too swift to dismiss a subordinate or aggressively show his teeth when faced with conflict? It's simply not practical to ask a past employer about the candidate's argumentative nature. Questions like "Is Peter apt to indulge in argument for argument's sake?" or "Is Peter unduly concerned about who is right rather than what is right?" could appear to attack the candidate unfairly and force the past employer to defend the candidate's actions.

Still, insensitivity in the executive suite could result in more than just hurt feelings and an angst-ridden staff. Verbal and sexual harassment, wrongful termination, and discrimination charges often occur when one manager is too liberal about his personal feelings or lacks sensitivity to and awareness of other people's personal rights. You can't afford to add a Bloody Mary to your staff in today's overly litigious employee-rights environment. And you certainly don't want to be in a position to have to temper a senior manager's impulsive inclinations in such a delicate area.

Analyzing the Response

How to Get More Mileage out of the Question. Assuming that the past employer admits that she's seen Peter take more of a personal stance in certain circumstances than was probably appropriate, you should logically follow up with:

➡ "Give me an example of a time when he prematurely reached a conclusion without having all the necessary details. How could he cultivate a greater sense of objectivity at this point in his career? Is it simply his style to shoot from the hip? Does his defensiveness stem from insecurity? Does he rule by intimidation and prefer to kick up all the dust so that he maintains control of the situation? Or is he just naturally a more abrasive and antagonistic person?"

These queries will no doubt unearth fairly negative examples of the individual's propensity to attack others or overzealously defend himself. Once again, though, being forewarned is forearmed because such information will put you in a better position for damage control once the inevitable surfaces—if you decide to hire such a candidate despite his weaknesses in this area.

17.

Preempting the Counteroffer

Steering Candidates Clear of Temptation

Counteroffers are simply enticements to keep employees aboard once they have given notice. Employers have historically been known to appeal to a departing worker's sense of loyalty, guilt, or fear to convince individuals to change their minds about resigning. It is not even uncommon to hear of offers of promotions, huge salary increases, and spousal perks to entice resigning employees to reject a new employer's offer.

It probably seems more logical to handle counteroffer issues with candidates *after* they've accepted your job offer. After all, most employers reason that they have to offer someone a job before the candidate will receive a counteroffer. However, it's critical to address counteroffer issues *before* extending an employment offer. Once you make an employment offer, you give total control over to the candidate. The individual then could very well use the counteroffer threat as leverage to negotiate more money from you. Remember, the counteroffer is just another variable in the employment process that you need to control.

What should you do if a candidate intimates he'll consider a counteroffer from his present employer? Simply advise him to address his needs with his boss right now: "Joe, why don't you go back and speak with your department head about your needs before we go any further? If you get the extra money that you're looking for, then you'll have to agree that my suggestion was good for your career. On the other hand, if you don't get the added compensation that you're looking for, then call me back and I'll address our offer a little more seriously." Excellent work. You have

249

proactively removed an arrow from the candidate's quiver that could have come back to hurt you later in the negotiation process.

Making employees counteroffers once they've given notice is a poor management practice. The strongest companies avoid subjecting themselves to counteroffer coercion. That's primarily because this strategy typically fails to solve the problems that made the employee want to leave in the first place. Statistically speaking, many companies that make counteroffers to resigning employees have experienced that counteroffers serve only to delay the inevitable. In a large percentage of cases, workers who accept counteroffers are gone within six months anyway. Indeed, keeping disgruntled workers aboard only hurts an employer's chances of shoring up weaknesses in the organization and making the necessary changes to move successfully into the future.

Besides, subjecting oneself to counteroffer coercion sends the wrong message to existing staff; throwing dollars at people to stay aboard once they've obviously shown themselves to be disloyal is a desperate move on the company's part and poor career management on the individual's part. In short, little good has historically come to either party from accepted counteroffers.

In contrast, companies that respect their employees' freedom to accept other employment offers send the right message to their remaining staff. The manager wishes the individual well and then swiftly joins forces with existing workers to reassign the current workload and fill the opening quickly. Employees leave those organizations with a minimum of friction and histrionics. No feelings are hurt, no undue pressure is exerted, and the corporate family has the chance to work together to rebuild from the loss.

This chapter addresses counteroffer issues from a resignation-drill or counteroffer preparation perspective. Although you know how dangerous it is for individuals to accept counteroffers, and even though your company may steer away from such practices, that doesn't mean that the candidate you're courting right now won't be subjected to counteroffer pressures once the individual returns to the office to give notice.

Resignation drills occur often in the recruitment industry when headhunters take their candidates through role-play scenarios of giving notice to the current boss. It makes sense for recruiters to spend some time preparing the candidate to resign so as to avoid surprises at the finish line that could wipe out all the work that has gone into the negotiations up to that point. So it's practical business sense that leads recruiters down this path. Resignation drills will benefit you as well as the hiring manager by dramatically increasing the chances that candidates will accept your employment offer and make a clean break from their current companies.

88

Tell me again: Why do you feel the position you're applying for meets your career needs, or why is working for our company so important for you?

Why Ask This Question?

Once you've concluded all the rounds of face-to-face interviews, thoroughly checked a candidate's references, and administered various tests and assessment tools, it's time to mentally prepare the candidate to accept your offer. The counteroffer prep and resignation drill function as a pre-closing technique to ensure that the candidate is aware that he will be propositioned once he returns to his current office to give notice. Therefore, the initial step in the process will require that the candidate voice out loud what benefits he'll gain by joining your company. This is specifically done by having him focus on how his personal or career needs are linked to the opportunity that your organization offers.

Analyzing the Response

Candidates typically join companies for one of three reasons. They are motivated because of:

1. The company and its growth plans, market niche, high-profile name-brand recognition, or reputation as a quality employer
2. The position's variety, pace, opportunity for self-expression, reporting relationship, or scope of authority
3. The people they met along with the way in the interview process who gave them the feeling that they would fit in, be appreciated, and be recognized for their contributions

Inviting candidates to reiterate what is most important to them serves as the foundation for going forward with the offer. Candidates must

251

convince you and themselves that their reason for leaving their present position won't come up again in the foreseeable future at your company. Don't assume that the benefits and the appeal of your organization are obvious to an outsider.

89

On a scale of one to ten—ten being you're really excited about accepting our offer, one being there's no interest—where do you stand?

Why Ask This Question?

If the previous query openly invites candidates to articulate their understanding of the benefits your organization has to offer them from a personal or career standpoint, then this follow-up query concretely qualifies their interest level. It forces candidates to come to terms with their own emotions and motives for job change as well as to volunteer any concerns they have about accepting your offer.

Analyzing the Response

This one-to-ten question is an absolute litmus test for gauging an individual's emotional state. If you ask the candidate where she falls on a scale of one to ten and she responds that she's an absolute ten, that's great. But beware: These are relative numbers, and it's the reasoning behind the numbers that counts, not the numbers themselves. For example, if Laura says she's a ten, your immediate comeback is, "Well, that's excellent, Laura. I'm happy to hear that. What makes you a ten?"

Good Answers. By qualifying the number, the candidate is forced to articulate her definition of a ten. If Laura is a ten because she's currently a management consultant for a Big 4 accounting firm who wants to move into a client company for her first controllership, then your offer makes solid business sense for both of you. The chances of her rejecting this offer are slim.

If, on the other hand, she's a ten because she's having difficulties getting along with her fickle boss, then she may be a fake ten. Interpersonal relationships change quickly with erratic supervisors, so that one day you're in and the next day you're out. Consequently, if the two kiss and make up, so to speak, or that boss leaves the company, then your motivated ten candidate might succumb to a counteroffer anyway. Beware the jilted subordinate.

How to Get More Mileage out of the Question. Let's say, however, that Laura answers that she's an eight. In that case, you need a threefold comeback:

1. "Why are you an eight?"
2. "What would make you a ten?"
3. "If that issue could be resolved, where would you then rank on a scale of one to ten?"

The key to this discussion obviously lies in closing the gap between the individual's perception of your opportunity and the reality of the job you're offering. Then it's simply a matter of confirming that no other roadblocks are in the way that could hinder the individual from accepting your offer. Here's how this scenario plays itself out:

You: Laura, why do you consider yourself an eight?

Candidate: Well, after doing my research, I really feel that a controllership in a company of this size should pay no less than $80,000. Your offer of $65,000 is somewhat less than I expected. I appreciate the fact that you're limited by internal equity in that you can't pay me more than your existing staff members who hold similar levels of responsibility. Still, we really didn't discuss salary until yesterday, and although I'm extremely interested in joining your company, I was somewhat disappointed because I feel you're paying below the market.

You: Okay, what would your compensation package look like to make you a ten?

Candidate: First, I'm currently earning $72,000 as a senior consultant, so I'd like a base of no less than that. On the other hand, if you really can't offer more than $65,000 in base salary, I'd like to receive a sign-on bonus that brings me to $72,000 and a management incentive package that exceeds the base.

253

You: I can't commit to you, Laura, that we could come up with a sign-on bonus or offer you participation in the incentive plan that you're requesting. I need to put a pencil to paper first. Now that I know what your expectations are, though, I have something concrete to work with. Let's put this issue aside for a moment. Assuming that I can create a compensation package that meets your needs, then where would you rank on a scale of one to ten?

Candidate: I'd be an absolute ten and would be ready to join the ranks by the middle of next month.

Notice how you've skillfully helped the candidate flesh out her arbitrary eight rating on the interest scale. You isolated her objection and then probed for other areas that concerned her. Finally, you preclosed her to accept your offer if her conditions were met. Voilà—you made a skillful employment offer that considered her needs and attempted to resolve her concerns before asking her to commit to you. Such practices will build goodwill in the preemployment process and convince new hires that your company sets people up to win by putting others' needs first.

90

**What would have to change at your present position
for you to continue working there?**

Why Ask This Question?

Whenever you're dealing with someone who's doing excellent work for a competing company, it is safest to spend some time analyzing what's going on in the person's current position so you understand how your offer stacks up against it. Of course, if a candidate is currently unemployed, this question has no application.

Analyzing the Response

Probably 70 percent of corporate Americans who willingly change jobs do so not because of technical matters but because of interpersonal conflict. When polled in survey after survey, U.S. workers rank recognition first among their top work priorities. This is usually followed by other emotional factors like enjoyable work and the ability to contribute to the team. Surprisingly, salary usually ranks fourth on the charts of reasons why employees stay with or leave a company. If recognition for a job well done ranks first, and it has direct linkage to interpersonal relationships with coworkers (and especially direct supervisors), then examining the level of recognition the individual currently receives is an important factor in the preemployment offer process.

Good Answers. When employing this query, look first for responses that are out of the individual's control. Pending layoffs, corporate relocations, and overall job insecurity will often result in the candidate responding, "Paul, nothing could change at my present company to entice me to stay." That points to a clean break with the current employer and a graceful transition into your firm.

In contrast, if the candidate responds vaguely, "Well, I can't really think of anything that could change at my present company and convince me to stay," then challenge her again by stating:

➡ "I've found that one or two changes could often make an individual think twice about leaving a company. What would those one or two areas be in your case?"

If that query still only generates a superficial or vague response, probe even deeper:

➡ "Tell me, Laura, about the recognition you get for a job well done. Do you feel that your contribution is properly recognized, or is it somehow diminished by your current supervisor?"

You're obviously leading the candidate down the path of coworker relationships. For the noncommittal candidate who is reluctant to address any shortcomings about her present company lest she weaken her negotiation posture, or for someone who hasn't given much thought to fixing relationship problems back at the office, this questioning pattern should force a critical issue to a head. After all, there is very likely a weak link somewhere in the chain that binds the candidate to her present company, and statistically there is an excellent chance that it stems from a people problem.

255

Even if the candidate feels she's properly recognized for her efforts, this add-on query regarding the individual's relationship with her boss will naturally segue into other reasons for leaving:

➡ "No, my relationship with my boss is fine. It's just that the company lacks state-of-the-art systems that would allow me to stay on top of the power curve in my field. Also, they brought in a new CEO about four months ago who's really changed the way things are done back at the office. All in all, I feel it's the right time for me to explore other career options. So there's really nothing that could change that would motivate me to stay."

Bravo. You've brought this issue to a logical conclusion and mandated that the candidate voice out loud that the situation is most likely beyond repair. That's an important psychological step to prepare the person to make the break. It also allows you to further understand how you should position your offer once the time comes.

91

Tell me about the counteroffer they'll make you once you give notice. If you gave notice right now, what would your boss say to keep you?

Why Ask This Question?

Ah, this is the heart of the resignation drill—no more beating around the bush. Our first queries in this session were roundabout probes to gently test for salient career issues that were pushing candidates out of their present companies' arms or, inversely, that could lead to counteroffer acceptance. This query mentally prepares the individual to deal with the counteroffer awaiting her. This way, when it comes, it won't be a surprise that catches the candidate off guard or otherwise lets her emotions cloud her better business judgment.

If, on the other hand, the company makes no counteroffer, then the candidate (who, because of your prompting, is preparing for one) may feel disappointed that she wasn't pursued more aggressively to stay aboard. Such an emotion will only enforce her conclusion that accepting your offer was the right thing to do all along. In either situation, your preclosing drill will have set the stage for a smooth transition out of her present company and into the new environment.

Analyzing the Response

Preparing for a concrete challenge to your potential offer makes practical sense and allows you to take sides with that individual by working together to plan her resignation and her successful exit out of her current company. A psychological good guy/bad guy contrast forms in the candidate's mind with the current boss playing the potential bad guy who is out to tempt her with perks that will only stand in the way of her succeeding at a new opportunity. Forewarned is forearmed for candidates too, and this brief exercise removes a snare that could entrap them.

 If you sense some danger in the candidate's response, revealing that a hefty counteroffer will be made or that it will be very hard for the individual to break the personal ties to her boss, follow this query up with an add-on corollary by asking, "What would change in your present position if you *did* accept a counteroffer? Would life six months down the road be any different than it is right now? Would you excel there as you could here?"

By allowing the candidate to play out this scenario in her head, you'll take her past the immediacy of the resignation counteroffer and further into the future. You know that statistics bear out a bleak reality for those who accept counteroffers, but you can't necessarily say that to the candidate, because you're a biased party in this negotiation. However, by pointing the candidate in this future direction, you're allowing her to reach the same conclusions about the limitations of staying with the current employer.

The bottom line to all this is that as a prospective employer, you are perfectly within your rights to find out what could entice the individual to stay with her current firm. That's not being nosy, and it's an effective way to gauge a candidate's interest level. After all, you have the job opportunity to offer. No matter how tight the labor market or how specialized a candidate's skills, one law will always remain firm in the land of employment hiring: The employer makes the calls. Use that guaranteed leverage to drill finalist candidates regarding their interest level in your company, their potential to accept a counteroffer, and their overall desire to make a positive impact on your organization. You'll simultaneously help them avoid becoming victim to the dangerous counteroffer syndrome.

257

18.

Making the Offer and Closing the Deal

Questions to Ensure That Candidates Accept Your Job Offers

Once the interviewing process is completed, candidates should be pre-closed on wanting to accept your job offer. Whether that's because you brought them through a questioning drill that helped them identify their own needs and tie their motives to your company's future or because you framed a real-life scenario of the limitations at their present company after their counteroffer acceptance, candidates should be much more receptive. After all, the worst time for them to be examining the pros and cons of leaving one company and joining another is now—at the actual time of the offer. Emotions run high at the finish line, and if they haven't played out this final scenario in their minds up until now, then they may fall victim to counteroffer temptation.

Of course, your job is not to coddle a candidate. As the employer, you don't want to have to convince someone to come to work for you. After all, if it's that much of a challenge just to get the prospective new hire to say yes to an offer, then this is probably a premature decision on the individual's part. Recall as well that the first decision you watch a candidate make is the acceptance or rejection of your offer. If the offer is accepted only half-heartedly, that may put a damper on this relationship's new beginnings.

Still, don't underestimate the tremendous pressure that most people feel while undergoing this significant rite of passage. In case it's been a while since you changed jobs, think back to the fears you experienced before saying yes to a new start date and good-bye to close friends at your last company. Remember that job change ranks right up there with fear of public speaking and fear of death in terms of causing anxiety in most of us humans. And rightfully so—severing the ties with a job where you know exactly what is expected of you, with your corporate family, the familiar restaurants where you have lunch, and the comfortable chair that you've broken in to fit your back conjures up intense fears in even the most confident people:

"What if the grass isn't greener on the other side? What if the new company experiences an unforeseen layoff? At least here I've got tenure and would probably survive the first few rounds of cuts. I've heard a lot about people getting axed because of the LIFO rule: Last in, first out means that I'd be the first one out on the street. Is my present job really so bad? I mean, at least I like the people and know where I stand. Help, I'm having buyer's remorse."

Which all points to the significance of making offers softly and delicately. Empathy for the job changer in the final decision process is crucial because while the new opportunity is exciting on the one hand, it requires disloyalty to the current employer on the other. So, saying yes to you means simultaneously rejecting the family and friends back at the office. In short, closing one chapter of your life and opening another is both exciting and scary. And no matter how much the candidate wants out, emotional twangs of fear and guilt remain. If you, therefore, approach the final offer (as in the counteroffer role-play) from a pull-sell rather than push-sell standpoint, you'll end up asking questions to make the candidate pursue you rather than vice versa.

The scenario is this: After conducting numerous rounds of interviews with multiple candidates, you boiled down your selection to two people. Both passed muster with everyone involved in the hiring process, both had solid references and test scores, and both were taken through a resignation drill as outlined in Chapter 17, "Preempting the Counteroffer: Steering Candidates Clear of Temptation," to ensure that they would accept your offer. You haven't spoken for two days while you've been deciding which candidate made the final cut. You're now about to make the offer to your primary candidate (of course, you're holding onto candidate number two just in case candidate one balks at the offer), and here's what it sounds like:

92

What's changed since the last time we spoke?

Why Ask This Question?

Simply stated, you should begin the candidate closing process with an assumption that if all the ingredients are there now that were there during the counteroffer role-play, then the candidate should accept your offer. If there is a change in plans on the candidate's part, now is the opportunity to share that with you. Again, the last thing you want to do is jump the gun and make an offer only to have it put on hold because of unforeseen circumstances. Controlling the offer process is, after all, the first thing that a candidate watches *you* do.

Analyzing the Response

Nine times out of ten, the candidate will respond that nothing has changed. In that case, you have the green light to move forward. And again, you'll have preclosed the individual via this conditioning process that you've been taking him through since your counteroffer drill.

On the other hand, if something has changed, like a sudden increase in responsibilities at the present company, a significant raise, or another job offer, or if the idea of relocating suddenly loses its appeal, then you're pushed back a step to the information-gathering stage that occurs in the counteroffer role-play. Find out what's changed, where the candidate stands on a scale of one to ten in terms of his interest in the position (see Question 89 in Chapter 17), and then go back to the drawing board to see if there is anything you could offer to fix the problem.

 Beware candidates who suddenly request long time frames to come to a decision. Ideally, the candidate will have had enough opportunity during the multiple rounds of interviews to research your organization, speak with the key players in his area, and determine what your performance expectations are. As a matter of fact, the resignation drill purposely surfaces questionable issues so that these last-minute delay tactics are avoided. Of course, there may be a legitimate reason why a candidate needs an additional twenty-four hours to determine his course of action. But asking for more than twenty-four hours can be problematic.

Candidates who request an additional week or more are usually waiting to hear from a different company about another offer. Putting you off is the only way to buy time to see whether they can generate the offer they *really* want. This is unfortunate timing for you because you're the backup job offer. If that doesn't hurt your feelings enough, keep in mind that, statistically, the chance of having your offer accepted, even if the individual's primary job doesn't come through, is marginal at best. People who tie their hopes to one job that ends up falling through usually decline the secondary job offer. That's simply human nature: Job number two most likely won't ever amount to the lost opportunities offered by job number one, reasons the candidate, so he passes on both.

How to Get More Mileage out of the Question. If you suspect that a candidate is stonewalling you in an attempt to wait for another offer, communicate your perceptions openly:

➡ "Dennis, I've found that people who suddenly need more time at the finish line typically haven't gathered enough information to make an informed decision. What's holding you back from saying yes to our offer?"

If you get a vague response, probe further:

➡ "Dennis, I want to start our relationship on the right foot, and I'd appreciate a candid response. My bet is you've got another offer on the table that might have more appeal to you than ours. If that's the case, I understand. You don't have to tell me who the other company is, but I'd like to know where we stand relative to another offer that you may be considering."

At that point, if your perceptions are correct, the candidate will admire your intuition and respond to your legitimate concerns. You'll learn what your chances are of landing this individual, and you can prepare either to wait out his decision or to line up other candidates.

What you don't want to do is attempt to convince the candidate at the finish line that your offer is superior. His focus is definitely on the other offer—otherwise, you would have heard an "I'll accept" already. So trying to convince him that you're better than his other suitor puts you at a disadvantage in the negotiation process: It will appear that you're begging as you shoot down the other company or try to resell your own. Again, by now, you've done all the selling you need to. Make a firm commitment to your own plan of action and respect the individual's right to plan his own destiny.

261

93

If you had to choose among three factors—(1) the company,
(2) the position you're applying for, or (3) the people you'd be
working with—which would you say plays the most significant
role in your decision to accept our offer?

Why Ask This Question?

This smacks of an exercise in the counteroffer drill (see Question 88 in Chapter 17)—namely, asking candidates to confirm why joining your company makes sense for them from a career or personal development standpoint. It bears repetition because when time passes between the interviewing stage and the final offer, it becomes critical to invite the candidate to redefine the benefits of joining your company—both for you and for him. You want to make sure this candidate has a clear understanding of what your organization is all about; he needs to hear again *out loud* what benefits and opportunities exist by joining your firm.

Analyzing the Response

Good Answers. You'll find that most people choose option one—the company—as the key reason why they change jobs. People look for the emotional recognition of a job well done, they want to work for a company that takes care of its people, and they want to know they can make a difference. Those emotional criteria are inherently found in the company and all of its manifestations: its people, its corporate culture, and its mission.

Don't be surprised, however, to find administrative support candidates linking themselves to option three. Workers who define themselves by the relationships they keep often see themselves via the people they report to. So an executive assistant reporting to a chief operating officer will probably base more of the decision to accept your offer on the perceived relationship with the COO. Likewise, bench scientists often leave one university, laboratory, or hospital to join the team of a principal investigator whom they've been following all of their careers.

Similarly, some aggressive corporate-ladder climbers may be more motivated by the increased responsibilities that the new position offers. The enticements of a greater span of control, budgetary responsibilities, or exposure to new areas of interest increase the individual's overall marketability. Such enticements lock the candidate into accepting the offer.

In short, any of these answers is fine. What's important is that you understand that key drivers that are motivating candidates to break ranks with their current employers and transition over to your team. That emotional connection will serve as the glue that binds the new hire to your organization for at least the first year. Beyond that, it's the hiring manager's and department's responsibility to create an environment in which the individual can thrive, motivate herself, and find new ways to add value, both to the organization and to her résumé.

94

If we were to make you an offer, tell me ideally when you'd like to start. How much notice would you need to give your present employer?

Why Ask This Question?

Notice the use of the subjunctive case in beginning this statement: *"If we were to make* you an offer." Even though you're about to make an offer within two or three minutes, there's no need to give away the farm. Keeping the candidate at arm's length only serves to heighten the individual's desire and to reinforce your control.

Analyzing the Response

Most candidates will need to give their current employer two weeks' notice. Of course, senior level managers may need to give several months' notice because of their broad responsibilities and the impact that leaving the company will have. Therefore, the first rule is: Don't pressure candidates to start tomorrow when they have to give appropriate notice. You could build a lot of resentment if you force individuals to walk away from their present company without giving that organization ample time to locate and train a replacement.

High performers are sophisticated consumers regarding the employment marketplace, and they realize that their current employers will be providing reference-check information about them for the next ten years.

No one wants to risk a negative future reference that says "Oh, Doris was a solid performer, but she left us without notice. That really stuck in my throat and was a very disappointing end to an otherwise excellent track record." In short, if you need someone immediately, hire a temp or a contractor. But let candidates determine their own timeliness for giving notice (as long as it's a reasonable amount of time for the amount of responsibility they hold).

The second rule is: Watch out for people who don't feel obligated to give their current employer any notice. After all, you don't expect to be left high and dry when this person decides to move on to greener pastures. More important, the decision to leave a company without giving any notice reveals little loyalty or character.

Consequently, the person's inclination to follow proper corporate etiquette may in itself play a role in your decision to extend the offer. Remember, you still haven't offered the job yet, and it's not too late to put the individual on hold, catch your breath, and then promise to call back later. Buying yourself some extra time at this point is perfectly acceptable.

Special note: Whenever possible, encourage the candidate to take an additional week off after the notice period expires. In other words, if someone needs to give two weeks' notice, encourage them to take an additional, third week off before they start with your company. The reason is simple: New hires likely won't have any vacation or paid time off for a year after they start, and it's very difficult to leave one job on Friday afternoon and start another on the following Monday morning. That extra week can go a long way in allowing new hires to have a short period of rest and relaxation, get their affairs in order, and generate some excitement about their new opportunity. From a practical standpoint, it's a very gracious and selfless move on the company's part, and new hires will appreciate it more than you know.

95

Can you share with me what final questions I can answer to help you come to an informed career decision?

Why Ask This Question?

This is the final setup before the salary negotiation. It gives you a chance to show yourself as a concerned and empathetic future employer. Such consideration will no doubt be very welcome to all candidates about to make a break with one company and a commitment to another. As such, this benevolent approach should be assumed in all final negotiations. More important, it invites airing of any issues or concerns that could botch the acceptance of the offer.

Analyzing the Response

If any issues other than salary beg for more consideration on the candidate's part, then go back to the drawing board and handle those concerns first before moving on to the final and most critical element of all: making the salary offer.

Candidates will typically ask for confirmations about the job responsibilities, reporting relationships, or benefits packages. Sometimes they'll mention that they have a four-day holiday already planned that can't be canceled and would like that time off without pay. Maybe they'll need to give three weeks' notice instead of two. Now is the time for such incidentals to surface.

What shouldn't occur, though, is that the candidate's demands suddenly skyrocket. For example, if an individual states that he forgot to tell you he has $25,000 worth of stock options that he expects you to include in his base salary, that smacks of extortion. Such take-it-or-leave-it propositions at the finish line are the ultimate show of poor negotiation timing. Be very leery of going ahead with an offer when such leveraging occurs in the eleventh hour.

96

At what dollar level would you accept our job offer, and at what dollar level would you reject it?

Why Ask This Question?

Well, if this isn't the million-dollar question. This is probably the most critical query in the entire employment process—and in this book.

Why? Because this is the first time you give all the power to the candidate. Up to this point, you've maintained control of the entire process: You've carefully guided the candidate and paced her through the interviewing process. You've preclosed her on accepting your offer during the counteroffer drill. And you've shown yourself to be a caring employer by bending over backward to address any questions or doubts so she could reach an informed career decision.

And now comes the showstopper. You've opened the curtain, and after the wonderful presentation you've done regarding the *potential* behind that curtain, the candidate finally comes face to face with the prize. So if she doesn't like it, it's all over. Still, you want to maintain as much control of this business negotiation as possible. Therefore, you phrase your question very carefully.

The key to the question lies in its tag: "at what dollar level would you reject [the offer]?" The reasoning, quite logically, is that this particular phraseology poses a fear of loss. It is exactly that fear that will keep the candidate from becoming too cocky and unmanageable at the finish line.

You may be thinking at this point:

➡ "Goodness, this is a lot of work to massage a job candidate into accepting an employment offer. I'm in the plastic-injection-molding business, not the headhunting business. Save this finesse stuff for the headhunters who make their livelihoods in staffing companies or finding people work."

The appropriate response to your argument is:

➡ "Hold on, there. Like it or not, you are in sales, and selling your company is the first order of the day. Furthermore, bending over backward to allay any candidate's concerns will only increase your reputation as a quality employer. And despite having emerged from the largest economic contraction since the Great Depression, finding qualified people is hard work. Therefore, you owe it to yourself to spend extra time at the finish line. Don't let weeks of work and recruitment expenses be wasted because of your haste in making an offer. Salary negotiations need to be finessed, and it's your responsibility to ensure that the candidate learns that you're putting her needs right alongside your own."

Analyzing the Response

How to Get More Mileage out of the Question. Let's run through a few common scenarios that have been known to snag even the best-prepared employers. No doubt you've been caught in one of these situations yourself at some point, so now's the time to give heed to the lessons you've learned.

Situation 1: The malleable candidate. Let's assume you're very straightforward in your recruitment advertising or the individual learned during the interview process that the salary range for technical writers at your company is $5,000 to $6,500 per month. The candidate is currently earning $5,200 per month, and your budget and internal equity analysis point to a 10 percent increase in base pay.

When it comes time to make the offer, you explain two things to the candidate in consideration:

➡ "First, Christina, I want you to know that we believe in making salary offers that reflect a candidate's experience, education, and skill level, whenever possible; second, please understand that we've got to look at internal equity before making any final decisions. If, for example, a 10 percent increase in base pay would end up paying you more than an existing employee who has more experience, then that 10 percent rule-of-thumb increase would no longer apply. Does that make sense?"

The candidate agrees, and the offer continues:

➡ "Christina, we've taken a look at your years of experience, educational credentials, and your performance track record, and we're happy to tell you that we can indeed offer you a 10 percent increase in your base salary. Therefore, we'd like to offer you the position at $5,720 a month."

Christina shrieks with excitement, accepts your offer, and wonders how she's going to be able to spend $520 more a month from now on.

Situation 2: The law of inverse gravity. Sometimes the story doesn't have such an amicable ending. One of the dangers of letting candidates know

267

the range of the position is that they hear only the top end of the range, while you may only want to pay at the bottom of the range. And there you have it: You're upside down in the deal. Should you let candidates know salary ranges in general? Probably not. The extra information will typically do more harm than good. In the last example, Christina was very understanding: She realized that just because the position had a maximum potential of $6,500 per month, that didn't mean she was going to get that amount. She accepted that fact readily.

Then again, remember that the laws regarding pay transparency and pay privacy are changing as this third edition is being written. Certain states, cities, or even industries (e.g., academia or the public sector) may be required to post salary ranges in all cases. If that's so, the transparency will likely help and hinder the process. On the positive side, candidates will know in advance of applying for a job whether it's in their salary range or not. On the not-so-positive side, candidates typically don't understand the mechanics of compensation: salary ranges, budgets, and internal equity are concepts that are unfamiliar to them. So they may see the top of the range and expect to be at or near it in all instances. In cases where employers don't offer the top of the posted range, candidates may walk away from offers, complaining that companies are cheap or simply don't see their worth.

In my opinion, if all companies in a given area (e.g., city or state) or industry are posting salaries alongside job openings, then it will be fairly easy for employers to adapt. More likely than not, however, salary-posting requirements will vary, and companies will not consistently adhere to the new rules, especially if those rules are being challenged in the courts on grounds of price fixing or other antitrust matters. In short, be prepared to demonstrate a good amount of flexibility, patience, and wisdom in all matters relating to compensation. It's likely to be the hottest area, along with independent contractor status and classification, in the employment space for the next decade.

But let's look at another candidate named Denise. When she was made the offer at $5,720 (and she had a very similar employment history to Christina), she felt insulted:

➡ "After all, aren't I worth $6,500 per month? Who works harder than I do? If the salary range goes to $6,500 and I'm being offered only $5,720, this company obviously feels that I'm not the best person for the job. I can't believe they're making such a big deal about such a small amount of money for the caliber of work I'll be doing for them. And if they thoroughly checked my references, they would have realized *how much I'm valued by my current employer.*"

Whoops. Now you're the bad guy, and the current employer is the good guy. Not an effective way to make employment offers.

So how do you avoid the law of inverse gravity? The answer is simply to not mention ranges to candidates at all during the interviewing process if that's allowed under your state or city's laws. Instead, once you've asked the person what her salary requirements are during the interview, say to her, "This position is in your salary range." This way, no target salaries are established, and the individual keeps an open mind throughout the negotiations.

Let's look at this, though, from the standpoint of having published the salary at the time of the job posting. How do you convince this person that $5,720 is a fair offer and that you're not a cheapskate? Well, it does put you at a disadvantage when you have to defend your offer. Still, there is a commonsense way to objectively explain the reasoning behind your decision. It's called *internal equity.*

Internal equity simply means that employees with like amounts of experience, tenure, and skill sets earn similar rates of pay. It wouldn't make sense to hire a new employee and pay her more than an existing employee who holds the same position unless there were extenuating circumstances (like the new worker has ten years of experience when the existing staff member has only three). Therefore, explain to the candidate:

➡ "Denise, we don't make salary offers in a vacuum. Although our ranges from low to high for a given position could be far apart, when it comes down to making the offer, we match the new hire's years of experience, skills, and abilities with the experiences of our existing staff members. Your final salary offer closely matches the salaries of the existing employees to whom you're benchmarked. That's the only fair way to handle this, and most employers handle the matter similar to the way we do.

"Of course, as a candidate, you can't know in advance whom you're going to be benchmarked to, and that's why offers are typically saved for the end of the hiring process. It takes a good amount of time to consider salary ranges, preapproved budgets, and internal equity analysis, but we do that once we've identified a finalist whom we feel can make an immediate and lasting contribution to our company. I know this is probably more information than you need, but I want to make sure you understand the logic behind how we approach salary offers. I'm happy to discuss this further to make sure you can come to an informed decision about our offer. What additional questions do you have at this point that I can answer for you?"

Such reasoning is clear, concise, and, most important, objective. It is absolutely critical that the candidate not perceive that there were any personal issues involved in your decision-making process. This strategy works 95 percent of the time. In situations where it doesn't work, the reason is because the candidate is unable to look at the issue from an objective distance and realize that the offer is based on valid business fundamentals. Losing that type of candidate at the finish line, however, may bode well for your company in the long run.

Situation 3: Making offers for newly created positions when you're not sure how much to pay. Creating new positions in your company and adding expertise because of the demands of increased business is exciting indeed. Don't feel, though, that you're the only employer who has ever run an online ad without any idea of what that job would be paying. It happens all the time. But what happens when you're down to the finish line and the vice president you're looking at hiring was making $265,000 a year in base salary at her last company but was laid off two years ago and hasn't been able to find work since? In other words, how do you decide how much to offer when all the rules of compensation law fall by the wayside?

Besides doing your own research as to market pay for similar positions requiring like skills, experience, and educational requirements, consider involving the candidate in the creation of a compensation package. No candidate will shy away from telling you off the cuff how much she should be paid. (It's usually a fairly high number relative to her past salary history.) But by engaging the candidate in developing a compensation plan relative to the position's impact on the corporate bottom line—its reporting relationship, scope of authority in terms of supervision and budgets, and the projected increases in company profitability that will result because of it—you'll get much more objective feedback from someone who probably knows that position's market worth better than anyone at your company.

Let's take an example. First, you have to give the candidate some parameters. Your position is paying in the $180,000 to $200,000 range. The candidate knows that coming in to this negotiation. Note that you should always tell someone the salary range if it's significantly *below* what she has been making. That's only fair since you don't want to waste anyone's time. (Sharing salary information up front may in fact be required under your state's law.) She's hungry to jump back into the market after two years on the sidelines, however, and she knows that she won't get the $265,000 base she had at her last company. She also knows that your company has done only retail home equity mortgage lending and that it desperately needs to gain access to the profitable wholesale market. Because she took her last company into wholesale and understands the pressures and pitfalls of developing new business lines, she's exactly what the doctor ordered as far as you're concerned in terms of prior experience.

So, step one sounds like this:

"Dorothy, now that you've studied our annual report, met with all the players in the decision-making process, and understand where we want you to go with this new wholesale product line, I'd like you to map out specific details regarding your expected base salary, bonus, options, perks, or whatever else is important to you. Bear in mind what our original salary range is, then make a case for your specific package. Email me an acceptable compensation package for your first two years so I can bring it to our senior management committee."

In explaining that this compensation proposal will be shared with the board of directors or executive committee, there is a lesser chance of exaggerated demands. Furthermore, sometimes executives will be fairly flexible in terms of base salary requirements when other nonmonetary or deferred-compensation awards could be added. It never hurts to ask, and you may learn of noncash perks that the person values at this point in her life that could cost you little in terms of up-front cash and gain you lots of negotiation leverage.

The candidate's proposal looks like this:

Base Salary	Bonus	Options	Total Comp.
Year 1: $200,000	10 percent first year	1,000 options @ $50 each	$260,000
Year 2: $205,000	20 percent second year	1,000 options @ $50 each	$296,000

In making this proposal, the candidate has set out to put a substantial portion of her pay at risk. After all, bonuses are discretionary on the basis of corporate and individual performance, and options may expire worthless if not exercised. So, in terms of pure payroll output, this individual is within your range.

Armed with the parameters that would make this candidate happy, you then have the option of perhaps cutting 10 percent off the first-year base but increasing the number of awardable options at the end of the second year. Whatever your final allocation, you're not shooting in the dark. Without this candidate's roadmap, you risk alienating her by making an insulting offer. Worse, you risk coming off as a naive employer because you're not familiar with wholesale compensation practices. On the upside, you may occasionally learn that certain noncash rewards carry a lot more weight in a candidate's mind, and that helps keep your payroll expenses down.

Therefore, involve the new hire in every aspect of the compensation plan creation. Few things in corporate America will work as well to build a shared sense of openness in information sharing, a greater sense of partnership, and increased accountability.

PART 3

KEY INTERVIEWING,
REFERENCE-CHECKING,
AND RECRUITMENT ISSUES

19.

Staying Within the Law

A Changing Legal Landscape, Plus Interview Questions to Avoid at All Costs

A Changing Legal Landscape

Major legal initiatives that can have significant impact on employers' future hiring activities are in play as of the writing of this third edition. Federal, state, and local laws continue to be introduced with the intention of creating a more level playing field where equal opportunity plays a greater role. These laws allow middle-class Americans to have a greater chance of regaining meaningful employment in an economy that continues to witness downsizing, outsourcing, and offshoring initiatives along with the significant impact of automation and technological change. Because the changing nature of work continues to impact the workforce in new and unforeseen ways, legislative attempts to slow and refine the pace of change are inevitable and predictable. How they reveal themselves upon rollout, however, will vary greatly, depending on political, social, and economic imperatives in play at the time.

These massive forces for change are occurring simultaneously as the rush for talent in a global, open market continues and while litigation potential skyrockets for employers who run afoul of the law. It's said that talent will remain any organization's ultimate success lever in an economy that depends upon intellectual capital. The balance between talent acquisition, social fairness, and legal compliance will likely continue to make headlines as we head into the third decade of the twenty-first century. The global race for qualified talent will impact everything from local education systems to international immigration programs, so keeping an eye on the employment marketplace from this point forward will remain a key component of business success.

Nowhere is this showing itself more than in new rules and regulations governing fair pay and gender pay equity, which may impact your ability to ask salary-related questions during the telephone screening, interviewing, or preoffer stages of the hiring process. The federal Equal Pay Act of 1963 was designed to amend the Fair Labor Standards Act by abolishing wage disparities between the sexes. However, it hasn't solved the problem of gender-based inequity in the world of compensation. Whether that has to do with loopholes and pitfalls relating to how the law was written or due to enforcement issues, census data and market data consistently reveal that the federal law hasn't had the teeth necessary to solve this age-old problem where female workers generally earn seventy-eight cents on the dollar relative to their male counterparts in the same or similar occupations.

Pay secrecy, pay transparency, and pay privacy are consequently new areas of focus that deserve your attention. While these laws are not a one-size-fits-all panacea to this issue because of legislative interpretations and differences at the state, county, and city level, it's important to understand how these three concepts interrelate and how they may impact your ability to discuss salary history or even salary expectations prior to the offer stage.

Pay Secrecy

Legislation surrounding pay secrecy has been introduced, permitting workers to discuss their salaries, benefits, and general working conditions with one another on a protected basis. Title VII of the Civil Rights Act of 1964 and the National Labor Relations Act already permit nonsupervisory workers to "act in concert" in discussing wages and other terms and conditions of employment, but current legislation intends to reinforce these rights under separate laws and ordinances.

Pay Transparency

Pending legislation aims to mandate that employers post wages or pay ranges for positions in job announcements, on job boards, and in job ads. Further, in Maryland, for example, employers must in all cases pay at least the minimum of the amount posted in the job announcement, advertisement, or posting—regardless of the new hire's skills, experience, or abilities. Pay-transparency legislation may inevitably raise antitrust issues since wages are a form of sales (i.e., the costs of labor), and sales lists may not be shared among competitors without violating current antitrust law. Still, you can expect to see similar legislation and regulations continue to expand, so remain vigilant in this emerging area of the law.

Pay Privacy

The third area of the pay-equity triumvirate—pay privacy—is the most impactful on your ability as an employer to discuss salary history and/or salary expectations with candidates prior to the point of actually offering them the job. What's the intent of such legislation? The goal is to withhold salary discussions until after a conditional employment offer is made (i.e., the point of "postoffer, prestart" status where background checks, preemployment drug screens, and preemployment physicals typically occur).

Why is this such a hot topic? Because in theory, if recruiters and hiring managers are basing starting salary offers primarily on applicants' current or historical compensation rates, then there's a substantial risk of perpetuating systemic pay disparities among genders. For example, if two candidates—one male and one female—are applying for the same position and the male currently earns $10 per hour while the female earns $8 per hour, then offering a 10 percent increase in base salary at the offer stage will simply prolong the pay disparity: the male will end up with an $11-per-hour offer, while the female applying for the same job—and arguably with the same level of skills, experience, and education—will receive an $8.80-per-hour offer.

The government's attempt to rectify pay disparity between the sexes will therefore rest on turning a temporary blind eye toward salary history and withholding compensation considerations until after a contingent offer of employment is made. Once that conditional employment offer is made, the company will then be permitted to ask about the candidate's current level of compensation, historical compensation levels, and desired compensation amount.

In the eyes of lawmakers, this attempt at blindfolding the compensation scales in favor of lesser-compensated female candidates who may likely possess the same skills as, or better skills than, their comparably experienced male counterparts seem to proffer a simple solution to the complex and long-term problem of gender-based compensation inequity.

277

Current laws and legislative initiatives go even further by declaring such inequities and inconsistencies to be a form of *discrimination*. In short, employers can expect to see increased judicial scrutiny of pay disparities between genders as these initiatives progress.

Therefore, be prepared to research and find answers to questions such as:

◆ Will it be permissible to ask job applicants what their *salary expectations* or *desired salaries* are? After all, even if you're not inquiring about their historical wage and salary levels, you have to know if their pay expectations are in line with your salary range so you're not pursuing candidates who wouldn't accept your job if you offered it to them.

◆ How do you distinguish between base pay, bonuses, and long-term incentives for more-senior candidates? Remember, total cash compensation or total cash plus incentive compensation is really what's at issue for senior leaders and executives—not just the base salary component. Will there be regulations that fine-tune exactly what compensation elements are included in the law?

◆ Can employers cap pay-transparency discussions for exempt workers or highly compensated employees? In theory, these types of laws are aimed at protecting those at the nonexempt, hourly levels of the workforce more than supervisors, managers, and senior executives. But we all know that pay disparities among male and female executives and board members are equally of concern, so will these types of rulings on pay discussions rise all the way up to the top of the corporate ladder or mainly focus on hourly workers?

It's not too far a stretch to imagine that companies may ultimately be required to remove the salary history box on their employment applications. The key point under fair-pay legislation is to ensure that whatever compensation a company agrees to pay someone will stand up to legal scrutiny when it is compared to the compensation paid to someone of the opposite gender who performs substantially similar work.

One thing looks to be for sure, though: Relying on past pay or superior negotiating skills will be unlikely to succeed in defending pay disparities in job offers. Therefore, as an employer, you may at some point be required to document and defend that any disparities in job offers between the sexes are job related, consistent with business necessity, and reasonably applied. To succeed in this rapidly changing arena, look to the laws of your state or city in addition to any federal legislation that may roll out. There are no clear rules or guidelines that provide specific direction in matters like these, so you're best off watching these matters unfold with the help of legal advisers and employment-law experts.

Caveat for This Book

Gender fair-pay initiatives aren't the only legal initiatives that may become law in your state, county, or city jurisdictions, but they deserve the most attention in our book because they speak directly to salary discussions during the telephone-screening interview, during the in-person interview, and prior to the employment offer (see Question 96). If they do become law in your area, you'll need to adjust your hiring practices to reflect these new mandates. Specifically, you may need to adjust your telephone screening form (see Chapter 20, "Telephone Screening Interviews: Formats and Follow-Ups for Swift Information Gathering") by eliminating the salary history and salary-expectations box. Likewise, you may need to eliminate any discussions during the onsite or video interview that follows. Finally, Question 96 may need to be postponed until after a conditional offer of employment is extended.

Then again, if you're a multistate employer, these restrictions and guidelines may be implemented in certain states, counties, or cities but not others. What's an employer to do? Considering customizing your telephone screening and interviewing forms by location. It's arguably not best to simply apply one rule across all company locations in this case. Yes, that may be easier to implement, but you'll want to retain your ability to discuss salary histories and pay expectations whenever possible because it's so practical and such a time saver to do so. In all cases, speak with qualified employment counsel for a site-by-site analysis of what will work best for your organization in terms of its interview questioning practices.

But wait—we're not done yet. Additional laws that may roll out and impact your hiring practices include:

◆ **Changes in minimum wage legislation**
 Minimum wage implementation is historically a straightforward exercise with little risk that applies uniformly to organizations in the same geographic area (typically a state or county). However, minimum wage issues are becoming a minefield of potential wage and

279

hour litigation as states, counties, and cities issue differing minimum wage schedules that require variable adjustments based on geographic thresholds. Specifically, minimum wage rates may be based on, among other things, where employees perform their work during the day. For example, in California, if drivers spend two or more hours per week in a jurisdiction covered by a higher minimum wage rate (think Los Angeles versus Pasadena versus Santa Monica), then the worker must be paid at the higher rate for those two hours that day. The time must be tracked and coded on the payroll statement, and significant penalties could apply if an hourly worker is compensated at the lower rate.

◆ **The use of noncompete clauses in onboarding new hires**
Noncompete clauses, which preclude working for a competitor for an extensive period (e.g., six months or one year), may be unenforceable, regardless of the level of the employee involved. As an alternative, you may want to drop noncompetes and focus on developing stronger nondisclosure or nonsolicitation agreements. If you have noncompete clauses in your employee handbook or include such language in offer letters, discuss their application and enforceability to ensure you're in compliance with local laws.

◆ **Ban-the-box legislation**
The purpose of the federal Fair Chance Act and so-called ban-the-box legislation (i.e., removing the check box that asks applicants to disclose whether they've been convicted of a felony or, in some cases, a misdemeanor) is to help former convicts find gainful employment while minimizing the nation's high recidivism rate. Proponents of ban-the-box legislation argue that without the chance to compete for work, these individuals often turn to crime and eventually return to prison. The legislation permits employers to conduct background checks and disqualify applicants from hire, but only *after* a conditional employment offer is extended. Further, the denial must be in writing and demonstrate why the former illegal activity is related to the job at hand.

Therefore, in theory, it would be harder for employers to rescind job offers if they met the candidate in person and found the individual otherwise qualified for the role. Further, ban-the-box legislation would provide employers with a safe-harbor defense against future claims of negligent hiring and negligent retention, which are defined as:

➡️ *Negligent hiring:* The employer knew or should have known of the employee's unfitness and failed to take action to prevent the alleged harm.

➡️ *Negligent retention/supervision:* The employer knew or should have known of action by the employee during the course of the worker's employment that placed the organization on notice of unfitness to continue in the position.

As of this writing, Hawaii, Massachusetts, Minnesota, Rhode Island, Illinois, New Jersey, Oregon, Connecticut, and the District of Columbia have adopted some form of ban-the-box rulings. Some cities and counties have done so as well, including New York City; Chicago; San Francisco; Los Angeles; Seattle; Philadelphia; Baltimore; Portland; Austin, Texas; Buffalo and Rochester, New York; and Montgomery County and Prince George's County, Maryland. Expect to see more on this hot topic as ban-the-box legislation initiatives continue to sweep the nation.

◆ **Fair Credit Reporting Act restrictions**
Companies can expect to see further attention given to the proper issuance of pre-adverse action letters (notifying candidates of background-check findings that may knock them out of consideration for a position) as well as adverse action letters (the document in letter form that says a company has decided to disqualify an application for the position at hand because of findings from a background check). Ongoing challenges to credit checks will likely remain a hot topic as worker privacy rights contend with companies' desires to conduct background checks in selection considerations. (Currently, CFOs and other senior executives as well as finance employees typically undergo credit checks, but extending credit checks to workers outside of finance or senior executive roles remains problematic.)

◆ **Worker misclassification challenges**
Employee versus independent contractor status remains one of the hottest and most controversial triggers for class-action wage and hour lawsuits. As the gig nation continues to make headlines, look for increased government scrutiny of independent contractors, freelancers, and anyone else from whom payroll taxes are not withheld and who is not allowed to participate in group benefit plans. This legal update

281

is not meant to scare you. But these types of regulatory initiatives may remain in play for years to come, only varying slightly according to legislative interpretations and case law results that help define them and create expectations around future hiring practices. In contrast, some of these initiatives may quickly fall by the wayside, replaced by newer ones that attempt to rectify an uneven distribution of wealth and opportunity among American workers. Whatever the case, be sure to vet your employment policies and employee handbooks regularly and work with qualified legal counsel to ensure compliance with the letter of the law as well as adherence to the law's spirit. In short, make recruitment and talent management a key organizational metric, standard, or key performance indicator to ensure that you have the talent available to thrive while insulating your organization from the compliance demands and litigation potential that may rise over the coming years and decades.

Interview Questions to Avoid at All Costs

No book on interviewing questioning techniques would be complete without an acknowledgment that certain queries could land you in hot water legally. You could get into trouble for the illegal use of the nonjob-related information that you obtained by asking a question in the pre-offer stage of the hiring process. If a candidate believes she was discriminated against because of improper information that you uncovered during the interview, for example, then she could bring suit against you for failing to hire her. The cost of *defending* such claims could be significant in terms of your company's monetary and time investments. The penalties for *losing* the suit typically include wages the applicant would have earned if hired plus the individual's attorney's fees. The average cost of an employment lawsuit, win or lose, can exceed $125,000 in attorneys' fees and settlement costs.

How difficult is it to steer clear of legal snares? Fortunately, it's not too difficult, especially if your staff is adequately trained and armed with the following information. As a matter of fact, with the number of people interviewing candidates in your company at any given time who could potentially be exposing your organization to unnecessary liability, this section of the book might well become a critical training module for your newly hired managers.

Although no one aims to blatantly transgress federal or state guidelines that bar various forms of discrimination, the intent is not at issue—only the form of the hiring manager's questions. So let's briefly look at some of the more common unacceptable preemployment inquiries that are floating around out there.

INAPPROPRIATE QUESTION 1: "What's your maiden name so that I can complete your background check?"

Asking for a person's maiden name can discriminate against her on the basis of marital status and possibly national origin. Instead, ask whether the candidate has used any other names in the past (not necessarily due to marriage) that will allow your company to verify the person's past work experience and education.

INAPPROPRIATE QUESTION 2: "How old are you? What year were you born? When did you graduate from high school?"

State and federal law protects those over forty years old. It promotes the hiring, promotion, and other terms and conditions of employment of older people based on their abilities rather than their age. There's no problem questioning the year of college graduation because people can graduate from college at any time in their lives, so there's no way to figure out the person's age. But nearly all high schoolers graduate at seventeen or eighteen, so an individual's year of birth could readily be determined by subtracting eighteen from the year of graduation. That's why asking for high school graduation dates must be avoided.

That might raise another issue in your mind, though. Are you still liable for information (written or spoken) volunteered by a candidate without your prompting? Yes. So to defend yourself, you have to remove anything written on an employment application that could compromise your adherence to proper interviewing guidelines. When a candidate mentions something out loud that doesn't belong in your meeting (e.g., "I'm forty-seven years old," "I'm so excited—I just found out I'm pregnant," or "I learned to speak English after I moved to America when I was eighteen"), immediately let the person know that such information isn't relevant to the interview. Move on to another issue and, by all means, don't write any of that information down on the employment application, résumé, or even on Post-it notes—all are subject to subpoena in the legal discovery process.

283

INAPPROPRIATE QUESTION 3: "Where were you born? Are you a U.S. citizen? Where did you learn to speak Spanish?"

These questions transgress guidelines regarding national origin, birthplace, and citizenship. Instead you should ask, "Could you, *after employment*, submit verification of your legal right to work in the United States?" Questions regarding a candidate's native language or acquisition of foreign languages in general should be avoided unless such language proficiency is an essential function of the particular job.

Is it legal to discriminate against someone because the person has an accent? No. Courts have held that accents are "immutable characteristics" innately tied to an individual's culture. Accordingly, discriminating against someone on the basis of a foreign accent can land you in hot water. However, be practical. You have the right as an employer not to hire a receptionist who is difficult to understand over the phone because the individual's English is difficult to understand. No jury would fault you for that practical business necessity, so you'd pass the "reasonable person" standard with flying colors. Still, when in doubt, speak with qualified legal counsel. An ounce of prevention is worth a pound of cure.

INAPPROPRIATE QUESTION 4: "Are you married? Are you planning on having children in the next few years? Can you make adequate provisions for child care?"

Whoops. A big no-no on your part. It's a legitimate concern to wonder whether a potential employee can meet overtime demands or report to work on time. However, you are limited by law to stating such things as the hours, any overtime demands, and company travel expectations and then simply questioning whether candidates would have any reason why they couldn't meet those requirements. The common mistake that hiring managers make lies in attaching some reason for a candidate's inability to meet the job's requirements.

For example, stating the following is fine: "This position averages approximately five hours of overtime per week, but that could include occasional Saturdays and holidays. Will that work for you?" However, stating your question with a lead-in causal connector like this would likely be deemed unlawful: "This position averages approximately five hours of overtime per week, but that could include occasional Saturdays and holidays. *Do you have any childcare or family commitments that would get in the way of being available for and flexible with that kind of schedule?"* If a candidate were to reason that she was rejected because of her response to this one question and then opted to pursue the matter legally, it could be difficult for a hiring manager to defend herself against such a claim.

INAPPROPRIATE QUESTION 5: "Would your religion prevent you from working weekends?"

Asking such a question discriminates on the basis of religious affiliation. It's just as easy and effective to state: "Weekend and holiday work is required, and members of our department must work one Saturday per month from 8 a.m. to 4 p.m. Is that acceptable to you as a condition of employment?" Similar to the example above, omit any type of causal connector that could appear discriminatory. For example, don't say, "Weekend and holiday work is required. Is that acceptable to you as a condition of employment, *or would your religion forbid you from working that kind of schedule?"* You can see how the tie-in to religion complicates the situation and could be difficult to defend against should your company be legally challenged.

INAPPROPRIATE QUESTION 6: "Are you disabled? Do you have any previous major medical problems? Have you ever filed for workers compensation? How many days were you sick last year? Do you have any serious health conditions that require you to miss work frequently? What prescription drugs are you taking? Have you ever been treated for alcoholism or mental health problems?"

The Americans with Disabilities Act (ADA) of 1992 requires businesses with fifteen or more employees to make their facilities accessible to the physically and mentally disabled and prohibits job discrimination on the basis of disability. The ADA says that a company can't exclude a qualified person from a job if that individual can perform the "essential functions" of the job either unaided or with "reasonable accommodation." The terms in quotation marks are, of course, subject to legal interpretation. To play it

285

safe, though, all you have to remember to ask after presenting a candidate with an accurate job description is, "Are you capable of performing the position's essential job functions with or without accommodation?"

Tying in causal connectors relating to workers compensation claims, sick leave taken, or diagnoses of physical or mental histories are another big no-no, especially with disability discrimination being one of the hottest subjects of lawsuits in the land. In short, there's no way around this: By law, you're limited to asking whether the individual is capable of performing the position's essential job functions, either with or without a reasonable accommodation. Period. If you venture any further than that into the individual's private medical history, you'll likely be exposing your company to significant liability.

INAPPROPRIATE QUESTION 7: "Have you ever been arrested?"

As explained earlier in this chapter, ban-the-box legislation is calling into question whether employers have the right to inquire about previous criminal histories prior to a conditional employment offer being extended.

If you're wondering what the difference is between being arrested and being convicted of a felony, it's that those arrested are presumed innocent until proven guilty. Moreover, categorically rejecting applicants on the basis of a felony record is a problem for two major reasons. First, the felony may have no relation to the essential functions of the job. Second, such a policy has been held to have an adverse discriminatory impact on certain ethnic and racial minorities. Therefore, you can see why legislation of this sort is making its way through various state and city courts and gaining traction: Fair-chance laws are intended to give those with criminal records an opportunity to reenter society as contributing members. That must be balanced, however, with employers' responsibilities of ensuring a safe workplace. As is always the case with pending legislative matters, seek the guidance of qualified legal counsel in terms of updating your employment application and training your front-line managers about how your organization handles this issue when evaluating candidates.

INAPPROPRIATE QUESTION 8: "What kind of discharge did you get from the military?"

Sorry, folks—military service questions must be limited to relevant skills acquired during service. Questions regarding the type of discharge the candidate received from the military are unlawful.

INAPPROPRIATE QUESTION 9: "Have you ever declared bankruptcy or had your wages garnished?"

There are no acceptable alternative questions that allow you to address these issues before the hire. You are, however, perfectly within your rights to make employment offers contingent on credit checks, provided (1) applicable state and federal laws are followed, and (2) good credit is necessary to perform the essential functions of the job. To this latter point, be aware that courts have taken a narrow interpretation in issues pertaining to credit checks; it's pretty clear why a company would want to do a credit check on a chief executive officer or chief financial officer. If you opt to conduct credit checks on candidates below that level, however, it would be best to vet your proposal with qualified legal counsel.

Further, keep in mind that a growing number of states, including California, Colorado, Connecticut, Hawaii, Illinois, Maryland, Nevada, Oregon, Vermont, and Washington restrict companies from making employment decisions based on an applicant's credit report. Their logic is that during tough economic times, when people are having difficulty making ends meet, using credit reports to screen out job applicants may be unfair and, on a more practical basis, not particularly useful, especially since these screens can be irrelevant to many positions and may be more likely to reflect economic hardship rather than a lack of judgment or overall responsibility. Again, when it comes to conducting credit checks, proceed with caution and gain appropriate guidance from qualified legal counsel.

INAPPROPRIATE QUESTION 10: "Who is the nearest relative we should contact in case of an emergency?"

It's fine for you to ask for *someone* to contact in case of an emergency. However, asking for the *nearest relative* could border on discrimination by national origin, race, or marital status.

Understand that these protections were set up nationally to level the playing field and give all citizens an equal chance to capitalize on employment opportunities. Seen in the optimistic light in which they were created, these queries help ensure that you (and every other U.S. company) run your business fairly and keep America working.

Other questions that might run you afoul of the law include:

➡ "You have a beautiful accent. Is English your first language?"

➡ "It appears that you're reading my lips. Do you have difficulty hearing?"

➡ "Have you ever been a victim of harassment or discrimination in the workplace?"

➡ "I see that you're pregnant. When are you due, and how much time will you need off?"

➡ "Have you ever sued one of your past employers?"

Allowable Preemployment Queries

Just so you don't get the impression that all questions bordering on personal issues are *verboten*, let's take a brief look at certain personal queries that are allowed under the ADA:

➡ "I see you broke your leg. You must be an avid skier."

➡ "I see you've been a manager for the past six years. How often have you taken training in preventing workplace harassment, and what are some of the key points you recall?"

➡ "We're very proud of our diverse staff. What role has diversity awareness played in your previous jobs as a hiring manager?"

➡ "Can you meet the attendance requirements of this job? How many days did you *take leave* last year?" (Note that the question doesn't say, "How many days were you sick or absent last year?")

➡ "Do you use illegal drugs? Have you used illegal drugs in the past two years?" (The ADA protects recovering alcoholics, but active users of illegal narcotics are not covered under any federal law.)

288   The bottom line regarding previous-preemployment inquiries is that they can indeed discriminate against a candidate's rights to privacy.

Although at first they seem somewhat burdensome in terms of hindering your ability to understand a candidate's work habits and reliability, the same information can usually be found out simply by asking questions a different way (e.g., "How many days did you take leave last year?" versus "How many days were you sick last year?"). In cases where no alternative questions are permissible (e.g., military discharge status or credit worthiness), you'll simply have to build a case for the individual's candidacy on other selection criteria. Forcing these forbidden issues tempts fate and simply isn't worth the legal exposure.

20.

Telephone Screening Interviews

Formats and Follow-Ups for Swift Information Gathering

Telephone screening interviews can be a practical defense to the sheer numbers of people applying for jobs these days. Telephone introductions attempt to determine candidate suitability in shorter time frames (roughly ten to fifteen minutes) with less commitment on your part (no courteous small talk or paying for candidate parking). Telephone interviewing skills are absolutely essential when setting up interviews across the country. With little time to meet with potential staff in faraway hotels for a remote office location, your initial candidate choices become critical. Hence, telephone profiling techniques will help you determine the optimal applicants to select for off-site interviews *before* you fly out of town. Many hiring managers who employ telephone screening say it cuts down on their in-person interviews by up to 40 percent.

Once you've shortlisted candidates based on their résumés, then line up your telephone calls accordingly. Your strategy for handling telephone interviews, similar to in-person meetings, is twofold: First, employ the matrix at the end of this chapter to gather adequate data regarding a candidate's suitability; second, once you've completed your initial questioning strategies, prepare to sell your company to the candidate. That typically includes forwarding all scheduled candidates an annual report or other company data (or at least pointing out to them locations online where they can research your organization) so they can familiarize themselves with your company before the meeting.

The ease of the candidate telephone evaluation will usually be determined by the scope and depth of a person's résumé or online profile. The more details, the easier the selection (at least from a technical standpoint). Still, not all candidates are masters at résumé writing or highlighting their achievements on LinkedIn, and you obviously don't want to screen out potential high performers because they're not great at selling themselves on paper. After all, most job candidates only briefly describe their primary job responsibilities without relating them to the achievements and accomplishments they gained for the company while working there. Furthermore, most people don't describe their companies' market niches or size as well as their own straight- and dotted-line reporting relationships. That information would obviously make the matching process a lot easier for you, so you'll have to cull it yourself.

There are five major segments of the candidate telephone screen, reflected in the matrix at the end of the chapter:

1. Keys to Hire
2. Candidate's Core Qualifications
3. Motivation for Change
4. Compensation Expectations
5. Scheduling Availability and Availability to Begin Work

All five are critical because any one area could knock a candidate out of contention. Remember, your goal during the telephone screen is to make sure that the big items are checked off: If salary expectations are out of whack, if travel restrictions are too limiting, or if the individual won't be available to start with your company for six months because of contractual or personal obligations, now's the time to find out. Furthermore, the information you develop in advance will go a long way toward further preparing for the in-person meeting still to come. Once you've completed a full round of telephone interviews and gained critical insights into individuals' core qualifications and career needs, you'll be better positioned to call back finalists and set up in-person meetings. Note that many of the condensed questions that follow are already profiled elsewhere in the book, so return to the source if you need more detailed explanations for using each question.

1. Keys to Hire

Every role is unique and contains specific qualifiers. An HR director opening, for example, might focus on recruitment, compensation, benefits,   **291** compliance, payroll, HR information systems, international HR, merger-and-acquisition due diligence, labor relations, and the list goes on. A generic HR director title means little, in fact, when its application can be so broad. If you're looking for someone, for example, who will focus on benefits and compliance, discuss that specific requirement in deep-dive fashion at the outset of the telephone interview. Candidates may have those search-engine-optimization terms on their résumés and in their LinkedIn profiles, but benefits and compliance specialists are cut very differently than recruiters and employee relations professionals. Further, your ad might not have specified a focus on benefits and compliance, so it's important to raise the issue at the beginning to ensure that the candidate is interested in an HR director role that focuses on those specialty areas.

The "Keys to Hire" section of the matrix should be completed in advance of the phone call and copied onto all questionnaire templates for a particular position. This will help hiring managers keep their eye on the ball and ensure consistent evaluations throughout the screening process. It's probably safe to assume that all positions have three keys to hire—requirements that will likely predict a candidate's chances of successfully transitioning into the role with minimal on-the-job learning needs. Whether you're looking for someone with qualifications in customer service, sales, programming and engineering, accounting and finance, or similar occupations, it should be a fairly straightforward exercise to identify the top two–three or three–five core requirements. Outline them in advance in the matrix to ensure that everyone's on the same page in terms of what you're looking for.

Automated screening is now a common part of applying online. Applicants are asked to respond to three to five questions, which then get reviewed by the recruiter before the individual is short-listed. The "Core Qualifications" section may then focus on someone who's led an HR transformation, implemented an HRIS system, merged with or divested from a competitor organization, or led large-scale downsizing efforts. Whatever the critical focus of the role, the automated screening process allows for focusing on accomplishments and achievements first with everything else second. Even if your organization doesn't use automated screening software, this approach to the "Keys to Hire" and "Core Qualifications" sections will help you narrow your criteria and conduct a more laser-focused evaluation of potential candidates.

2. Candidate's Core Qualifications

This is your opportunity to match the keys to hire to the individual's core qualifications. Make specific note of any mismatches that may be critical in the selection process: an inability to speak fluent Spanish, the lack of a bachelor's degree, a lack of knowledge of Photoshop or Adobe Creative Suite, and the like. Generally speaking, if a candidate can't cover two of the top three or three of the top five keys to hire, it may be better to continue looking rather than schedule an in-person interview.

The "Current Company Demographics and Role Specifics" section is likewise important when it comes to each candidate's qualifications. Being an HR director means very different things when you're working in a privately held company with 200 employees versus a publicly traded one with 20,000. This is your chance to assess such issues as:

- Publicly traded versus privately held company (include stock symbol/ exchange for publicly traded companies)
- Company size, either in terms of revenue or the number of employees (or both)
- Reporting relationship (supervisor title, direct versus extended reports, size of department)

Remember that even though most candidates don't provide this level of detail on their résumés or LinkedIn profiles, it's important for you to assess these factors to maximize the chances of a solid match (and justify the time you'll take for an in-person interview). It's not to say that you can't hire someone who's an HR director out of a Fortune 1000 company to work in your small, privately held, nonprofit organization, but it would sure be nice to know that up front before you invite the individual to an in-person meeting. Simply stated, you won't know unless you ask. And it's fairer for candidates as well. This way, they have a clearer understanding of the organization and the role before they opt to take time off from their current position to come in for an interview.

Likewise, be sure to distinguish between straight- and dotted-line reporting relationships, and clarify the numbers and titles of subordinates. It's not enough to note that the facilities manager you're speaking with oversees a staff of four people; you have to identify the roles those subordinates play in the company. For example, supervising two building maintenance technicians and two facilities engineers is different from overseeing four office support clerks.

293

3. Motivation for Change

We discuss the importance of aligning candidates' motivations for changing roles throughout the book. Chapter 4, "Questions About Career Stability," Chapter 17, "Preempting the Counteroffer," Chapter 18, "Making the Offer and Closing the Deal," and other areas of the book address the importance of ensuring that the opportunity your organization offers makes sense for the candidate in the near to intermediate term. Without a healthy match between the candidate's career needs and your company's desire for high performance, consistency, and sustainability, the new relationship may fail.

While we address this key issue in these chapters and delve into conversations in much more depth during the interview and offer-preparation stages, it makes sense to touch on it lightly during the telephone prescreen. Keep an eye out for any red-flag responses at this initial stage that may concern you (e.g., "My company is considering promoting me, but I'm not sure I want to stay"). Make special note of any hesitations the candidate may have about timing, location, or other pending offers on the table. When it comes to career management and filling jobs, after all, timing is everything.

4. Compensation Expectations

As we mentioned in Chapter 19, "Staying Within the Law: A Changing Legal Landscape, Plus Interview Questions to Avoid at All Costs," discussions surrounding compensation history and salary expectations are under debate and changing as of the time of the writing of this third edition. Pay-privacy legislation is being introduced and adopted (although not uniformly) to avoid perpetuating systemic pay disparities among genders. Its intent is to rectify pay disparities between the sexes and may rest on turning a temporary blind eye toward salary history and withholding compensation considerations until after a contingent offer of employment is made. Therefore, whether you can discuss salary history up front or must wait until a conditional employment offer is made will likely depend on the rules of your state, city, or municipality. Further, while you may not be able to discuss salary *history* prior to a contingent employment offer being made, you may be able to discuss salary *expectations*. Be sure to customize this section of the telephone screening template, therefore, to match state and local laws in this important and changing area of talent selection and hiring.

Also, assuming you're free to discuss historical compensation, be sure to consider more than just the base salary. Hourly workers often earn a lot of additional money via overtime, turning a $36,000 base salary into a $45,000-per-year position when it comes to total cash compensation. Offering that individual a $42,000-per-year salary—assuming there is little overtime at your organization—would in effect represent a $3,000 cut in overall compensation for that candidate. Ditto for bonus targets: While bonuses are typically discretionary, a bonus target of 10 percent represents something totally different than a target of 33 percent. In other words, you may have a lot more discretion to offer a lower base salary if your bonus target has triple the compensation potential. Reciprocally, if your bonus target is low, you'll likely have to increase the base salary component to make an equitable offer.

For more senior-level candidates, equity, deferred compensation, and long-term incentives may make up a critical piece of the overall compensation package. If they're scheduled to receive a huge payout in the next six months, it's best that you find that out up front. It will likely indicate that you either have to come up with a significant signing bonus to make up for their lost equity distribution (often in the form of stock options or restricted stock units), or the candidate won't be able to start with you until the equity tranche is paid out. While none of these issues would necessarily preclude moving forward with the interview, you'll want to know up front where the timing stands relative to the candidate's next merit increase, bonus, or long-term equity incentive payout. This will help set expectations appropriately on both sides.

Yes, it may sound premature to discuss salary during the initial telephone screening stage since you've neither met the candidate nor had the chance to discuss other critical factors beyond compensation. Still, telephone interviews are meant to crystallize the entire prequalification process, so it's wise to surface this important issue, if permitted by law, before proceeding to schedule an in-person or video interview or to arrange for a candidate's plane ticket to visit your office.

In fact, some employers simply outline the base salary and other compensation factors (e.g., overtime, bonus target) up front during this first phone call so that neither party is wasting time by interviewing. Compensation budgets are often preset with no flexibility to go above the stipulated maximum, so it may make sense to get this critical issue off the table right from the start. Your approach will depend on state and local laws, your company's philosophy regarding hiring practices, and the talent demand in your market. Be sure to confirm in advance how your organization prefers to handle salary discussions specifically during the telephone screening stage and in general. The new laws have teeth that can bite hard in terms of penalties and damages, so this is something you must get right before you pick up the phone to make your first call.

5. Scheduling Availability and Availability to Begin Work

This one's fairly self-explanatory and obvious, but it's always a good idea during a telephone screen to make sure that the candidate has the appropriate amount of flexibility to match your expectations regarding schedules, shifts, and travel requirements. For more junior-level workers, you'll also want to discuss if the location of your office, warehouse, or laboratory is within a reasonable traveling distance. Be especially careful here: Non-exempt workers who are eager to find a job and earn their next paycheck may be quick to say yes to a job that's fifty miles from home or that will take ninety minutes and three buses to reach one way. Despite their eagerness to join your ranks, longer commutes may not make sense for them over the longer term, and once a similarly paying position becomes available closer to home, they may resign for it. What's a reasonable commute, time to spend in the car, or percentage of air travel will clearly depend on the nature of the role and the potential compensation. It's always worthwhile asking, however, since this can be a deal breaker in the first six months to one year.

Question 94 in Chapter 18, "Making the Offer and Closing the Deal," discusses the importance of candidates' timing in accepting your offer and making themselves available to begin. Please refer to that chapter for more information on the topic.

TELEPHONE INTERVIEW SCREENING QUESTIONNAIRE			
Name		Date	
Position		Source	
Keys to Hire (complete in advance) 1. 2. 3.			
Candidate's Core Qualifications 1. 2. 3.			

TELEPHONE INTERVIEW SCREENING QUESTIONNAIRE (cont.)	
Current company demographics and role specifics (company size and reporting structure)	
Motivation for Change	
"Why are you considering leaving your current company?"	
"What initially attracted you to our position?"	
"Why do you feel you're particularly qualified for this role, and why would this be a good move in career progression for you?"	
Compensation Expectations	
"What is your current compensation?" (Base pay versus overtime, bonus target, long-term incentives, etc.)	Base $_____ + _____ Total cash compensation: $_____ Total deferred compensation: $_____
Timing of next merit increase, bonus, or long-term equity incentive payout:	
"What's your desired salary?"	Base $_____ + _____ Total cash compensation: $_____ Total deferred compensation: $_____
Scheduling Availability and Availability to Begin Work	
Schedule/Shift/Location Match	❑ Yes ❑ No
Travel Availability/Restrictions	❑ Yes ❑ No
Availability to Interview	
Availability to Begin Working	
Overall Assessment on Telephone Screen	
❑ Technical Skills Match ❑ Communication Style/Respectful and Appropriate Tone of Voice ❑ Realistic Career/Role Expectations ❑ Acceptable/Logical Reason for Leaving Current Position ❑ Appropriate Level of Career Introspection and Business Maturity	Interviewer Notes

A Special Note About Applicant Disposition Codes for Internet-Related Recruitment

The Office of Federal Contract Compliance Programs (OFCCP) is a division of the Department of Labor and is responsible for ensuring that employers doing business with the federal government comply with the laws and regulations requiring nondiscrimination. The OFCCP uses the Uniform Guidelines on Employee Selection Procedures to define a "traditional" applicant, an individual who applies in person using a paper application. Additionally, the OFCCP has adopted a definition for an Internet applicant, which applies whenever an employer uses the Internet or related technologies, such as email or fax, to recruit for a position. Under this definition, an individual is considered an applicant when four specific criteria have been satisfied:

1. The individual submits an expression of interest in employment through the Internet or related electronic data technologies.
2. The contractor considers the individual for employment for a particular position.
3. The individual's expression of interest indicates the individual possesses the basic qualifications for the position.
4. The individual, at no point in the contractor's selection process prior to receiving an offer of employment from the contractor, removes himself or herself from further consideration or otherwise indicates he or she is no longer interested in the position.

Detailed disposition codes should be used to identify which applicants should be included in the required analyses of hiring activity. Disposition codes should identify the reason each candidate was not selected (e.g., did not meet basic qualifications, was not considered, withdrew from process) and the step of the hiring process where this decision was made (e.g., phone screen, interview). The following chart provides a list of sample disposition codes that federal contractors may use for Internet-related recruitment.[1]

Selection Process Step	Disposition Code/Reason	Internet Applicant Solicit Race/ Gender/ Vets/IWD*
SAMPLE APPLICANT DISPOSITION CODES		
Hired	1. Hired: external applicant	√
	2. Hired: internal applicant	√
Applicant Declined Offer	3. Offer Declined: no reason/other	√
	4. Offer Declined: compensation/benefits	√
	5. Offer Declined: working hours or location	√
	6. Offer Declined: accepted another offer	√
Offer Extended, Not Hired	7. Offer Extended, Not Hired: background check	√
	8. Offer Extended, Not Hired: did not show for first day	√
	9. Offer Extended, Not Hired: unsatisfactory I-9 doc	√
	10. Offer Extended, Not Hired: medical screen or other test	
Interview	11. Rejected After Interview: not best qualified education	√
	12. Rejected After Interview: not best qualified experience	√
	13. Rejected After Interview: not best qualified skills	√
	14. Rejected After Interview: poor interview	√
	15. Rejected After Interview: internal candidate selected	√
Hiring Manager Review	16. Rejected by Hiring Manager Following HR Review: not best qualified (may want to include sub codes to specify education/experience/skills)	√
Phone Screen	17. Rejected After Screen: not best qualified education	√
	18. Rejected After Screen: not best qualified experience	√
	19. Rejected After Screen: not best qualified skills	√
	20. Rejected After Screen: poor interview	√
Does Not Meet Internet Applicant Definition/ Exclude from Affirmative Action Plan	21. Jobseeker Withdrew: no response after 2 contacts	√
	22. Jobseeker Withdrew: accepted another position	√
	23. Jobseeker Withdrew: did not show for interview, test, etc.	√
	24. Jobseeker Withdrew: not interested in hours, location, salary/benefits	√
	25. Jobseeker Withdrew: other	√
	26. Rejected: basic qualifications not met	√
	27. Not Considered: incomplete application	√
	28. Not Considered: résumé/application not reviewed	√
Position Not Filled/ Exclude from AAP	29. Position Not Filled: filled next AAP year	√
	30. Position Not Filled: requisition cancelled	√
	31. Position Not Filled: requisition not filled	√

*IWD: Individuals with Disabilities

21.

Getting Real Information from Reference Checks

It is often said that no matter how skilled the interviewer, interviewing is at best a limited activity with restricted potential to predict on-the-job performance. And I agree that this is perfectly true. While you're at it, you could throw references into the same argument. Past employers rarely share performance problems with you, nor will they reveal patterns of inconsistencies or obstacles that workers experienced. And don't forget about aptitude tests: Capacity for analytical problem solving has limited bearing on daily performance or street smarts gained from the school of hard knocks.

So why don't you just hire whoever happens to walk in the front door? Because experience bears out that taking interview feedback, references, and tests into consideration paints a much more reliable picture of an individual's probable performance on the job. Although no one exercise in the employee-selection process can guarantee future work performance, multiple evaluations and assessments will increase the probability of locating high-performance individuals whose business and personal styles match your organization's corporate culture.

References are critical elements in the candidate-selection process. Unlike interviews, reference checks provide objective, third-party feedback of what it's like working with the candidate on a day-to-day basis. Who better than the individual's past supervisor to comment on strengths, weaknesses, pace, interpersonal communications, and aptitudes? And unlike tests, reference checks have real-world application—they're not just measurements of pure intelligence in a vacuum. Indeed, making employment offers without having spoken to past supervisors is like having a loose cannon on the deck of your ship. Without that human-evaluation element, you risk missing the historic dimension of working side by side with the candidate. You also risk getting snared by the so-called *professional interviewer* who interviews much better than he or she performs on the job.

These questions are designed to provide you with critical insights regarding a candidate's historical work performance. Up to now, you've asked candidates to evaluate themselves in comparison with their peers. You've measured their abilities to reduce operating expenses, save time, and improve the work flow. You've gauged their understanding of how their jobs met their departments' key strategic objectives and what roles their departments played in making their prior companies successful. And you've consistently employed behavior-based interviewing questions to ensure that candidates put their initial responses into a real-world context, thereby avoiding canned, superficial answers.

Still, you have only a one-sided argument until you bounce your findings off the other key player who has the ability to confirm the information you've developed: the candidate's immediate past supervisor. This individual is the only person in the universe capable of verifying your insights into this prospective new hire's ability to make an impact on your company and rectifying, if you will, any distorted images of the candidate's history. So if it sounds as if you have a few more rounds of interviews lined up once you've gotten your finalist candidate in sight, congratulations—you understand where we're going with this topic.

Reference checks are fairly quick, easy, and painless to perform. Compared to the hours that go into interviewing and testing candidates, reference checks have the biggest payback in terms of reward to effort. The questions that follow could be used during the interview, but they lend themselves better to third-party evaluations than they do to direct communication with a candidate. After all, few if any candidates would admit to having problems accepting constructive criticism, handling interruptions and breaks in their routine, or hustling to meet deadlines.

Of course, if you would like to employ some of these questions during an interview, you could phrase them in a behavioral format during your meeting like this: "Tom, tell me about the last time some outside influence negatively affected your job performance." And you'd likely get an honest answer that was grounded in reality. Still, the nature of that issue is better judged by a past supervisor than by the candidate sitting in front of you during an interview.

301

Special note: If the candidate's past company is out of business, or if former supervisors can't be found to share insights about the individual's performance, request a recent annual performance appraisal instead. It should provide you with fairly objective feedback regarding the individual's strengths, weaknesses, and areas for further training.

Furthermore, beware of past employers who refuse to comment on a candidate's performance. One neutral reference who verifies only dates of employment and last title held may merely be following the company's official reference policies, but too many such employers "taking the fifth" may indicate there were problems with the individual's work. Human nature dictates that past supervisors will help former subordinates whom they liked find other jobs. When minimum-disclosure patterns begin to occur, on the other hand, it's sometimes because past supervisors would rather say nothing than say something negative about an employee. If you find that more than one or two former employers refuse to take your calls, or they strictly quote dates and title, proceed with caution: At best, the individual may be burning bridges; at worst, the candidate may have engaged in egregious misconduct that resulted in a summary termination or lawsuit.

Some additional thoughts and considerations:

◆ References should be conducted prior to the employment offer. Some organizations state that "an offer is contingent upon reference checks," but that could land your organization in hot water legally. After all, if you extend a conditional employment offer, inform the candidate that you still have to check references, and then tell the candidate that she's no longer under consideration, she could logically reason that's because her past employer provided a poor reference. That could incentivize the candidate to seek legal counsel, and both your company and the past employer could become subject to legal action. Remember, reference checks come *prior* to the offer; in comparison, background checks, preemployment drug screens, and preemployment physicals occur *after* the conditional offer (but before the candidate officially starts work). It would be a mistake to treat reference checks like background checks, preemployment drug screens, and preemployment physicals that all occur postoffer. In short, don't extend an employment offer without having conducted the reference checks first.

302 ◆ You probably need no more than three references, on average, to gain insights into a candidate's relatively recent work history. Assuming the

average job lasts roughly two to three years, then three references will cover ten years of work experience, and you typically wouldn't need to go back more than ten years in checking references. (That will depend, of course, on the role in question: CEOs and C-suite candidates are typically vetted much more thoroughly than other rank-and-file applicants.)

◆ Never jeopardize a candidate's current position by insisting that you speak with the current supervisor. Candidates typically keep their job searches confidential for obvious reasons, so when it comes to checking references with current employers, show appropriate flexibility. For example, ask the candidate for two or three of the most recent performance reviews in place of a reference. Performance reviews will highlight strengths, weaknesses, and the individual's overall performance level for that particular performance year. Unlike letters of recommendation or LinkedIn endorsements, which only show strengths and positives, performance reviews demonstrate shortcomings and areas for improvement as well and therefore are more objective and balanced. Likewise, ask to speak with a former supervisor from that company who's no longer there. Or else ask to speak in confidence with someone currently at the company whom the candidate trusts and who can speak to the individual's strengths, accomplishments, and areas for development without divulging the individual's job-change intentions.

◆ Avoid speaking with peers and subordinates unless the situation calls for it (e.g., if the candidate is a CEO, speaking with her subordinates as well as board of director members makes sense). Likewise, avoid personal references who can speak to the individual's character: While that could be nice to know, it adds little value to the reference-checking process. After all, you'll always want to speak with former immediate supervisors who directly oversaw the candidate's work and who can share insights into the individual's style, talents, and shortcomings. Your goal in the reference-checking process, after all, is to gain direct insights into how to provide the appropriate amount of feedback, structure, and direction to the individual on a regular and ongoing basis.

◆ If you're a member of your company's talent-acquisition team and work as an internal recruiter, consider having your hiring-manager clients join you for reference-check calls. Share with the referent that you're both on the phone, and encourage the hiring manager to speak directly with the former supervisor—peer to peer—to gain a much

303

broader and more thorough understanding of the candidate's style and technical knowledge.

◆ Always have candidates set up the reference-checking calls in advance with their prior supervisors rather than attempting to make cold calls. For example, if a candidate hasn't worked for a particular supervisor for three years and you make a cold call, you'll likely get hit with responses like "All reference checking calls must be referred to HR" or "We're only allowed to verify dates of employment and last title held." Instead, place the burden on the candidate to open up the lines of communication with the prior supervisor like this: "Sally, I'd like to speak with the following three supervisors at your last three employers: Mark Tomlinson, Susan Harris, and Maureen Farber. Would you please call them and tell them I'd like to speak with them? We take references fairly seriously here, and they're critical to the hiring process. If you could tell them that I'd like to speak with them for about 15 minutes, I'd appreciate it. They can call me if that's easier for them, or else I can call them at whatever time is easiest for them. Please get back to me with their updated contact information and the best time for us to reach each another."

By making candidates responsible for bridging the reference, you should be able to get prior supervisors speaking with you the majority of the time. Again, if they're still unwilling to discuss the candidate in question, proceed with caution. One employer who refuses to speak with you may not raise any red flags or serve as a deal breaker, especially since you can ask for a performance review to cover that gap. But if none of the three prior supervisors is willing to take your call, be especially careful to weigh the candidate's pros and cons before welcoming that individual into your corporate home. There may be a valid reason behind their refusal to speak with you, but that's usually more the exception than the rule. Personally, as a recruiter myself, no references equal no hire. Proceed with appropriate caution when facing similar circumstances.

Finally, remember that this book is not a treatise aimed at addressing the legal subtleties surrounding confidential communications between employers regarding candidates' references. Nor is it a forum for discussing employee privacy rights and the potential for accusations of libel, slander, defamation, and negligent hiring. Such issues go beyond the scope of this book. However, failure to check references could result in negligent-hiring or negligent-retention claims, so refusing to check references altogether may not be a wise and appropriate policy. When in doubt, speak with qualified legal counsel about your organization's approach to this critical part of the hiring process.

How to Get Employers to Open Up to You During the Reference-Checking Process

The keys to checking references in today's cautious business environment lie in (1) taking past supervisors out of the judgmental past and placing them in the evaluative future regarding the candidate's abilities and (2) removing the perception of potential liability associated with judging a past subordinate's performance and replacing it with advice on how to manage this person in order to bring out the best in his or her abilities. This goal is accomplished in three steps.

Step 1: When opening a conversation with a past supervisor of the employee in question, spread honey on the situation. The appeal of flattery often gets people talking freely:

➡ "Susan, Sally said some excellent things about your managerial abilities in terms of giving her clear direction and structure in her day. I was hoping that, reciprocally, you could share some of your insights into her ability to excel in our company."

Step 2: When beginning the first reference questions, avoid asking generic queries regarding the candidate's job duties, greatest strengths, and areas for improvement. Instead, paint a picture of your corporate culture and its unique pressures so this supervisor can do some evaluative decision making regarding the individual's "fit factor" within your organization. For example:

➡ "We're a mortgage banking firm in an intense growth mode. The phones don't stop ringing, the paperwork is endless, and we're considering Sally for a position in our customer-service unit that deals with our most demanding customers. Is that an environment in which she would excel?"

Step 3: If the employer is hesitant about sharing performance feedback, replace the notion of "What you tell me will determine whether we hire this person" with an appeal to the employer's managerial expertise:

➡ "Susan, I won't ask you to address anything you'd rather keep confidential. And I also want you to know that I'm not burdening you with the responsibility of judging this person's past. We're simply at an evaluation stage right now where several candidates are in contention for the job, and we want your advice in terms of how to manage this person most effectively by not having to reinvent the wheel with her. So my questions to you will be in terms of the kind of structure we should provide to give her the most support from day one and make her a success. Are you okay with that?"

Because these questions focus more on future suggestions for supervision and development than do traditional queries that pass judgment on past performance, much of the stigma attached to the legal liability issues of sharing reference information will be removed. But what if the employer still won't talk? Hard liners who insist that corporate rules are not to be broken are the ultimate challenge in the reference-checking process. Of course, the impact of one employer's refusal to participate must be kept in perspective; if other employers are giving rave reviews and this one supervisor refuses to provide feedback under any circumstances, then that silence shouldn't necessarily become a negative swing factor to ultimately disqualify the candidate.

Your last-ditch strategy would be to call an employer back and state:

➡ "I appreciate your adherence to your corporate reference-checking guidelines. Still, I can't help but assume that no news is bad news since most employers will give a good reference to help a former worker land a new job if that person was a solid performer. My assumption at this point, therefore, is that there were very likely problems with Sally's performance or conduct, which you'd rather not share. That's understandable, but again, it could really help her if you'd be willing to discuss your insights about what it's like supervising her. I'll keep what you say totally confidential and off the record, but it may negatively impact her candidacy if we can't develop appropriate references."

This appeal to guilt may seem like an unfair stratagem, but there's nothing to lose at this point. Besides, once you've framed your concerns so explicitly, you should rest assured that further silence on the employer's part represents a tacit agreement with your stated concerns. Finally, close the reference check by asking if the candidate is considered rehireable.

A "no comment" response or flat-out "no" should dictate your course of action in evaluating other more suitable individuals.

Special note: Don't forget that prior supervisors are potential candidates. Once you complete your reference call, leave your phone number and contact information with the reference. If appropriate, consider closing with a statement like, "Susan, please hold onto my contact information, and if you'd ever like to talk about your own career-path needs or learn more about our organization, I'd always be happy to speak with you again." It certainly plants a seed, and seeds never hurt.

22.

Background Checks

Many employers who consider using background investigation firms think only of liability protection. Courts have ruled that companies have a general duty to check criminal records for prospective employees who interface with the public or who could have an opportunity to commit a violent crime while in the course of their employment. After all, damages against employers are being awarded where the company was deemed negligent because it failed to perform a reasonable search into an employee's background prior to hiring. Therefore, a background check is seen as a simple way to minimize the exposure of a wrongful-hire or wrongful-retention lawsuit.

That's certainly a valid reason to employ background investigation firms. Here's a more sobering statistic: According to the U.S. Department of Justice, almost seven million Americans were on probation, in jail, in prison, or on parole—that is, approximately 3 percent of the adult population, or one in every thirty-three adults. In addition, according to recent figures from the Bureau of Justice Statistics, recidivism is high: Some 67 percent of prisoners are rearrested for a new offense within three years of release from prison.

Moreover, every year billions of dollars are lost by businesses nationwide because of employee theft, so the odds are that convicted thieves will steal again when the opportunity presents itself. Finally, keep in mind that homicide is one of the largest causes of workplace deaths and that almost a dozen people are murdered in the course of doing their jobs every week. This is serious stuff, and employing workers without completing background checks can be a source of major liability to your company—both financially and in terms of compromised workplace safety.

On a more practical basis, background investigation firms will help you hire better employees by steering clear of candidates who have falsified their employment applications. Since industry experts approximate that 30 percent of all résumés contain some misrepresentation (most commonly in the education section), a sound background check will help you screen out individuals with compromised work ethics, reduce turnover, and provide you with greater peace of mind regarding your hiring decisions. And no matter how good your reference checks are, you won't have the time, resources, or authority to check into candidates' criminal backgrounds.

What do you look for in selecting a background investigation firm, and how much do their services cost? Depending on the position being applied for, employers should begin with a basic five-point search and add background-checking criteria as necessary. The basic five-point search will typically cover a candidate's:

1. Criminal history in all counties where the applicant resided, at least for the past seven years, along with any initial alias ("a.k.a.")
2. Motor vehicle report
3. Social Security verification
4. Federal district court search
5. Multijurisdictional database search

The basic criminal search should be completed by the background investigation firm at the source (as opposed to via the Internet or via CD-ROM database retrieval), with criminal searches performed at the local superior and/or municipal court for the most up-to-date records. That said, a search of a criminal database along with searches at the local jurisdiction cast a wider net and may identify crimes in a county where the subject never lived. Just be careful not to use a database as the only method and tool for your criminal search. Various industry experts agree that database searches, although helpful, may offer a false sense of security if not used in tandem with investigations at the source of the original record (e.g., at a courthouse or hall of records). In fact, if you rely solely on a database to conduct your criminal search and that particular database misses a conviction, you could be held liable for a negligent-hiring claim.

In his book *Sleuthing 101: Background Checks and the Law,* author Barry J. Nadell states:

> The information derived from public record databases may be outdated and/or inaccurate. The National Criminal Database Search should be used as a "conviction locator" only as it may provide additional criminal information not found by researching the county or state of residence or all counties found on the subject's Social Security trace or credit report. When using the National Criminal Database Search, it is crucial to conduct county criminal searches to perform proper due diligence and comply with the law. Identification of individuals is based on name and limited identifiers; consequently, misidentifications may occur.[1]

The number of years of criminal history that can typically be investigated depends on the laws of your state. The motor vehicle report is important because warrants for arrest may appear on them. Driving records can likewise include driving under the influence, possession of drugs, and failures to appear before a court. The Social Security trace is not absolute in verifying the accuracy of the individual's Social Security number but is primarily used to identify counties (and aliases) where the subject has lived.

Additional searches, for extra fees, may include a candidate's:

- Credit report
- Education verification
- License verification
- Military records verification
- Workers compensation filings (postoffer applicants only)
- Sexual offender/child molester identification requests (e.g., for school employees, home health employees, workers at childcare centers, or in any cases where companies have "parties at risk")

Credit reports should generally be conducted only when applicants have a fiduciary responsibility to your company or handle cash. Accounting, finance, and senior-management candidates typically should have their credit histories checked. In those types of roles and positions of trust, the applicant's financial condition is likely to be relevant to the position, and a credit check can be justified. By acting responsibly in evaluating candidates' credit histories, you'll mitigate risk by protecting yourself not only from in-house loss or theft but also from actions brought by others if the employee acts wrongfully on your behalf.

The cost of a basic package ranges from $25 to $100 per search. You may be able to create your own package deals for a discounted fee by guaranteeing the firm a certain number of searches per year. Ancillary services like credit checks or education verifications may cost from $10 to $25 per search. Court fees may apply as well. Turnaround time is typically twenty-four to seventy-two hours; however, education verification or out-of-country searches may take longer.

In addition, it is critical that your background investigation firm follows the laws established under the Fair Credit Reporting Act (FCRA) as amended by Congress in 1997 and the Consumer Reporting Employment Clarification Act of 1998, as well as applicable state laws. Penalties for noncompliance include actual and punitive damages as well as costs and attorneys' fees. In some cases, civil or criminal penalties may apply.

Legal Limitations on Background Checks

Under federal law, employers must ensure that any background check is job related and consistent with business necessity. The U.S. Equal Employment Opportunity Commission (EEOC) takes the position that improper use of background checks may create a disparate impact on certain protected classifications, such as race. There should be a direct connection between the type of background check performed and the applicant/employee's job duties. The background-check process also must be consistent: The same type of background check should be conducted for all applicants in similar job positions, unless there are specific reasons to limit the search to only some applicants.

This job-related component is important to a defensible background-check process. For example, while there would be a strong business justification to conduct a credit check on an accountant or CFO, it would be a larger leap to justify a credit check on a custodian or engineer. With its no-more-background-checks-than-absolutely-necessary philosophy, the EEOC is particularly focused on the job-related requirement.

Furthermore, the EEOC takes the position that even if an employer uses a targeted screening process, the employer should still provide "an opportunity for an individualized assessment" before taking adverse employment action based on criminal history information. Although the EEOC stops just short of actually requiring employers to conduct individualized assessments, the agency's guidance repeatedly stresses that a screening process that does not include individualized assessments is more likely to violate the federal law antidiscrimination provisions found in Title VII.

A number of states restrict employers' abilities to request certain types of background checks at all. Thirteen states and the District of Columbia limit employers' ability to request credit-background checks: California, Colorado, Connecticut, Hawaii, Illinois, Maryland, Minnesota, Nevada, Ohio, Oregon, Pennsylvania, Vermont, and Washington. (Minnesota, Ohio, and Pennsylvania have guidance or advice, not statutory prohibitions.) In addition, five local governments—New York City; Chicago; Cook County, Illinois; Philadelphia; and Madison, Wisconsin—have passed laws limiting employers' ability to conduct credit checks.

There is a movement among states and some municipalities to enact ban-the-box or comparable legislation. Depending on the jurisdiction, ban-the-box statutes make it unlawful for an employer to (a) inquire about criminal history, (b) require completion of a background check consent form, and/or (c) conduct a background check before a certain point in the application process.

FCRA Disclosure Rules

Your background investigation firm should provide you with legal disclosure forms (updated pursuant to any Federal Trade Commission staff opinion letters) in English and Spanish that require candidates' signatures to demonstrate their consent to being investigated. (The Fair Credit Reporting Act makes it legal to procure a consumer report for employment purposes only if the consumer has been notified in a clear and conspicuous written disclosure before the consumer report request, and only provided that the consumer has given written authorization.) In addition, the firm should provide you with sample rejection letters to applicants should your decision not to hire be based wholly or in part on information contained in the report.

Under the FCRA, the disclosures must consist "solely" of the disclosures. For example, the Federal Trade Commission has opined that a disclosure is unlawful where it includes a "release of liability" or "liability waiver" sentence—in which the employee/applicant releases the company or the consumer reporting agency—because it adds more to the disclosures than is statutorily allowable.

Please note that a number of states also regulate the disclosure-and-authorization process and provide job applicants with additional rights. It is important that your company and the background investigation firm are familiar with these state requirements.

FCRA Adverse Action Rules

Note that subjects of background checks have the right to dispute the information discovered by the background checking agency. Your agency will be able to assist you in those cases. However, a practical response on your part, as the employer, would be to acknowledge the job applicant's disagreement with the findings and notify him of the agency that provided the information along with the specific information itself. At that point, simply explain that the candidate may pursue clarifying his record on his own time, and that once he does, if (a) the position is still open and (b) he is still clearly the most qualified candidate for the position, you would be very happy to consider his candidacy further. Don't be too surprised, however, if you never hear from that individual again.

Finally, be sure to include information regarding your company's practice of conducting background checks in your preemployment literature. There's definitely a preventative value to stating your intentions up front. After all, if candidates learn from your recruitment brochure, employment application, or posters in your office that you conduct criminal background checks (or drug screenings, for that matter), they will typically walk out before taking the time to fill out an application if they know they can't meet your requirements.

Dollar for dollar, background checks are an excellent preemployment tool. Expect 3 to 5 percent of all candidates to be knocked out of the running. That could save you significant time and money depending on the number of hires you make every year. The added time to the hiring process is minimal because you can begin background checks at the same time you conduct reference checks. Most important, your employees will appreciate your due diligence in assuring them a safer workplace.

Civil Records Checks

Whereas criminal records checks have become commonly accepted in corporate America, civil records checks remain controversial. The

Internet has provided greater access to employers in terms of researching candidates' backgrounds, and private information that extends beyond the criminal realm is fair game in many companies' eyes.

Civil records checks might cover such areas as divorce, discrimination and other civil lawsuits, trade-secret and intellectual-property violations, and breaches of fiduciary duty. Whether you believe that such issues might impact your decision to hire a candidate is up to you. However, because the trend to conduct civil background checks appears to be on the rise, it may be worth discussing with your background checking provider as well as your employment counsel.

Before broaching the topic, however, keep the following two caveats in mind:

1. Civil lawsuits, unlike criminal cases, do not generally provide an applicant's address, date of birth, or other identifying criteria. Therefore, you may be conducting this search based solely on a candidate's name, which clearly makes this a challenging task with somewhat limited usefulness.
2. Because few states possess statewide civil records databases, the consistency of the investigator's research and data-mining efforts may be compromised.

More significantly, the relevance of the information that you develop may be challenged by candidates who are denied employment. How will they find out that you used the civil information in your employment decision? Because under the Fair Credit Reporting Act, you're obligated to inform them of any adverse employment action that was based on the data you collected. It's not much of a stretch to assume that applicants may claim that you improperly relied on information that was neither job related nor a valid predictor of potential job performance.

Finally, remember that courts have debated the use of criminal background checks and their application in the workplace. That means that workplace standards and legal interpretations are fairly well documented and predictable. However, there has been little discussion in the courts up to now regarding the appropriate use of civil records in the preemployment process. Therefore, what constitutes appropriate company behavior in matters such as the misuse of civil records in hiring decisions is fairly undefined.

Generally speaking, you don't want to become a footnote in the case-law books just to prove a point. If you move forward with civil background checks, define the parameters of your program, discuss in advance the relevance of the information you're seeking to uncover, and, as always, seek appropriate legal counsel.

Social Networks as a Form of Background Screening

Professional and social networking sites like LinkedIn, Facebook, and YouTube are proliferating at an exceptional rate. Consequently, many employers are now looking online at the social networking profiles of prospective candidates. And if online profiles display provocative comments relating to alcohol consumption, drug use, and or sexual exploits, few employers would ignore the information.

Candidates may question the ethics behind such character checks, and although the legal and privacy ramifications of using social networks for background checks are currently being debated in the workplace and no doubt in the courts, the bottom line is that self-published information on the web is generally considered to be in the public domain and fair game for any onlookers—employers included (as long as an adverse employment decision doesn't violate workplace-discrimination laws).

In essence, in a world of user-generated content, which the web has created, every consumer is now a publisher (think blogs), expert (think Wikipedia), critic (think Amazon.com), and broadcaster (think posting videos on YouTube). And, according to TMP Worldwide, a global digital recruiting technology company, whereas web 1.0 connected people to information and web 2.0 connected people to people, web 3.0 represents an open source where everybody is connected to everything. Therefore, all sources of free information can be seen now as fair game.

Candidates, especially earlier-career millennials and generation Z workers, are well advised not to publish anything on the Internet that could reflect poorly on them in the foreseeable or distant future. That's because web entries and blogs, much like email, can't really be destroyed once they've made their way into the Internet's intricate and endless web of connections. On a positive note, candidates can use blogs and social networking sites wisely to affirmatively build their visibility and credibility as expert resources in their fields.

Yes, there will always be the challenge of entity resolution: Is the John Smith you're now researching online the same John Smith you're planning on hiring? However, the trend is clear: Companies will increase their use of online searches, including personal information they're not supposed to have access to. As a result, many employers may end up using non-job-related information about candidates' private lives in making employment decisions, whether they are conscious of it or not.

The how-to of conducting social networking and blogging checks on prospective candidates will depend on each website's instructions and membership rules. It may be as simple as doing an online search for someone's first and last name using a common search engine like Google to see what organic search results surface. Most companies would agree that that's fair because it's open territory. On the other hand, you'll have to decide for yourself whether you'll want to create accounts on some of the more popular social networking sites in order to participate in the social network background checking game.

In addition, before you rush to create accounts on some of the more high-profile boutique sites, like LinkedIn, Facebook, and Twitter (all accessible by employing a www.com protocol), remember that they all have privacy notices limiting use. Your company will therefore need to consider whether the manner of obtaining such material is consistent with privacy laws. Furthermore, it's an ethical question whether the company or its recruiters choose to formally register with such sites (i.e., create user names and passwords) in order to access membership information versus simply relying on the open Internet (e.g., using Google search toolbars) for general data mining.

Finally, employers have an obligation to be reasonable in terms of how they use and collect information that may be available to them. Simply speaking, it is the employer's duty to not use any information that the company should not have. An employer should likewise consider whether such online content is reasonably related to the requirements of the job. Otherwise, the consideration of extraneous information that is not a valid predictor of job performance may create a source of liability.

Proceed with caution, therefore, so as not to unfairly jeopardize an individual's candidacy via mistaken cyberidentity, privacy violation, or possible discrimination. And remember that people do indeed learn and grow from past mistakes and indiscretions.

23.

Interviewing and Evaluating Freelancers and Remote Workers

The New Frontier of Hiring Just-in-Time and Virtual Talent

This additional chapter to the third edition of *96 Great Interview Questions to Ask Before You Hire* is critical because of changes in the economy, the nature of our society's work patterns, and demographic shifts that influence the way work gets done. The gig economy is changing the corporate landscape in terms of just-in-time professional services that individuals can provide to companies as needed—providing freedom to portfolio workers and flexibility to employers but challenges in terms of workplace regulations, worker protections, and benefits portability. Likewise, remote employment is on the rise because of technological improvements that allow for distanced service delivery, bringing with it greater flexibility in corporate hiring practices and workers' career-management goals, yet requiring a different set of interviewing, onboarding, and leadership skills.

Where this chapter differs from the rest of the book is that the many questions listed will not go into detail or follow the "Why Ask This Question" and "Analyzing the Response" format. Instead, we'll attempt to take a broad-brush approach to the questions to help you define what is key to the hires you're making in these large and growing subdisciplines of corporate America. This is intended to be a starting point to help you formulate ideas for interviewing and reference-checking scenarios, but our goal is to save you time and help you home in on the key attributes that will help you hire more effectively across this broad spectrum of workers.

Freelancers

It's been called the on-demand economy, the 1099 economy, the peer-to-peer economy, and freelance nation, but both the government and commerce sectors seem to be settling in on the term *gig economy* to describe the large-scale trends in employment that are defining the current generation. You'll hear terms like *solopreneurs, free range humans,* and *portfolio careers.* Whatever nomenclature you opt for, this tectonic shift in the social contract between workers and the companies that employ them could be viewed as either inherently freeing and positive or insecure, vulnerable, and downright scary. What we do know is that some 53 million Americans—one in three workers—derive some form of income outside of the traditional nine-to-five setting and are considered freelancers.

The first picture these terms conjure up is of skilled professionals opting to pick and choose the work they engage in: well-educated millennials looking for creative outlets for their productive talents and measuring themselves in terms of their concrete contributions and results; individuals willing to forego job security for the possibility to choose where, when, and how they work, while having enough time and opportunity to travel and otherwise disengage from the workplace. This optimistic snapshot of solo contributors feeling fully engaged in their work and making just-in-time, creative contributions to the employers they choose to support is accurate for some. The counterreality is that far too many U.S. workers were displaced after the Great Recession of 2008 and are having tremendous difficulty regaining traction in their careers because of massive cuts in middle-class jobs—traditional roles that defined prior generations and that offered job security, benefits, and retirement options that have now disappeared due to outsourcing, offshoring, and mergers and acquisitions, created primarily by technological advances and globalization.

However you define it, freelancing is part of a huge economic and cultural shift. Whether you see this as helping U.S. businesses or gutting the fabric of American society, this part-time work model and on-demand workforce is a new fact of life and force to be reckoned with. Depending on the types of projects you need completed and the types of independent contractors you may need to bring aboard temporarily in order to complete your project or at least particular aspects of it, employ some of the following questions to help you define and determine who might best meet your project-specific needs on a finite, short-term basis.

Initial Considerations and Prequalification

➡ How much time do you have to dedicate to the project demands of a program like this?

➡ In terms of your availability, do you anticipate having any competing projects or priorities while working with us over the next [ninety] days?

➡ Based on your understanding of our needs, how can you help our project succeed and what, if any, obstacles or roadblocks can you foresee?

➡ What is your general approach toward launching a project in terms of strategy, effectiveness, and efficiency?

➡ What's the typical-size company you support, and what niches (types of industries, nonprofit, international, startup, and the like) do you generally serve?

➡ Which elements from your portfolio bear closest resemblance to the project we'll need you to work on for us?

➡ What do you think of the current marketing and creative materials on our website?

Communication Style and Performance Expectations

➡ How do you ensure that communication, collaboration, and accountability are part of the freelancer-client relationship?

➡ If you win this project, what will be your general approach to crafting a roadmap to success? What would you do on your first day of work for us?

➡ How would you describe your design style? How do you help clients determine if your design aesthetic will complement the organization's branding?

➡ How would you generally handle it if you suspected that you might miss a deadline? How much advance notice can we expect? Likewise, do you feel our timeline is realistic?

➡ How do you typically measure and communicate results, especially in terms of key performance indicators (KPIs) and intermittent milestones that you set for yourself?

➡ How would prior clients grade you in terms of your balance between quality and volume? How about your working relationships and communication style?

Measurement, Accountability, and Fee Structure

➡ Of all the projects you've worked on, which one mirrors this one most closely? What were the end results of that particular project, and what types of similar challenges could we expect?

➡ On a scale of one to ten, ten being the highest, how challenging is this project relative to others you've worked on? Is there any part of this project that you're not that familiar with or where you might need to rely on additional resources or subcontractors?

➡ How comfortable are you with troubleshooting connectivity issues? How do you generally troubleshoot problems on your own?

➡ Tell me about your remote project tracking experience. How do you tend to stay on top of your work and remain committed to your project milestones?

➡ What are the go-to technical tools that you use on a daily basis? [Follow-ups] We use Skype/Hangouts/Slack, etc. How familiar are you with that? How do you typically use these tools to increase productivity and build relationships when working remotely?

➡ How do you structure the pricing for your services, and what is generally included or excluded from your basic fees? [Alternative] Here's how we set our fees and accounts-payable processes. [Describe.] Does that sound reasonable to you?

Successful Completion and Follow-Up

➡ What percentage of your projects comes in on time and under budget?

➡ How would you envision the finished product if you're fully successful in this assignment?

➡ Who will own the intellectual rights to the finished product? [Alternative] Our agreement would need to stipulate that we own the intellectual property for the work you create for us. Is that agreeable to you?

➡ On a scale of one to ten, ten being the highest, how interested are you in pursuing this project timing-wise and in terms of building out your project portfolio?

➡ How do you tie payment installments to interim project-completion signposts? When is the remainder and full amount due? [Alternative] This is how we schedule installments and final payment. [Describe] Is that acceptable to you?

Remote Employees: How to Measure and Manage the Unseen

When hiring for a remote role, the requisite skills, knowledge, and experience aren't enough. The general nature of working with a distributed workforce makes hiring and managing more complex, requiring different sets of leadership skills and worker attributes. Of course, not all remote work is the same. Hiring someone to work exclusively from home is different than hiring that person to work in a different building or even a different part of the same building. Expecting workers to come to the office two or three days per week is different than hiring people exclusively to work from their homes who may never visit the corporate office. Still, technology is driving this change in workplace flexibility, and arming yourself with sets of questions that best ferret out individuals who can thrive in this unique working relationship is critical.

Likewise, some workforces are hybrids of in-office and distributed (a.k.a. remote) workers, while others comprise only remote team members. These dispersed employees may work in different cities, states, countries, and time zones, and all rely heavily on technology to communicate. Determining the best strategy to manage remote teams depends on a variety of factors: the company's business model, its culture and values, the strength of its leadership team, and the employees' needs and attributes.

On the positive side, employers that offer remote working opportunities can benefit from greater flexibility in their hiring practices and service-delivery models, lower overhead costs, and a greater pipeline of applicants to choose from. Workers likewise benefit from the freedom and flexibility of being their own boss (well, almost), eliminating commute time, and finding a greater work-life balance between their career and personal needs. This doesn't mean, however, that there aren't unique challenges and disadvantages to remote-reporting relationships. Managers fear that they cannot account for workers' time and efforts, while workers can come to feel isolated because of their out-of-sight-out-of-mind status, which may trigger feelings of insecurity and disengagement if they see that their career options may be limited.

Hiring and selecting remote workers, therefore, involves special considerations that don't come into play when hiring people who work in the office, side by side with their supervisors. In fairness, it's usually not the remote part of the equation that's problematic; it's the misalignment between talents and interests. After all, workers may think they've won the lottery if they're fortunate enough to get the opportunity to work from home. It doesn't take long, however, before they realize that they miss the social element of work and the general camaraderie with peers that make the day go by. Your goal in hiring remote workers, therefore, lies in maximizing the advantages and minimizing the disadvantages of the unique nature of remote working relationships.

If Candidates Have Prior Remote Working Experience (Preferred)

➡ Why do you like to work remotely, and what does a successful remote working relationship look and feel like in your experience?

➡ Share with me what the specific working expectations were for the prior positions where you've worked remotely.

➡ Paint a picture for me of your working environment at home in terms of your office or workspace where you provide customer service.

➡ I've always found that the best remote team members are self-starters who are able to motivate themselves and work independently. How close is that to describing you? Can you give me an example of how you typically motivate yourself to feel engaged about your work?

➡ Aligning people's talents with their core responsibilities in the job is always an important part of a good match. Of the following five characteristics of a top performer, which two do you associate with most and why?

- Collaborative
- Independent
- Organized
- Reliable
- Results oriented

➡ In your experience, is it more difficult to feel engaged if you're remote? If so, how have you successfully overcome that?

➡ As a remote customer-service specialist, how have you demonstrated creativity and innovation in terms of customizing solutions for clients with special needs?

➡ If you accept this job and you're successful in it one year from now, what will that success look and feel like?

If Candidates Have No Prior Remote Working Experience (Not Preferred/Riskier)

➡ Having not worked remotely before, what are some of the advantages and disadvantages that you suspect may be at play in terms of a long-distance working relationship?

➡ What interests you most about the possibility of working remotely?

➡ What are your biggest concerns about not being collocated with your boss and peers?

➡ Without getting too specific or providing me with concrete examples, are you concerned about any particular distractions at home that may impact your ability to hold longer conversations with customers or remain engaged on the line for uninterrupted periods of 20 minutes or more?

➡ Tell me about your ability to put work aside at the end of the workday, when it is so close by. Do you suspect that you'll have any challenges in disengaging or disconnecting from your work when it's right at your fingertips?

➡ Most people don't have the organization, focus, or motivation to be productive working remotely, and successfully working from home is a skill that takes time and commitment. How do you see yourself succeeding in this if you've never done it before?

➡ What do you think it takes to deliver A-level performance on a consistent basis when you're working remotely?

➡ We care more about customer loyalty than we do about customer satisfaction here at XYZ Company. How does customer loyalty show itself when the entire working relationship is by phone, email, texting, or occasionally video chats?

Establishing a Rhythm and Cadence of Feedback and Communication

➡ Share with me how you've maintained a sense of community and connectedness through virtual and in-person meetings and get-togethers at your prior companies.

➡ How do you go about establishing relationships and communication hubs with your peers to keep from feeling alienated or disconnected from the group?

➡ Some leaders worry about being effective in a virtual environment because if they can't physically oversee what's happening, they can't know that work is getting done. How could you allay that concern that many managers have when it comes to hiring remote employees?

➡ How do you ensure that you never leave your manager flying blind when it comes to important customer updates or changes in plan?

➡ How often would you prefer to have feedback when it comes to updating me about your work? In other words, what's the right amount of structure, direction, and feedback that you prefer from your supervisors regarding your workload?

➡ If you believe that communication and accountability go hand in hand, how would you structure your communications with me to ensure that I feel confident in your work and in your meeting and exceeding expectations?

Technical Skill Acumen

➡ What would you add or subtract from a technical standpoint to your last remote working experience that could have helped you connect better with your manager and peers or provide a stronger customer-delivery experience?

➡ When it comes to customer interaction, are you more comfortable on the telephone, with email, in person, or using video chat? What tools do you typically rely on to increase connectivity and communication?

➡ If there were one app or other piece of software you could create to enhance remote workers' abilities to do their jobs more effectively, what would it be?

➡ As you know, our company relies on [brand/type] software for all client communications. Would you consider your skills basic, intermediate, or advanced in that area? On a scale of one to ten, ten being highest, how proficient are you in that particular software?

➡ Do you have any concerns or hesitations about the software and technology we use or your ability to work with it?

Setting Expectations Correctly and Measuring Results

➡ How do you hold yourself accountable in terms of the performance expectations you set for yourself?

➡ What kinds of measurement standards—scorecards, KPIs, or customer-satisfaction surveys, for example—have you been accountable for in the past? Which ones work best for you?

➡ Job descriptions outline what you're supposed to be doing; performance expectations outline when you're doing something well. What kinds of performance expectations have you been held to in the past, and how did you quantify your results?

➡ When it comes to local versus remote performance, I find that successful remote workers create goals for themselves: checklists, personal metrics dashboards, quarterly achievement calendars, and the like. What have you used in the past to gauge your performance? [If none] "What could you see yourself creating to demonstrate your results?"

➡ In terms of prior reviews or one-on-one feedback you've received from past supervisors about your ability to perform and excel in a remote environment, what were your strongest attributes and your key areas for development?

➡ When was the last time one of your supervisors engaged in a surprise review of your work? What did the random evaluation reveal, and what takeaways or advice did you gain from their feedback?

Employee engagement, self-motivation, and accountability are standards that strong interviewers set for those they evaluate at all levels— whether full time or flexible and contingent. Look for no less among those who fulfill just-in-time roles to help your organization tackle timely challenges or who work independently and provide remote support. After all, depending on your company's primary product line and service-delivery model, such flexible workers and working arrangements can provide you with significant advantages and opportunities in the burgeoning virtual workplace.

24.

Effective Onboarding to Maximize the Chances of Initial Success and Create True Believers

When it comes to effective onboarding practices, many companies fail by a wide margin. They spend significant amounts of time sourcing and attracting candidates, interviewing and reference checking, background checking and drug screening, but once the person shows up for the job on day one, companies often underwhelm them. Few organizations dedicate appropriate resources to the overall onboarding experience, which, unlike new employee orientation on day one, should occur over thirty-, sixty-, and ninety-day periods, with a one-year look back for good measure.

In fact, many companies do little more than new employee orientation on a hire's first day. Some dedicate a full day to it, while others try to limit it to a half day or even to one hour. That's a critical oversight on their part. Transitioning new hires into your company has multiple cascading events that take place over time for the leader, the new hire, and the organization. Much more than simply enrolling people in benefits and setting up their payroll, it's your first chance to make a good impression and truly integrate the individual into your culture. Let's discuss various aspects of onboarding to ensure that your investment in your new hires is well spent and appropriately planned.

New employee orientation typically introduces hires to company policies and codes of conduct, safety requirements, organization charts, and, with some luck, introductions to key leaders within the organization. The onboarding process, which should be stretched over at least the first ninety days, provides you with an opportunity to follow up, fine-tune, and orient new hires to ensure maximum engagement and productivity right from the start. On a very broad level, onboarding provides you with an opportunity to:

♦ Address what your organization "overmanages." In other words, what you emphasize, value, and pay particular attention to needs to be clearly explained and demonstrated over time because it defines who you are at your core and what differentiates you from your competition.

♦ Create true believers and sell your company's story while highlighting your history and achievements. No, not everyone needs to understand your company's financial statements or analysis of its strengths, weaknesses, opportunities, and threats, but all new hires should truly understand what your company does, how it does it, and what it wants for its employees. This is a very special opportunity to sell your organization's uniqueness, and trying to unload everything in one day will surely miss the mark in helping your employees appreciate and value your culture and heritage.

♦ Set expectations around the customer service experience. What do you expect from your new hires in terms of servicing internal and external customers and clients? What are your rules of engagement so everyone knows what you value and what you model? How do you inspire customer loyalty rather than mere satisfaction, and who are some of the internal heroes who have gone above and beyond in terms of winning and engaging the hearts and minds of some of your key clients or customers?

♦ Set appropriate standards for how you want new hires to value their work and see their connection to the bigger picture. Give them a reason why they should not only spend their time but their discretionary effort. As Walt Disney Company aptly puts it, do you teach your employees to lay bricks or build cathedrals? Do your employees understand their connection to the broader picture? Do they know why the founders created the organization and how? Do they recognize the value your organization brings to its customer base and to the community overall?

♦ Explain how new hires are assessed via ninety-day performance reviews, quarterly and midyear performance discussions, and annual reviews that are tied to merit increases. Do you have special technology or programs in place to provide real-time feedback and recognition to peers inside and external to your department when they exceed expectations? New hires can use this opportunity to better understand where they are now, where they want to be, and how to get there. Likewise, use this opportunity to share performance review templates, goal-setting worksheets, and self-review forms as well as individual development plan templates to set their sights on longer-term achievements right from the start.

In short, how you handle the employee's first hour, first day, first week, and first three months on the job provides you with multiple opportunities for touch points, feedback, suggestions, and clarifications. Compared to the sink-or-swim onboarding method used by many companies during new employee orientation, this strategic approach to new hire onboarding will drastically increase your chances of success and long-term retention.

Better yet, assign a mentor. Weekly one-on-one follow-up meetings with someone more senior to the new hire but on the same team can provide a fabulous return on investment for both the mentor and the mentee. The new hires have someone to guide them through the ins and outs of the organization, the hidden land mines that could otherwise derail an early career, and a resource for getting to know the players and their personalities and penchants that much better. Such relationships build trust and camaraderie, but more than that, they help new hires integrate into your company with more confidence because of the safety net they provide.

And what a great stretch assignment for more-senior or tenured (non-manager) teammates. Placing people into stretch roles on an intermittent basis increases their sense of self-worth. It provides them the opportunity to grow and develop new team members—a great strength to add to someone's personal brand and reputation. And it provides a healthy sense of accomplishment where the more-senior member has skin in the game to ensure the new hire's success. These are all very important elements of a healthy working environment that focuses on employee engagement and development while capitalizing on the organization's investment in the new hire.

What should you focus on in your follow-up meetings? Your primary focus should be on developing your new hire's understanding of the business, its key players, and its current initiatives. What are the high-level goals that your company is focusing on, and how does each person's role contribute to those goals? What opportunities exist where new hires can make a difference? Further, these segmented and extended onboarding programs provide you with opportunities for one-on-one feedback with a member of management outside of the new hire's immediate team or department. For example, the recruiter, HR representative, or a department head may want to spend one-on-one time with a new hire at various intervals conducting a pulse check to see how their onboarding experience is progressing. According to the editors at Business Management Daily, some questions you might want to ask include:

Thirty-Day One-on-One Follow-Up Questions

➡ What do you like about the job and the organization so far?

➡ What's been going well? What are the highlights of your experiences so far? Why?

➡ Now that you've had a month to roll up your sleeves and get your hands dirty, what don't you understand about your job and our organization?

➡ Have you faced any surprises since joining us?

➡ What could we have done differently during the interviewing process to realistically prepare you for your new role?

Sixty-Day One-on-One Follow-Up Questions

➡ Do you have enough, too much, or too little time to do your work? Do you have access to the appropriate tools and resources? Do you feel you haven't been sufficiently trained in any aspects of your job to perform at a high level?

➡ How do you see your job relating to the organization's mission and vision?

➡ What do you need to learn to improve? What can the organization do to help you become more successful as you transition further into your role?

➡ Compare the organization to what we explained it would be like when you initially interviewed with us. Have you experienced any surprises, disappointments, or other aha moments that you're comfortable sharing?

➡ How does it go when your supervisor offers constructive criticism or corrects your work?

➡ How would you describe the general tenor or tone from your co-workers? Do you find that they've been supportive of your success or somewhat critical or pessimistic?

➡ Do you see a particular pivot point coming? In other words, after two months in the role, do you feel that you'll need to make a major adaptation to what you originally imagined you'd be doing or a critical change in your focus or expectations to remain successful?

Ninety-Day One-on-One Follow-Up Questions

➡ Which coworkers have been particularly helpful since you arrived? [Goal: pinpoint which employees can be influential in retaining new hires.] Would you recommend anyone to become a mentor to new employees?

➡ Who do you talk to when you have questions about your work? Do you feel comfortable asking? Has anyone gone out of their way to make you feel welcome or included in social or work-related events?

➡ Have you had any uncomfortable situations or conflicts with supervisors, coworkers, or customers? Did you feel inclined to escalate matters to your supervisor or to human resources on any particular occasions?

➡ Does your supervisor clearly explain what the organization expects of you? How would you rate leadership communication overall on a scale from one to ten (with ten being highest)?

➡ Do you believe your ideas and suggestions are valued? Can you give me an example of some type of change you've recommended that's been implemented?

➡ In retrospect, what could we have done differently in setting your expectations appropriately for working in our company overall and for your job specifically?

➡ [If the new hire supervises leaders] Have you engaged in any skip-level meetings with your extended reports to gauge how they're feeling about their immediate supervisors? Is there anything you'd recommend reinventing in terms of how your department or team functions?

➡ How would you grade us in terms of our extended onboarding program, and what suggestions can you share that would make our program stronger?

The end result: better performance, improved engagement, and stronger retention. After all, it only stands to reason that employees who are engaged in these types of activities from the first day will feel a stronger connection to your organization over time. They'll feel acknowledged, included, and more excited about their prospects for long-term success, so they'll likely demonstrate greater loyalty and productivity. What's interesting is that it won't even take that much time. While traditional new employee orientation may still last one full day, follow-up meetings on days thirty, sixty, and ninety may be scheduled for four hours, two hours, and one hour, respectively. All in all, your total hour commitment may be little more than sixteen, but because the meetings are spread wisely over the new hire's ninety-day introductory period, the constant follow-up and ongoing contact help cement a relationship that will stand the test of time. And of course, you can extend this initial contact period to six months and then the one-year anniversary if you agree that the feedback you're getting is worthwhile.

Is there an opportunity cost for removing the individual from the field at these various intervals? Of course there is—after all, both the supervisor and new hire will be away from their desks or worksites while these discussions and minitraining programs are going on. But think of all you'll be gaining: You'll have a chance to identify your top performers, provide special assignments to those looking for more, spot individuals who may be challenged and need to course correct, and flag others who may not have been cast in the right role during the hiring process. Your extra attention will help new hires incorporate new concepts and skills into their natural learning process when the timing is right for them, and your extra sets of eyes will identify opportunities that your organization may not have otherwise been aware of.

There are few opportunities that will help your organization maximize its investment in new hires and catapult the chances for success like an extended onboarding program. Employ this low-hanging fruit strategy for the next six months and measure your new hire retention results as a before and after. Don't be surprised to see a superior return on this particular investment in your new hires' futures because of the time you'll save, opportunities you'll identify, and ongoing commitment that will benefit your organization over the long haul.

25.
Maximizing Your Recruitment Resources

Selecting outside organizations to help you identify and approach high-performance job candidates can be highly effective if you know how best to utilize their services. Contingency and retained search firms are constantly looking for new clients to add to their rosters, but at what salary level does contingency stop and retainer start? What options do you have for blending the two types of services? What niches have recruitment process outsourcing (RPO) firms filled relative to traditional search firms? And how can outplacement firms help you identify top performers who may be in transition through no fault of their own? Let's take each of these issues one at a time and then provide you with resources for further research.

RECRUITMENT OPTION 1: Contingency Search Firms

Contingency recruiters come in two basic flavors: (1) professional/technical search and (2) administrative support recruitment. You're probably well aware of traditional administrative support agencies that place secretaries, staff accountants, customer services representatives, and the like. Such organizations typically place job candidates earning $70,000 a year and under. Professional/technical agencies, in comparison, usually specialize in individual disciplines like accounting and finance, data analytics and

---

This chapter is based on Paul Falcone's book *75 Ways for Managers to Hire, Develop, and Keep Great Employees* (AMACOM Books, 2016).

IT, retail, software engineering, and pharmaceutical sales. Such candidates typically earn between $65,000 and $125,000 a year.

What these firms have in common is that they operate on contingency, meaning they get paid only if you, the client, hire one of their candidates. A contingency recruitment firm is a high-volume, brokerage type of business that achieves economies of scale by placing candidates with similar skills, knowledge, and abilities into organizations with like needs. That's why they specialize in particular technical disciplines. In searching for candidates with a predetermined profile, agencies develop candidates who simultaneously meet multiple client companies' needs. In short, it's a business set up to prove capitalism right: Those search firms that are the most successful at meeting clients' demands flourish. Therefore, working with contingency recruiters is a win-win situation: You pay only if you hire their candidate.

Contingency recruiters earn a fee based on a percentage of a candidate's annual salary. The typical formula is 1 percent per thousand dollars of the candidate's first-year earnings, to a maximum of 33 percent. For example, if you're a semiconductor manufacturer looking for an early-career sales engineer who earns $75,000 a year, then your fee to a contingency recruiter who successfully finds someone for you is $24,750, or 33 percent of $75,000. Contingency search firms also offer a safety-net guarantee period in case a candidate doesn't work out in the first quarter. Those guarantees usually come in the form of a thirty-day free trial period (where the fee you paid is totally refunded) and a ninety-day candidate-replacement period (where the agency replaces the candidate at no additional cost). Fees and guarantee periods may be negotiable, depending on your market and the demand for the particular types of candidates you're pursuing. For example, depending on the talent demand for a particular position, you may be able to negotiate a 20 percent fee. Likewise, you might be able to negotiate a ninety-day, money-back guarantee (rather than a candidate replacement) if the new hire doesn't work out, so it's definitely worth discussing these options at the onset of the search assignment.

RECRUITMENT OPTION 2: Retained Search Firms, or Headhunters

The retained search business, in comparison, is a much more exclusive game. Retained recruiters typically target candidates earning $100,000 and up. For example, if a semiconductor manufacturer is looking for a general manager with an MBA and ten or more years of power electronics experience in the international arena to become part of a $20 million company with 800 employees, then a retained recruiter would bid for the business and begin the search.

Of course, there might only be fifty or one hundred qualified people in the whole country who meet your exacting criteria. That means that the headhunter would have to spend a great deal of time researching your competition, developing names and profiles of candidates, approaching those individuals with your opportunity, and then qualifying them in terms of their willingness and ability to do the job, fit your company's corporate culture, and potentially relocate.

The whole process is obviously not cost-efficient if done strictly on a contingency basis. So these recruiters work on retainer and traditionally get paid in three installments: one-third of the fee initially to begin the search, one-third after thirty days, and one-third after sixty days—regardless of whether the search is completed.[1] You are, in essence, paying for their time and expertise in researching, sourcing, and proactively qualifying candidates who are not currently on the job market.

The executive recruiter acts as an aggressive third party to scout the best talent at competing companies and to persuade them to consider a career-advancing move with your firm. You also benefit from their years of networking experience and contacts, in addition to their ability to coach candidates through the hiring process and assist them in understanding the full opportunity that your organization offers. In-house recruiters and social media sources are great, but they typically lack the firepower, time, and resources you may need in urgent situations for executive level talent. Likewise, they may not have the experience or expertise to land such senior-level candidates. When the urgency is great and your company needs an expert in the field who can dedicate full attention and resources to identifying executive candidates with specialized backgrounds, then an executive search firm can serve as an excellent resource in filling that need.

Unlike contingency recruiters who must place a candidate to earn a fee, the retained recruiter gets a fee that is guaranteed up front. Because of that financial arrangement, there is little financial bias to preclude a pure consulting relationship. The best retained recruiters focus on the right candidate at the right time who is the right fit for their client company. They seek to understand candidates' personal and career drivers, what motivates them personally, and how this opportunity addresses their

335

longer-term career needs. This ensures the best and most authentic outcome for all parties. Consequently, executive search recruiters serve as management consultants who attempt to shift the competitive balance of management power in their client company's favor.

The bottom line: Employ a retained search firm for six-figure positions with exacting criteria when your sense of urgency is great and your need for dedicated attention is critical. If you find it difficult to pay a retainer when contingency recruiters will apparently do the same work for free, remember that it wouldn't make as much sense for contingency recruiters to work a search assignment that's too difficult when they have other, more fillable openings to tend to. Retained recruiters, in comparison, will be beholden to you until the assignment is completed because they will already have been paid their fee.

RECRUITMENT OPTION 3: Recruitment Process Outsource (RPO) Providers

Recruitment process outsourcing is becoming a prominent alternative to in-house staffing as well as contingency and retained search. RPO is a form of business process outsourcing whereby an organization outsources its recruitment function to a third party. This makes most sense in cases where high-volume openings make it more cost efficient to source, interview, and onboard candidates with the help of an external provider (think procurement warehouses where hundreds of new hires may be required at any given time).

However, RPO doesn't only come into play when hundreds of hires are required within short time frames. In general, any company that hires ten or more workers per month could potentially benefit from the services of an RPO provider. RPO firms attempt to offer more efficient recruitment services for their client companies, and their ultimate goal is to lower your company's cost per hire and allow your organization to focus on its core strengths and business competencies.

Recruitment outsourcing services can also make sense if you work in an industry that has fluctuating hiring demands or in cases where you want to be prepared for a volatile labor market. For example, when a business downturn hits and recruiting needs suddenly drop, so does a company's need for recruiting staff. Likewise, when a business finds itself suddenly expanding, recruiting needs may suddenly spike. Outsourcing the recruitment function allows your company to pass along the cost risk of those resources to the RPO provider, which offers flexibility, economies of scale, and greater access to potential talent pools.

RPO differs greatly from providers such as staffing companies and contingent/retained search providers in that it assumes ownership of the design and management of the entire recruitment process and the responsibility for results. An RPO provider functions as your internal recruitment department. Your contract can spell out specific recruitment-related functions that you want to outsource (e.g., sourcing slates of candidates, passing them to internal recruiters or entering them into your organization's applicant tracking system, performing testing or credential verifications, and even coordinating interviews, checking references, and extending offers). The provider allows you to just as easily outsource the entire recruitment function as a package offering (although this can have cultural implications and negatively impact employees' sense of job security and well-being).

RPO providers can use their own employees or your company's staff, technology, methodologies, and reporting. Therefore, it's difficult to approximate their costs; it all depends on how much of the process you intend to outsource and whether you choose to retain recruiters on your payroll or outsource them. Generally speaking, RPO costs follow five models:

1. *Management Fee*—A monthly fee is paid to the RPO provider for handling an agreed-upon number of positions. The agreement may include escalation factors if the number of hires increases over a certain threshold or over a specific period.
2. *Cost Per Hire*—A fee is paid for each candidate who is successfully brought through the program and hired. The cost-per-hire model works best with shorter-term projects, where the service may be needed for only a few months or for a specific assignment.
3. *Management Fee + Cost Per Hire*—This combines the first two. The management fee covers the processing of applicants, with additional fees paid for successful hires.
4. *Cost Per Slate*—Best suited for short-term projects and recruiting assignments, this model includes a fee for a fixed number of sourced, screened, and qualified candidates for each open position. Candidates are then formally pipelined to internal recruiters and hiring managers for interview consideration.

5. *Cost Per Transaction*—A set fee is charged for a specific process to be completed by the RPO provider (e.g., initial screening, testing, or reference checks). In such cases, the RPO vendor charges a fixed hourly rate or for each process or successful candidate.

Whether an RPO solution makes sense for your organization will depend on whether you're comfortable working under an exclusive agreement for outsourcing recruiting for your entire organization, a specific hiring drive, or a known project length. It will require an exhaustive, holistic look at your current cost per hire, retention and turnover statistics, and overall caliber of talent hired. As a broader trend gaining momentum in corporate America, it could be worth a closer look for additional consideration.

RECRUITMENT OPTION 4: Outplacement Firms' Job Development Departments

Outplacement firms are paid by companies that are downsizing to assist displaced workers in finding jobs. When companies demonstrate concern for hastened reemployment of laid-off workers, they foster a sense that people are well taken care of, and that automatically minimizes the traumatic impact on remaining employees. As far as the company is concerned, the cost of outplacement (typically 10 to 15 percent of the displaced executive's base salary for a nine-to-twelve-month program) is far outweighed by the altruistic and practical benefits that allow it to continue its business operations without undue interruption.

It's in the outplacement firm's best interests to get their candidates placed as quickly as possible. That's because it costs outplacement firms lots of money to provide services for displaced executives, such as office and telephone access, word-processing support for cover letters and résumés, administrative support, and the like. It's estimated that if a senior-level candidate remains on the outplacement firm's books for more than six months, the outplacement firm loses money on that transaction. (That up-front 10 to 15 percent fee gets more than consumed once the individual has used up more than six months of services.)

While originally established in the 1960s by Challenger, Gray & Christmas, Inc., as an executive perk that focused on senior-level career support at a time when layoffs were less prevalent, outplacement services today are typically offered at all levels on the employment spectrum.

When companies downsize because of mergers, acquisitions, or bank-ruptcies, for example, all impacted workers may be offered some form of outplacement services in exchange for signing a full release of claims (typically including severance packages and benefits continuation for a limited time). Fees are often tiered depending on the level of the employee involved and the length of the outplacement program:

◆ At more junior levels (e.g., nonexempt, manufacturing, and produc-tion positions), a typical program might include web and virtual fa-cilitation only and include must-have tools and techniques needed to conduct an effective job search. Such assignments typically cost as little as $500 per person, depending on the number of individuals im-pacted and the specific services offered.

◆ Professional, technical, and higher-level individual contributors might be offered a one-to-three-month program that includes monthly one-on-one meetings with a counselor, classroom workshops taught by career experts, and virtual video support to help with résumé prepa-ration, interviewing techniques, and company research resources. Individual career and marketplace exploration is common, including alternative career paths like self-employment, franchising opportuni-ties, and transition programs into retirement. Costs for a typical six-month package for a professional or technical worker generally range from $2,000 to $7,000.

Why is all this relevant? Because outplacement firms employ job de-velopers and researchers to help their candidates find work. Those job developers are constantly soliciting job openings from other companies and encouraging their candidates to seize the opportunities available. Re-member that because the outplacement firm is paid by the candidate's old company, not by you (the potential new employer), this free supply of talent could significantly reduce your cost per hire. If you're unsure of this source because you feel that the candidates from outplacement firms are the ones who couldn't make the cut, don't be. Companies have downsized entire divisions in this era of mergers, acquisitions, and divestitures, and many of the candidates now in outplacement's care were being placed by retained search not so long ago. Outplacement firms are an incredible source of free, highly qualified candidates, and it would be an absolute mistake not to list your openings with them.

Following are some of the largest outplacement firms in the nation. Their job banks are national, so listing a job opening will give you vast exposure. Also, if you want to keep the identity of your company confidential or if you want only those résumés that meet certain criteria, the job developers will typically do the initial screening for you. Take advantage of this free and effective service immediately by contacting the following industry giants:

Challenger, Gray & Christmas, Inc.
Corporate Headquarters
150 South Wacker Drive, Suite 2800
Chicago, IL 60606
312-332-5790
www.challengergray.com

Lee Hecht Harrison
Corporate Headquarters
50 Tice Boulevard
Woodcliff Lake, NJ 07677
800-611-4544
www.lhh.com

Right Management
Global Headquarters
100 Manpower Place
Milwaukee, WI 53212
800-237-4448
www.right.com

Interviewer's Checklist: The 96 Questions

Bonus Question A: Walk me through your progression in your career, leading up to how you landed in your current role at your present company.

Bonus Question B: What's your primary reason for leaving your current organization, and what criteria are you looking for in terms of selecting your next role, company, or industry?

Bonus Question C: Let's say you were to get this job with our organization. If you were happy in your role and excelling in your job one year from now, what would it look and feel like?

1. Tell me about your greatest strength. What's the greatest asset you'll bring to our company?
2. What's your greatest weakness?
3. What was your favorite position, and what role did your boss play in making it so unique?
4. What was your least favorite position? What role did your boss play in your career at that point?
5. Where do you see yourself in five years?
6. What makes you stand out among your peers?
7. What have you done in your present/last position to increase your organization's top-line revenues?
8. What have you done to reduce your department's operational costs or to save time?
9. What has been your most creative achievement at work?
10. What would your current supervisors say makes you most valuable to them?
11. What are the broad responsibilities of a [job title]?
12. What aspects of your job do you consider most crucial?
13. How many hours a week do you find it necessary to work in order to get your job done?
14. How does your position relate to the overall goals of your department or company?
15. What area of your skills do you need to improve upon in the next year?
16. How many employees were laid off simultaneously?
17. How many people survived the cut?
18. How many waves of layoffs did you survive before you were let go yourself?

19. What does growth mean to you?
20. What will you do differently at your present company if you don't get this position?
21. Can you describe how you've progressed through the ranks and landed in your current position at ABC Company?
22. How have you added value to your job over time?
23. How have you had to reinvent or redefine your job to meet your company's changing needs? What proactive steps did you have to take to increase the output of your position?
24. Can you distinguish between your vertical progression through the ranks at your last/present company and your lateral assumption of broader responsibilities?
25. What would be your next logical move in progression at your present company?
26. What kind of mentoring and training style do you have? Do you naturally delegate responsibilities, or do you expect your direct reports to come to you for added responsibilities?
27. Every company has its own quirks—its "dysfunctionality quotient," so to speak. How dysfunctional was your last company, and how much tolerance do you have for dealing with a company's shortcomings and inconsistencies?
28. How would you describe the amount of structure, direction, and feedback you need in order to excel?
29. In terms of managing your staff, do you "expect" more than you "inspect," or vice versa?
30. How do you approach your work from the standpoint of balancing your career with your personal life?
31. Paint a picture of the corporate culture you'll create if we hire you. Do you operate under a more centralized and paternalistic agenda with power centralized in the hands of a few, or do you constantly push responsibility and accountability down the line?
32. Why did you choose your [college/major]?
33. How does your degree prepare you (a) for a career in [industry] or (b) to excel as a [job title]?
34. What qualifications do you have beyond academics that qualify you to make a successful transition into business?
35. Do you think your grades are a good indicator of your ability to succeed in business?
36. What other types of positions and companies are you considering right now?
37. If you were to accept this position with us today, how would you explain that to a prospective employer five years from now? How would this job provide a link in your future career progression?
38. What was the most difficult ethical decision you've ever had to make in your career or during your education, and what was the outcome?

342

39. How would you describe "professional behavior" in the workplace?

40. I see you've had a tango or two at the Job Hoppers' Ball. Let's discuss how you plan on building your résumé from a longevity standpoint.

41. Who is your typical reading audience when you're writing something, and what level of language do you use?

Bonus Question 8A: Where do you relate best: up one level, down one level, or with your peers?

Bonus Question 8B: How would you grade yourself in terms of face-to-face communication, especially in terms of negotiation or confrontation? Do you consider that a strength or an area for personal development?

42. How do you rank competitively among other account executives in terms of your production?

43. What are the two most common objections you face, and how do you deal with them?

44. Role-play with me, if you will, presenting yourself to me over the phone as if you were a headhunter. Can you convince me that this "product" you're selling is worth my time?

45. How do you define your closing style?

46. All salespeople need to find equilibrium between (a) high-volume production numbers and (b) quality. Which philosophy drives your sales style more?

47. Tell me about the last time you failed to meet quota. How many times did that happen over the past year, and what plan of action did you take to get back on track?

48. With no undue flattery, if you will, grade me on how well I'm conducting this interview: What can you tell me about my sales and management style on the basis of the questions I'm asking you?

49. How important is the base salary component to you? Would you prefer a straight commission if it offered you the potential for an additional 35 percent in aggregate earnings over the base salary?

50. Tell me about your quality ratios: How many prospects do you typically see before closing a sale?

51. How much does production vary from desk to desk in your office?

Bonus Question 10A: From a self-assessment standpoint, where might you be lacking in terms of being a perfect match for this position? What's your most critical self-assessment of your strengths and weaknesses for this position and in terms of your overall fit?

Bonus Question 10B: Tell me about your approach to goal setting. How do you measure progress and quantify your achievements?

Bonus Question 10C: What's one thing about your career that's guaranteed to make you smile?

Bonus Question 10D: Are you satisfied with your career to date? What would you change if you could? Do you think you've had too many job changes or too few?

Bonus Question 10E: Would you classify yourself as a "born leader," or is leadership something that you've focused on and developed over time?

Bonus Question 10F: Most jobs at your level require the ability to deal with ambiguity and shift gears quickly, even without having all the information. Give me an example of a time when you had to adjust for and lead through a sudden change in plans with no blueprint to guide you. What were the circumstances and how did you handle it?

Bonus Question 10G: How would you describe yourself in terms of your personal brand? How do you model the behaviors that you espouse?

Bonus Question 10H: What career advice would you give someone getting into the field right now?

Bonus Question 10I: Tell me about the difference between leadership and management. Is it necessary to supervise someone to establish your reputation as a leader?

52. Can you give me an example of your ability to facilitate progressive change within your organization?
53. Tell me about the last time you inherited a problem unit—one suffering from poor productivity or low morale. What was the scope of the problem, and how were your direct reports affected?
54. Did you create a culture of open information sharing and increased accountability by giving responsibility to your subordinates, or did you focus more on establishing their parameters and controlling the decision-making process?
55. How do you typically stay in the information loop and monitor your staff's performance?
56. How do you typically confront subordinates when results are unacceptable?

Bonus Question 11A: What kinds of organizational transformations have you led? What lasting value have you created for your organization?

Bonus Question 11B: Tell me about your approach to strategic change management. How do you approach change yourself, and how do you get your people's buy-in?

Bonus Question 11C: Have you ever considered starting your own business?

57. Tell me about your last performance appraisal. In which area were you most disappointed?
58. In hindsight, how could you have improved your performance at your last position?

59. Where do you disagree with your boss most often? How did you handle the last time she or he was wrong and you were right?

60. How would your supervisor grade your ability to cope with last-minute change without breaking stride?

61. Why do you want to work here?

62. What do you know about our company?

63. Can you tell me about your understanding of the job you're applying for?

64. What can you do for us if we hire you, and when should we expect to see concrete results?

65. How structured an environment would you say this individual needs to reach her maximum potential?

66. Does this individual typically adhere strictly to job duties, or does he assume responsibilities beyond the basic written job description?

67. Can you comment on this person's ability to accept constructive criticism?

68. How much do outside influences play a role in this individual's job performance?

69. Would you consider this individual more of a task-oriented or a project-oriented worker?

70. How does the candidate handle interruptions, breaks in routine, and last-minute changes?

71. How would you grade the candidate's commitment to project completion?

72. How would you grade this candidate's capacity for analytical thinking and problem solving?

73. Does this individual need close supervision to excel, or does she take more of an autonomous, independent approach to her work?

74. How global a perspective does this candidate have? Do you see him eventually making the transition from a tactical and operational career path to the strategic level necessary for a career in senior management?

75. How would you grade this candidate's listening skills?

76. How effective is the candidate at delivering bad news? Will the person typically assume responsibility for things gone wrong?

77. Please grade the individual's capacity for initiative and taking action. Does this person have a tendency to get bogged down in "analysis paralysis"?

78. Is this candidate's management style more autocratic and paternalistic or is it geared toward a more participative and consensus-building approach?

79. In terms of this individual's energy level, how would you grade his capacity for hustle?

80. How does this individual approach taking action without getting prior approval?

81. Is it this person's natural inclination to report to someone else for sign-off, or does the candidate operate better with independent responsibility and authority?

82. After so many years in the business, is this candidate still on a career track for which she can sustain enthusiasm?

83. How effective is this person at orchestrating a corporate ensemble of functional areas?

84. Can you address the candidate's ability to cope with the significant pressures associated with senior management?

85. Does this person ever delay the inevitable in terms of disciplining or dismissing employees?

86. Is this individual inclined to maintain smooth and amicable relations at all costs, or is she more likely to show her teeth when faced with adversity?

87. Does the candidate stay open to all sides of an argument before reaching a decision, or does he get personally involved in conflicts?

88. Tell me again: Why do you feel the position you're applying for meets your career needs or why is working for our company so important for you?

89. On a scale of one to ten (ten being you're really excited about accepting our offer, one being there's no interest), where do you stand?

90. What would have to change at your present position for you to continue working there?

91. Tell me about the counteroffer they'll make you once you give notice. If you gave notice right now, what would your boss say to keep you?

92. What's changed since the last time we spoke?

93. If you had to choose among three factors—(1) the company, (2) the position you're applying for, and (3) the people you'd be working with—which would you say plays the most significant role in your decision to accept our offer?

94. If we were to make you an offer, tell me ideally when you'd like to start. How much notice would you need to give your present employer?

95. Can you share with me what final questions I can answer to help you come to an informed career decision?

96. At what dollar level would you accept our job offer, and at what dollar level would you reject it?

Notes

The Anatomy of an Effective Interview

1. Legislation in the areas of salary inquiries and discussions was under debate at the time of this writing. Depending on the laws of your state, you may need to delay specific salary discussions until after a conditional employment offer is extended. See the legal update in Chapter 18 for additional information.

Chapter 10

1. *Occupational Outlook Handbook,* Bureau of Labor Statistics, U.S. Department of Labor, www.bls.gov/ooh.
2. In 1970, Greenleaf published his first essay, "The Servant As Leader," which introduced the term *servant leadership.* His later book was *Servant Leadership: A Journey into the Nature of Legitimate Power and Greatness* (New York: Paulist Press, 2002).

Chapter 11

1. Steve Bates, "Retail Revolution Challenges HR: While Stores Close, Growth in E-Commerce Creates New Positions," May 4, 2017, Society for Human Resource Management, http://bit.ly/2qULvAd.

Chapter 20

1. Special thanks to Berkshire Associates, Inc., in Columbia, Maryland, for generously sharing these proposed applicant tracking codes with us. Berkshire Associates is a human resource consulting and technology firm that specializes in solutions in affirmative action, applicant management, compensation, diversity metrics, and professional training.

Chapter 22

1. Barry J. Nadell, *Sleuthing 101: Background Checks and the Law* (Chatsworth: Barry Nadell, 2004), 29.

Chapter 25

1. In highly competitive markets where middle-market search firms are vying for business, they may be willing to make the final one-third of the placement fee contingent upon completing the search. Again, this is a point for negotiation. Note, however, that the largest executive search firms likely won't negotiate that final one-third of the fee.

Index

349

About the Author

Paul Falcone (www.PaulFalconeHR.com) is a human resources executive in Los Angeles and has held senior-level positions with Nickelodeon, Paramount Pictures, and City of Hope. He has extensive human resources experience in entertainment, healthcare/biotech, and financial services, including in international, nonprofit, and union environments.

Falcone has dedicated much of his professional life to advancing the human resources profession, both as a member of the Extension HR Advisory Council of the University of California at Los Angeles and as an instructor in the UCLA Extension School of Business and Management, where he teaches courses on recruitment and selection, legal aspects of human resource management, workplace ethics, and international human resource management. He is a long-time contributor to *HR Magazine*, *SHRM Online*, and *AMA Playbook* and is a nationally recognized speaker for the Society for Human Resource Management (SHRM). He has been interviewed and quoted by prestigious news organizations like the *Harvard Business Review*, *Forbes.com*, the *Financial Times of London*, *U.S. News and World Report*, *CBS Money Watch*, and Bloomberg's *Money News*.

Falcone is the author of a number of bestsellers with AMACOM Books, a division of American Management Association. His newest book, *75 Ways for Managers to Hire, Develop, and Keep Great Employees*, focuses on in-the-trenches leadership wisdom, helping front-line managers master leadership offense and leadership defense strategies to propel their careers while protecting themselves and their organizations from employment-related liability. His book *101 Tough Conversations to Have with Employees: A Manager's Guide to Addressing Performance, Conduct, and Discipline Challenges* provides leaders with the strategies and scripts to address substandard job performance and inappropriate workplace conduct while maintaining workers' respect and dignity and holding them fully accountable for results. His most popular book, *2600 Phrases for Effective Performance Reviews*, has sold over 200,000 copies and remains one of AMACOM's bestsellers. His book *101 Sample Write-Ups for Documenting Employee Performance Problems: A Guide to Progressive Discipline & Termination*, now in its third edition, is one of SHRM's all-time bestsellers and remains the paradigm for documentation in the employee performance-improvement process.

Falcone obtained his bachelor of arts and master's degrees from UCLA. He lives in Valencia, California.

More classic bestselling titles by Paul Falcone

2600 Phrases for Effective Performance Reviews

Packed with ready-to-use phrases and words, action items, and descriptions that managers, supervisors, and HR professionals can use to evaluate performance, prepare development plans, and address performance problems. Covers the twenty-five most commonly rated factors, including productivity, time management, decision making, and teamwork, as well as specific roles such as customer service, finance, sales, and more. The book provides hundreds of phrases to use in performance-improvement plans, plus an appendix of helpful individual words.

9780814472828 $10.95

101 Sample Write-Ups for Documenting Employee
Performance Problems, Third Edition

These ready-to-go documents eliminate the fretful second guessing about what to do and how to say it. Expertly written, they cover every kind of problem: substandard work quality, absenteeism, insubordination, sexual harassment, social media misuse, cyberbullying, medical marijuana, Family and Medical Leave Act abuse, and more. In addition, readers will find a complete explanation of the entire disciplinary process and (as a last resort) eighteen sample termination letters.

9780814479773 $39.95

101 Tough Conversations to Have with Employees: A Manager's Guide
to Addressing Performance, Conduct, and Discipline Challenges
9780814413487 $17.95

75 Ways for Managers to Hire, Develop, and Keep Great Employees

The Performance Appraisal Tool Kit: Redesigning Your Performance Review
Template to Drive Individual and Organizational Change

Available at your local bookstore, online, or call 800-250-5308.
Savings start at 40 percent on bulk orders of five copies or more.
Save up to 55 percent.
Prices are subject to change.
For details, contact AMACOM Special Sales.
Phone: 212-903-8316, email: SpecialSls@amanet.org.